TED TALKS

MW00830503

Keynote

ADVANCED

Lewis Lansford
Paul Dummett
Helen Stephenson

NGL.Cengage.com/Keynote

PASSWORD keynoteStdt#

Contents

PRONUNCIATION	READING	LISTENING	SPEAKING	WRITING
Vowel sounds at word boundaries	Why do we sleep?	Planning a trip	Luxury and necessity Talking about things we need Hedging	A statement of opinion Writing skill: Hedging expressions
Weak *of* Sounding encouraging	Image, identity and clothing	Preparing for a job interview	Evaluating data Talking about image Making suggestions	Giving feedback Writing skill: Being diplomatic
Sentence stress in cleft sentences Stress in expressions of disagreement	How groupthink closed the 'flying bank'	Choosing a logo	Evaluating teamwork Dealing with groupthink Dealing with disagreement and reaching consensus (Choosing a logo)	Emails dealing with disagreement Writing skill: Encouraging cooperation
Approximations Intonation in questions	One man's meat …	Asking how something works	Using approximations Talking about sales potential Asking for clarification and repetition (Giving and receiving instructions)	Information for a house guest Writing skill: Instructions
Softening negative statements	Eureka moments?	Planning a party	Talking about life experience Where my ideas come from Brainstorming and choosing the best ideas	A to-do list Writing skill: Abbreviations
Stress in content and function words	The parable of the stones	Discussing options for solving a problem	Talking about why things are useful Describing a solution Finding solutions	Online advice form Writing skill: Softening advice or recommendations

PRONUNCIATION	READING	LISTENING	SPEAKING	WRITING
/ŋ/ sound Contraction with *have*	The power of visualization	Speculating about a mystery	The benefits and drawbacks of daydreaming Talking about visualization Speculating	A news story Writing skill: Neutral reporting
Voicing in final consonants Emphasizing the main focus of the sentence	Bad team building	Reviewing a project	Cause-and-result relationships Work issues Taking part in a meeting	Debriefing questionnaire Writing skill: Linking devices
Stress with intensifying adverbs Polite and assertive intonation	Can stress be good for you?	Dealing with awkward situations	Holiday lessons learned Talking about stress Having difficult conversations	A record of a meeting Writing skill: Reporting verbs
Saying lists	Understanding risk	Assessing risk	A TV news story Facing risks Discussing alternatives (Health and safety issues)	A consumer review Writing skill: Using qualifiers
Intonation in subordinate clauses Sure and unsure tones	Visionaries	Life coaching	Looking after what matters Talking about visionaries Sharing dreams and visions of the future (Talking about a vision of the future)	An endorsement Writing skill: Persuasive language
Sentence stress in explaining outcomes Sentence stress in making arrangements	Is pessimism really so bad?	Arranging to meet	Past views of the present Talking about financial decisions Making arrangements	A group email Writing skill: Impersonal language

Communication activities 172 and 183 | TED Talk transcripts   173

Featured TED Talks

Unit 1
Less stuff,
more happiness
Graham Hill

Unit 2
Who am I? Think
again
Hetain Patel and Yuyu Rau

Unit 3
Making peace
is a marathon
May El-Khalil

Unit 4
How I beat
stage fright
Joe Kowan

Unit 5
I'm not your inspiration,
thank you very much
Stella Young

Unit 6
How to make
filthy water
drinkable
Michael Pritchard

1 Necessities

BACKGROUND

1 You are going to watch a TED Talk by Graham Hill called *Less stuff, more happiness.* Read the text about the speaker and the talk, then answer the questions.

   1 Hill's website promotes a lifestyle that doesn't harm the planet. What sorts of actions or choices do you think he recommends/discourages?

   2 Hill believes that we can be happier if we have fewer possessions. Do you think he's right?

   3 How easy do you find it to get rid of stuff?

TEDTALKS

GRAHAM HILL is a North American journalist who studied architecture and design. He founded TreeHugger.com, a website dedicated to promoting a lifestyle that doesn't harm the planet and to making complex environmental issues easier to understand. He's currently the CEO of LifeEdited, a project devoted to living well with less. Graham Hill's idea worth spreading is that we can actually be happier with fewer things, so long as we are able to edit our lives in smart, practical ways.

A family's possessions outside a traditional yurt in Xinba'erhuzuo Qi, Mongolia

KEY WORDS

2 Read the sentences (1–6). The words in bold are used in the TED Talk. First guess the meaning of the words. Then match the words with their definitions (a–f).

1 Even though I had everything money could buy, my happiness **flat-lined**.

2 I **crowdsourced** advice on the best green holiday options.

3 Deleting my old photographs **cleared the arteries of** my computer.

4 The simple design avoided **extraneous** elements that would detract from the clean look.

5 The recycling campaign has helped to **stem the inflow** of waste into our local landfill site.

6 The bowls are three different sizes, so they **nest**, making them easy to store.

a reduce the inward movement
b via the Internet, asked a lot of people for
c not relevant or related
d stopped increasing, but didn't decrease
e removed unnecessary stuff from the inner workings of
f fit one inside the other

AUTHENTIC LISTENING SKILLS Relaxed pronunciation

When some words combine with *of, have* or *to*, some sounds in the word may be lost or changed in speech. In addition, the *of, have* or *to* is reduced to a weak /ə/ sound, for example *kind of* → *kinda*; *should have* → *shoulda*; *want to* → *wanna*.

3a ⌂ **1** Look at the Authentic listening skills box. Then listen to sentences 1–3. Underline the expressions with *to* and *of* that are reduced and changed.

1 So I'm going to suggest that less stuff and less space are going to equal a smaller footprint.
2 First of all, you have to edit ruthlessly.
3 We've got to cut the extraneous out of our lives, and we've got to learn to stem the inflow.

3b ⌂ **2** Read extracts 4 and 5. Which expressions do you think will be reduced or changed? Listen and check.

4 … we combine a moving wall with transformer furniture to get a lot out of the space. My bed just pops out of the wall with two fingers.
5 Most of us, maybe all of us, are here pretty happily for a bunch of days with a couple of bags …

1.1 Less stuff, more happiness

TEDTALKS

1 ▶ **1.1** Watch the TED Talk. Number the five topics (a–e) in the order Graham Hill discusses them.

a examples of situations where we live comfortably with less
b three ways to 'live little'
c the personal storage industry
d the contents of the box discussed
e Hill's 420 square foot (39 m²) apartment and how he got it

2 Work in pairs. Check your answers to Exercise 1.

3 ▶ **1.1** How much of the talk can you remember? Answer the questions. Then watch the first part (0.00–2.55) of the talk again and check your answers.

1 How much has the typical living space in the USA increased in the past 50 years?
2 In addition to having more space, what other two things have increased for the average North American?
3 What, significantly, *hasn't* increased for North Americans in the past 50 years?
4 What three benefits of having less stuff and living in a smaller space does Graham Hill name?
5 Hill talks about having an 'edited' set of possessions. What does he mean by that?

▶ dorm **N AM ENG**
▶ hall of residence **BR ENG**

▶ digitize / organize **N AM ENG** / **BR ENG**
▶ digitise / organise **BR ENG**

4 ▶ **1.1** Watch the second part (2.56–4.42) of the talk again. What examples does Hill give for his three main approaches (1–3) to life editing?

1 Edit your possessions – cut the extraneous and learn to stem the inflow.
2 Repeat the mantra: small is sexy.
3 Use multifunctional spaces and housewares.

5 ▶ **1.1** Watch the third part (4.43 to the end) of the talk again. Answer the questions.

1 How much does Graham Hill suggest we could reduce our living space by?
2 What does he point out about the people who are attending the TED Talk?
3 What does he say 'life editing' will give us more of?
4 What does the symbol < = > mean?

6 Hill uses a lot of examples from the USA in his TED Talk. How do you think issues of living space / amount of material possessions compare in your own country?

VOCABULARY IN CONTEXT

7 ▶ **1.2** Watch the clips from the TED Talk. Choose the correct meaning of the words.

8 Complete the sentences in your own words. Then discuss with a partner.

1 If I had to edit my possessions ruthlessly, I'd start by getting rid of …
2 My personal mantra is …
3 My … is/are digitized.

CRITICAL THINKING Identifying aims

9 Look at this list of reasons for giving a talk. Which most accurately describes the main aim of Graham Hill's TED Talk?

1 to entertain by telling an interesting and sometimes funny personal story
2 to give the listener new information
3 to persuade using objective facts
4 to inform and ask the listener to make a specific decision or choice
5 to persuade by making an emotional appeal

10 Read the comments* about the TED Talk. Which one of them mentions details that show what Hill's main aim was?

Viewers' comments

P **Paolo** – The box is so familiar. Everyone has one, right? Bringing it on stage and talking about it really made the point.

K **KMJ** – It's hard to argue with smaller utility bills, more money and a smaller environmental footprint. I think < = > ('less equals more') is a really useful equation.

E **Erica** – Great talk, and completely true. And I love his apartment. I want one!

The comments were created for this activity.

PRESENTATION SKILLS Using props

TIPS

Props can be an extremely useful tool for presenters. A well-chosen prop:

- stimulates the audience's curiosity or builds anticipation.
- provides a visual focus.
- helps clarify or reinforce an idea.
- may help the audience relate to your ideas.
- can help the audience visualize a complex idea or process.
- serves as an example.
- isn't distracting.
- makes your talk memorable.

11 ▶ **1.3** Look at the Presentation tips box. Then watch how Graham Hill uses his cardboard box in the TED Talk. Answer the questions.

1 How does Hill's box both build anticipation and reinforce his ideas?
2 Hill stands in front of the box for most of the talk. Do you think the box is distracting to the audience? Why? / Why not?
3 What other props might Hill have used to make the same point?

12 Work in pairs. Prepare a two-minute mini-presentation. Make some brief notes on one of these topics. Think of a simple prop you could use to illustrate each of the talk topics.

1 air pollution
2 the benefits of regular exercise
3 money spent by the public on holidays abroad
4 a comparison of the size of homes and living space around the world
5 the working lives of factory employees

13 Work with a new partner. Take turns to give your presentation. Remember the advice from the Presentation tips box to help you use your prop effectively.

▶ burner **N AM ENG**
▶ hob **BR ENG**

▶ a bunch of **N AM ENG**
▶ quite a few **BR ENG**

1.2 Luxury or necessity?

DO YOU REALLY **NEED** IT?

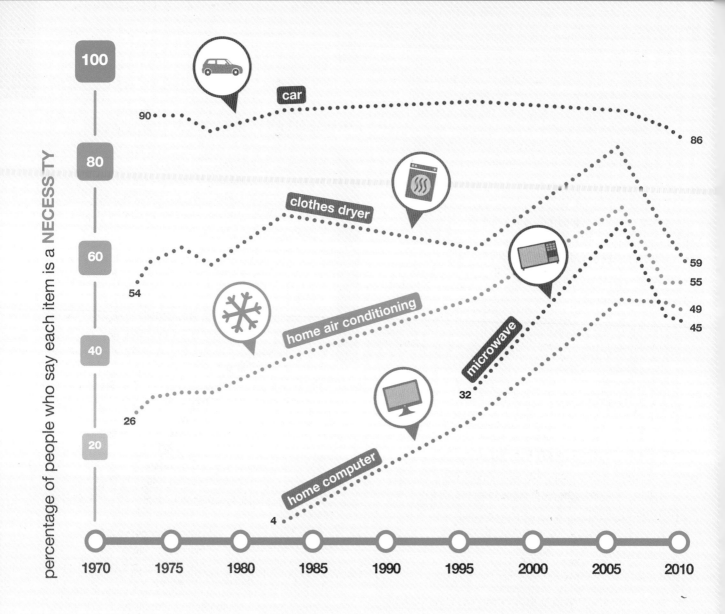

percentage of people who say each item is a NECESSITY

100
80
60
40
20

90 · · · · · · car · · · · · · 86
clothes dryer
54
home air conditioning
microwave 59
55
49
45
32
home computer
26
4

1970 1975 1980 1985 1990 1995 2000 2005 2010

GRAMMAR The perfect aspect

1 What's a luxury? What's a necessity? Think of two or three examples of each in your own life.

2 Write N (necessity) or L (luxury) for each the following. Explain why.

1 car N
2 clothes dryer L
3 home air conditioning L
4 microwave oven L
5 home computer L
6 Internet access N

3 Look at the graph showing changing ideas about necessities and luxuries in the USA. Then answer the questions.

1 When the lines on the graph go up from left to right, does it show that more people considered the item a necessity or more people considered it a luxury?

2 Do the lines between 1980 and 2005, show a generally healthy economy or a weak economy?

3 Sometime after 2005, people suddenly change their minds about what is a luxury and what is a necessity. Why do you think this happened?

4 Read the text in the Grammar box. Match the verbs in bold to the letters (a–e) on the time line.

THE PERFECT ASPECT

What we consider to be a luxury **has changed** in sometimes unexpected ways over the years. Up until 2005, people's expectations of home comforts such as microwaves and clothes dryers **had been increasing** steadily. However, some time after 2005, the trend reversed and by 2010 the percentage of people considering these items a necessity **had fallen** to levels not previously seen since the 1970s. This downwards trend **has been continuing** and shows no sign of bottoming out. Though numbers of cars and computers don't fall as sharply in the data compared to air conditioning and clothes dryers, our attitude to these **will probably have changed** again in the next ten years.

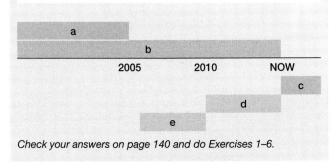

Check your answers on page 140 and do Exercises 1–6.

5 Work in pairs. Explain the difference between the pairs of sentences.

1 a When my car broke down, I had decided to sell it.
   b When my car broke down, I decided to sell it.

2 a By this time next year, I will have moved to a smaller flat.
   b This time next year, I will move to a smaller flat.

3 a I've been thinking about getting rid of my TV.
   b I'd been thinking about getting rid of my TV.

4 a I've used my travel hairdryer a lot.
   b I used my travel hairdryer a lot.

5 a Had you been trying to think of ways to save money?
   b Have you been trying to think of ways to save money?

6 Match the two parts of the sentences.

1 I've been spending a lot of time   C
2 I'd been thinking for years about trying to simplify my life   F
3 I will have spent thousands of dollars making improvements to my home   E
4 I've been working full time for ten years,   A
5 I hadn't used a computer for several years   D
6 I will have owned three cars in my life   B

a and now I want to work less and have fewer luxuries.
b after I get the new one next week.
c reading about how to live more simply.
d when I was given one to use for work.
e by the time I sell it next year.
f when I finally decided to do something about it.

7 Choose the best options to complete each sentence.

1 My phone has become a necessity. I don't think I'll ever *be able* / *have been able* to get by without it.
2 Before last year, I *hadn't played* / *didn't play* the guitar since I was a teenager. Now I play every week, but I do think of it as a bit of a luxury.
3 Running has become a necessity for me. I *ran* / *'ve run* in eight marathons so far. I'd go crazy without it.
4 My luxury has always been reading. I *spend* / *'ve been spending* three hours a day reading.
5 Until recently, I *hadn't ever used* / *wasn't ever using* an alarm clock, because my dad always woke me up. But since I started university, an alarm clock has been an absolute necessity for me.

8 Complete the sentences. Use the correct (simple or continuous) present perfect, past perfect or future perfect form of the verbs.

1 He _has never owned_ (never own) a clothes dryer because he doesn't mind hanging out the washing.
2 I _had driven_ (drive) to work for years before I finally decided last year to start walking.
3 For the past year, you _'ve been trying_ (try) to convince me to buy a new laptop, but I don't want one!
4 By the time we retire, we _'ll have saved_ (save) thousands of pounds by living in a smaller flat.
5 If they _had not installed_ (not install) air conditioning, they could have saved a lot of money.
6 I _have lived_ (live) in a computer-free house for ten years next January, and I don't plan on changing that!
7 She _has used_ (use) her bike as her main form of transport for the past fifteen years.
8 I _have been working_ (work) all day to try and finish this report, but I wish I'd done it sooner!

SPEAKING Luxury and necessity

9 **21st** **CENTURY OUTCOMES**

Work in groups. Think of one luxury in your life – something you could do without, but would miss – and one necessity. Tell the group.

10 Take turns asking and answering questions. Explain how each came into your life, and the role they play in your life now. Use perfect constructions.

11 Are your ideas about luxury and necessity the same as the other members of your group? Or is one person's luxury another person's necessity?

1.3 I'm wide awake

READING Why do we sleep?

1 Work in pairs. Discuss the questions.

1 About how many hours do you sleep per night?
2 Would you prefer to sleep more or less, or do you sleep the right amount?
3 Do you tend to wake up early and feel alert in the morning, or do you feel alert at night and stay up late?

2 Read the article. Which of the following are included?

1 An explanation of what happens when a person is deprived of sleep
2 Some reasons why people have difficulty sleeping
3 A list of physical and emotional problems caused by working at night
4 Descriptions of how to fight sleep and how to encourage it
5 An explanation of some of the dangers of exhaustion
6 Some famous people's bad experiences with being unable to sleep

3 Find a sentence in the article that either supports or contradicts each of these statements.

1 Randy Gardner is the world-record holder for staying awake.
2 Sleep deprivation causes people to lose touch with reality.
3 The brain basically shuts off when we fall asleep.
4 Experts say that a healthy adult should have a minimum of eight hours' sleep each night.
5 Light can have a strong effect on the natural sleep cycle.
6 Not getting enough sleep could shorten your life.
7 It's impossible for anyone to function for more than a few days without getting a solid night's sleep.
8 The only documented instances of sleep deprivation lasting more than two or three days are experiments carried out by scientists.

4 Work in pairs. Match the expressions from the article with the definitions (a–f).

1 Gardner was **wide awake**.
2 Gardner began to **nod off** uncontrollably.
3 He needed to **sleep on it**.
4 She **drifted off to sleep**.
5 He **hadn't slept a wink**.
6 He didn't **oversleep** in the mornings that followed.

a wait until the next day to make a decision
b gradually fall asleep
c had no sleep
d fall asleep when you don't mean to
e wake up later than you mean to
f completely alert

VOCABULARY The prefixes *over-* and *under-*

5 When attached to a verb or adjective, the prefix *over-* can be used to mean *more than necessary* and *under-* can mean *less than is necessary* or *not enough*. What's the meaning of these words from the article?

1 Sleep is **undervalued** in the modern world as a means of staying healthy, happy and productive.
2 The dangers of being too tired are often **underestimated**.
3 Being **overworked** and exhausted slows brain function.
4 But don't **overdo** it!
5 Eleven- to seventeen-year-olds are probably **undersleeping** if they don't get an average of 8.5 to 9.5 hours a night.

6 Complete the sentences. Use words with *over-* and *under-*

1 We needed more staff in the office.
The office was _____.
2 People use the word *awesome* far more than is necessary.
Awesome is _____.
3 It's easy to spend too much money on luxuries.
It's easy to _____ on luxuries.
4 My idea isn't developed enough.
My idea's _____.
5 The bus was so crowded that it was unsafe.
The bus was _____.
6 We estimated that 500 people would visit, but only 300 came.
We _____ the number of visitors.
7 I'm surprised this restaurant isn't more highly rated.
This restaurant is _____!
8 The price of the movie was too high.
The movie was _____.

7 Work in pairs. Discuss the questions.

1 What places in your area are frequently overcrowded?
2 Can you think of a product or resource that is underused?
3 What products or services do you think are overpriced?
4 Can you think of a book, film, restaurant, or something else that you feel is underrated?
5 Can you think of a book, film, restaurant, or something else that you feel is overrated?

SPEAKING Talking about things we need

8 **21st CENTURY OUTCOMES**
Sleep is a necessity for a healthy, happy life. Make a list of other human necessities.

9 In small groups, compare your lists. Then try to agree on the five most important necessities for daily life.

Why do we sleep?

Adults spend, on average, a third of their lives asleep. But ask the question above, and you'll find that there isn't a clear or simple answer. But there are plenty of other interesting questions ... and answers.

How long can a human go without sleeping? In 1965, seventeen-year-old Randy Gardner of San Diego, California stayed awake for 264 hours and 24 minutes – just over eleven days – breaking the then world record of 260 hours. Gardner's record has been broken several times since, though not by much, and it remains the best-documented sleep-deprivation experiment ever conducted.

What happens when you stay awake for eleven days? On the first day of the experiment, Gardner was wide awake and ready to go at six in the morning. By day two, however, his thinking showed signs of becoming less clear. When asked to identify simple objects by feeling them with his hands, he found it difficult. By day three, he had become unusually moody. On day four, he began to hallucinate, imagining that he was a famous American football player. Nights were difficult, as Gardner began to nod off uncontrollably. His friends kept him awake by driving him around in the car and playing pinball and basketball with him. As the days passed, Gardner's speech became less clear, he felt dizzy, his vision was blurred and his memory began to fail. He also continued to hallucinate.

Amazingly, after Gardner finally fell asleep he slept for only fourteen hours and forty minutes and awoke refreshed and alert and he didn't oversleep in the mornings that followed.

How much sleep do we need? Sleep is undervalued in the modern world as a means of staying healthy, happy and productive. But there's no 'magic number' of hours you need to sleep each night. According to the Sleep Foundation, people who are eighteen and older usually need between seven and nine hours per night, and eleven-to seventeen-year-olds are probably undersleeping if they don't get an average of 8.5 to 9.5 hours. Younger kids need more sleep, and infants the most – fourteen to fifteen hours daily – to stay healthy.

What tricks do people use to try to stay awake? One of the most common tricks for staying awake is drinking coffee, tea or soft drinks that contain caffeine, a naturally-occurring chemical found in the leaves, seeds, nuts and/or berries of various plants. It stimulates the brain, makes us feel more alert and even helps us think more quickly. Other techniques include getting up and moving around regularly, listening to lively music, splashing cold water on your face, and pulling on the bottom part of your ears. Soldiers have been kept awake – and focused – by wearing special goggles that shine a light the colour of sunrise into their eyes, keeping their brains in 'wake-up' mode. But don't overdo it! Eventually, mind and body need a rest.

Can sleep deprivation cause any problems? The dangers of being too tired are often underestimated. Tiredness has been a factor in big disasters, such as the Chernobyl nuclear accident in 1986, and in countless road accidents all over the world every day. Being overworked and exhausted slows brain function, negatively affects judgement, contributes to depression and makes you forgetful. And there are physical problems, too. Chronic sleep deprivation can increase the risk of heart disease and other serious health problems.

Why do we sleep? The best answer may be 'Because we're tired'.

HE NEEDED TO SLEEP ON IT

Albert Einstein, probably one of the greatest minds of all times, is said to have required ten hours' sleep each night. The reason is likely to be that he did a lot of problem-solving while sleeping. Research has found that as we sleep, our minds are able to continue working, and as a result, it's possible to fall asleep with a problem and wake up with a solution.

SHE DRIFTED OFF TO SLEEP

In 2005, Ellen MacArthur broke the world record for the fastest solo round-the-world sailing boat voyage. As part of her training, a sleep expert trained MacArthur to take ten half-hour naps each day, resulting in a total of five hours sleep in every twenty-four. Judging by her successes, this approach appears to have worked well for MacArthur.

HE HADN'T SLEPT A WINK

The 2001 TV game show *Touch the Truck* featured twenty contestants competing to win a brand new pick-up truck. The set-up was simple. Each person put one hand on the truck. They weren't allowed to lean on it or to sit down at all, but were allowed a ten-minute break every two hours and a fifteen-minute break every six hours. The winner was the person who could keep a hand on the truck for the longest period of time. That was Jerry Middleton, who stayed awake for 81 hours, 43 minutes and 31 seconds without letting go of the truck.

1.4 Keep it to the bare minimum

LISTENING Planning a trip

1 If you were planning a canoe and camping trip of several nights, what four or five necessities from home would you bring with you?

2 🎧 **3** Listen to four friends planning a canoeing trip. What do they decide to bring? What do they decide not to bring?

3 🎧 **4** Listen to the statements from the conversation. Circle P for the more polite ones and D for the more direct ones.

1	P	D
2	(P)	D
3	P	D
4	P	D
5	P	D
6	P	D
7	P	D
8	P	D
9	(P)	D
10	P	D

4 What makes the more polite expressions sound more polite?

5 🎧 **5** Complete the sentences with these words and phrases. Then listen and check your answers.

don't know	just suggest	know
might not be	might possibly want	no expert
personally	wonder	

1 I'm _____, but I don't think that we can expect to have a phone signal.

2 _____, I feel that we don't want to be weighed down with too much stuff.

3 I _____ about you, but I don't think we'll want a lot of devices on this trip.

4 Can I _____ we leave our other electronics at home?

5 All I _____ is that I'm going to want at least three pairs of socks.

6 I _____ if we should consider leaving the camping stove behind?

7 We _____ it if we have rainy weather.

8 It _____ a bad idea for all of us to look at it together.

Pronunciation Vowel sounds at word boundaries

6a 🎧 **6** Look at the words that are written with consonants at the end. When spoken, do they end with a consonant sound or a vowel sound? Listen to check.

1 know
2 wonder
3 personally

6b 🎧 **7** What happens when the word is followed by a vowel sound? Listen to check.

1 All I **know is** …
2 I **wonder if** …
3 **Personally I** feel …

6c 🎧 **8** Listen. What sound do you hear between the words in bold?

1 I'm **no expert** …
2 It might not **be a** bad idea to …
3 I don't think there's a **law against** fires.

6d Practise reading aloud the sentences in Exercise 5.

SPEAKING Hedging

7 Work in small groups. You're planning a two-week stay on a tropical desert island. There is fresh water and plenty of fruit to eat and there are trees for shade, but nothing more. Talk about what you'd need to take with you. Use the hedging expressions in the Useful expressions box.

HEDGING

I think it's reasonable to assume (that) …
It seems to me (that) …
I don't know about you but …
I'm guessing …
I'm no expert, but I (don't) think (that) …
Can I just suggest …
Personally, I feel (that) …
All I know is (that) …
I wonder if … ?
It might not be a bad idea to …
maybe / probably / might possibly

WRITING A statement of opinion

8 **21st CENTURY OUTCOMES**
Read the two short statements of opinion. Do you agree or disagree with either of them?

Writing skill Hedging expressions

9a In the first text, find:

1 two adverbs that mean *maybe* or *possibly*.
2 an adverb modified by another adverb, meaning *very likely*.
3 two phrases that mean *probably*.
4 An expression that says one thing probably makes another thing true.

9b What six hedging expressions are used in the second text?

10 Who would you take on a one-year desert island adventure? A farmer or a fisherman? Write your answer. Use hedging expressions.

11 Work in pairs. Exchange statements of opinion. Which hedging expressions has your partner used?

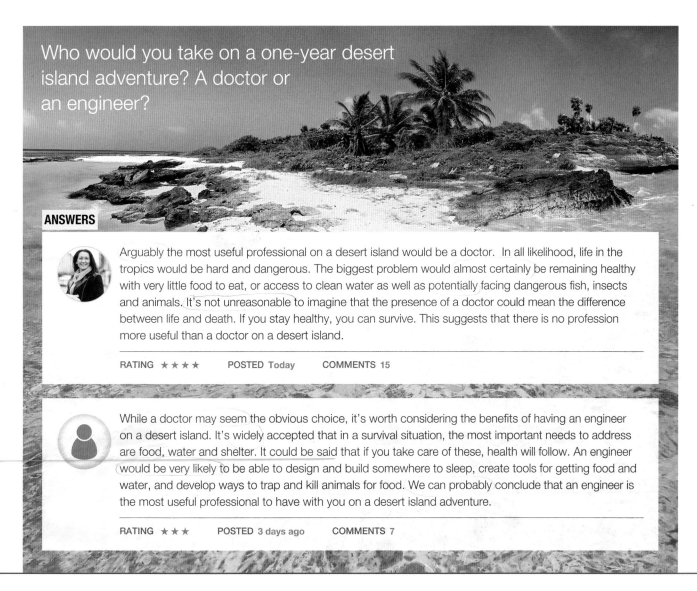

Who would you take on a one-year desert island adventure? A doctor or an engineer?

ANSWERS

Arguably the most useful professional on a desert island would be a doctor. In all likelihood, life in the tropics would be hard and dangerous. The biggest problem would almost certainly be remaining healthy with very little food to eat, or access to clean water as well as potentially facing dangerous fish, insects and animals. It's not unreasonable to imagine that the presence of a doctor could mean the difference between life and death. If you stay healthy, you can survive. This suggests that there is no profession more useful than a doctor on a desert island.

RATING ★ ★ ★ ★   POSTED Today   COMMENTS 15

While a doctor may seem the obvious choice, it's worth considering the benefits of having an engineer on a desert island. It's widely accepted that in a survival situation, the most important needs to address are food, water and shelter. It could be said that if you take care of these, health will follow. An engineer would be very likely to be able to design and build somewhere to sleep, create tools for getting food and water, and develop ways to trap and kill animals for food. We can probably conclude that an engineer is the most useful professional to have with you on a desert island adventure.

RATING ★ ★ ★   POSTED 3 days ago   COMMENTS 7

2 Image and identity

A woman in carnival
costume in Venice, Italy

TEDTALKS

HETAIN PATEL, a performance artist, and dancer **YUYU RAU** give a surprising performance that plays with identity, language and accent – and challenges us not to judge by surface appearances. Patel has used photography, sculpture, installation and performance to explore cultural identity. Yuyu Rau, who trained in ballet and contemporary and Chinese classical dance, has toured with Patel and often acts as his translator in performances. Hetain Patel and Yuyu Rau's idea worth spreading is that gender, race, and class are only a few of the factors that define a person's identity.

BACKGROUND

1 You are going to watch a TED Talk by Hetain Patel and Yuyu Rau called *Who am I? Think again.* Read the text about the speakers and the talk, then answer the questions.

  1 What do you think 'Think again' in the title means?

  2 Rau and Patel talk about accent. In your native language, what do you think people can tell about you based on your accent?

  3 For you, which is the most important to your identity:
- your language?
- your ethnicity?
- your nationality?

KEY WORDS

2 Read the sentences (1–6). The words in bold are used in the TED Talk. First guess the meaning of the words. Then match the words with their definitions (a–f).

  1 When I heard his accent, I **made the assumption** that he was from India.

  2 My grandparents **emigrated from** their native country many years ago in the 1920s.

  3 My brother **does a** very good **imitation of** Bruce Lee's way of moving.

  4 When I was a kid, I loved reading Spider-Man **comics**.

  5 Chinese is a **tonal** language, which means the rising and falling of the voice is important.

  6 I doubted the **authenticity** of his accent.

  a where meaning is related to the high or low quality of the sound

  b permanently left

  c copies

  d truth, genuineness

  e illustrated books

  f formed an opinion that something was true without proof

AUTHENTIC LISTENING SKILLS
Dealing with accents: voiced and unvoiced sounds

The sounds /b/, /d/ and /g/ are voiced in English, but in Chinese are unvoiced, so Chinese speakers often say /wʊt/ rather than /wʊd/ for *would* and /bɪk/ for *big*. For examples of changing consonant sounds in native speech, please see the Authentic listening skills on page 53.

The Chinese language doesn't use consonant clusters at the end of words. As a result, /ɑːskt/ can become /ɑːsk/ or have a vowel added /ɑːskɪd/. Knowing about the different ways of saying consonants may help you understand other people better.

3a 🎧 **9** Look at the Authentic listening skills box. Then listen to sentences 1–3 from the TED Talk. Circle /t/ or /d/ sounds at the ends of words that are silent or almost silent.

  1 Hi, I'm Hetain. I'm an artist. And this is Yuyu, who is a dancer I have been working with. I have asked her to translate for me.

  2 If I may, I would like to tell you a little bit about myself and my artwork.

  3 I'm not going to say it in English to you, because I'm trying to avoid any assumptions that might be made from my northern accent.

3b 🎧 **10** Read sentences 4 and 5. How do you think they will be spoken? Listen and check your answers.

  4 As a child, I would hate being made to wear the Indian kurta pyjama, because I didn't think it was very cool.

  5 My dad never wore it, so I didn't see why I had to.

2.1 Who am I? Think again

TEDTALKS

1 ▶ **2.1** Read the sentences. Then watch the TED Talk. Choose the correct word to complete each sentence. Then work in pairs to check your answers.

1 Patel says he doesn't speak English at first because he doesn't want people to *hear his accent / understand him*.
2 Patel *speaks / doesn't speak* Chinese fluently.
3 Patel *doesn't usually wear / usually wears* traditional Indian clothing.
4 Patel believes that copying others *is usually a bad idea / helps shape our identity*.
5 Patel grew a moustache *as an art project / to please his father*.
6 Patel's father speaks English with *an Indian / a British* accent.
7 Patel's Chinese is *incorrect / correct but a bit strange*.
8 Patel believes that we become who we are *through imitation / only when we stop imitating others*.

2 ▶ **2.1** Complete this extract from the talk with these words and phrases. Then watch the first part (0.00–3.33) of the talk again and check your answers.

this baggy trouser part	Chinese Mandarin	different tones
a dress	the embarrassment	
the Indian kurta pajama	the robes (tai butai)	

'The only problem with masking it with [1]_____ is I can only speak this paragraph, which I have learned by heart when I was visiting in China. So all I can do is keep repeating it in [2]_____ and hope you won't notice.

As a child, I would hate being made to wear [3]_____, because I didn't think it was very cool. It felt a bit girly to me, like [4]_____, and it had [5]_____ you had to tie really tight to avoid [6]_____ of them falling down. My dad never wore it, so I didn't see why I had to. Also, it makes me feel a bit uncomfortable that people assume I represent something genuinely Indian when I wear it, because that's not how I feel.

Actually, the only way I feel comfortable wearing it is by pretending they are [7]_____ of a kung fu warrior like Li Mu Bai from that film, *Crouching Tiger, Hidden Dragon*.'

▶ side parting **BR ENG**
▶ side part **N AM ENG**

▶ mum **BR ENG**
▶ mom **N AM ENG**

3 ▶ **2.1** Watch the second part (3.34–6.14) of the talk. Read the questions then watch and answer.

1 What two things is Patel's artwork concerned with?
2 What five things do people make assumptions about?
   appearance, _____ , *gender*, _____ , _____
3 When Patel imitates Hong Kong martial arts star Bruce Lee, what language does he speak?
4 What two things happened when Patel grew his hair and moustache?
5 When Patel says people yelled the Spanish words *Arriba! Arriba! Ándale! Ándale!* at him, is he suggesting that:
   a people thought he spoke Spanish?
   b he looked like people's idea of a Mexican person rather than an Indian?
   c people tried to make him feel uncomfortable?

4 ▶ **2.1** Watch the third part (6.15 to the end) of the talk. Decide if the sentences are true (T) or false (F). Correct the false ones.

1 In China, women and men have distinctly different styles of speaking.
2 Patel sounded a bit like a woman because his teacher had been a woman.
3 Patel says that when he imitates his father, he discovers who his father really was.
4 Patel says that trying to be authentic sometimes makes his art turn out in unexpected ways.
5 Patel learned his style of sitting in the video from his parents and grandparents.

5 When you were young, who were your heroes? Who did you look up to or imitate?

VOCABULARY IN CONTEXT

6 ▶ **2.2** Watch the clips from the TED Talk. Choose the correct meaning of the words.

7 Complete the sentences in your own words. Then discuss with a partner.

1 Recently, I seriously underestimated the time it would take to …
2 When I was a kid, I learned … by heart.
3 I strive for …

CRITICAL THINKING Constructing an argument

8 Which sentence best explains the main argument of Hetain Patel's TED Talk?

1 Patel doesn't want people to judge him negatively because of how he speaks or dresses.
2 Chinese women speak their language very differently from Chinese men.
3 Our identity is formed not only by who we are at birth, but also by what we do in life.

9 Read the comments* about the TED Talk. Which one best explains how Patel constructed his argument?

Viewers' comments

D Daniel – Patel makes his point very creatively. He shows us that his father was his most important influence and how his attempts to copy his heroes like Bruce Lee and Spiderman were a big waste of time.

H Helena – I love the way Patel builds up to the main point. He talks about his childhood heroes Spiderman and Bruce Lee, then tells us about imitating his father and a Chinese woman. These stories show how multiple influences shaped him, sometimes in unexpected ways.

M Malcolm – Patel starts out making the point that he never really felt at home in Britain wearing 'foreign' clothes and then tells us about a variety different people he tried to become before finally realizing that he'd basically lost his identity. Interesting!

*The comments were created for this activity.

PRESENTATION SKILLS Using humour

TIPS

Humour can be an extremely powerful tool for presenters. Humour can:
• grab and hold the audience's attention.
• help you and your audience relax.
• make your audience more receptive to your ideas.
• help your audience remember your ideas.
• leave everyone feeling better.

10 ▶ **2.3** Look at the Presentation tips box. Then watch how Patel and Rau use humour. Match each clip (1–4) with a description (a–d).

a Patel and Rau do something visual and physical.
b Patel pretends to have an accent other than his own.
c Patel impersonates (pretends to be) a famous person.
d We hear something surprising and unexpected.

11 Work in pairs. You are going to give a two-minute mini-presentation with a partner about image and identity. Choose one of the topics below or think of your own idea. Make some brief notes on the topic and think of an unexpected or highly visual way you could you present it.

• A study has found that tall people tend to earn on average 10% more money than short people.
• Research has found that school uniforms improve attendance and academic performance.
• Psychologists have discovered that people with certain accents are judged to be more intelligent than speakers with other accents.

12 Work with another pair. Take turns to give your presentation. Remember the advice from the Presentation tips box. Did you come up with similar ideas?

▶ pyjamas **BR ENG**
▶ pajamas **N AM ENG**

▶ moustache **BR ENG**
▶ mustache **N AM ENG**

2.2 Cyber crime

IDENTITY THEFT

A WHAT ARE THE MOST COMMON TYPES OF IDENTITY THEFT?

Type	Percentage
Goverment Documents / Benefits Fraud	27%
Credit Card Fraud	14%
Phone or Utilities Fraud	13%
Employment Fraud	9%
Bank Fraud	8%
Loan Fraud	3%
Other	26%

B HOW OLD ARE THE VICTIMS OF IDENTITY THEFT?

Age	Percentage
9 and under	8%
20–29	23%
30–39	21%
40–49	18%
50–59	15%
60–69	9%
70 and over	6%

C WHAT PERCENTAGE OF PEOPLE IN EACH AGE GROUP HAVE THEIR MOBILE PHONES STOLEN (OR LOSE THEM)?

Age	Percentage
18–24	45%
25–34	37%
35–44	30%
45–54	30%
55–64	26%
65 and over	20%

GRAMMAR Amounts and comparisons

1 Do you know identity theft is? Have you known or heard of someone who was a victim of it? What happened?

2 Look at bar graph A. Answer the questions.

1 What are the most and least common types of identity theft?

2 Which type of identity theft do you think involves getting electricity services for your home in someone else's name?

3 Which type of fraud involves pretending to be someone else for the purpose of getting a job?

3 Read the text in the Grammar box on page 23. Answer the questions (1–5) about the expressions in bold in the text.

AMOUNTS AND COMPARISONS

A little over a quarter of identity crime – twenty seven per cent – involves government documents or benefits. This is fraud where someone pretends to be someone else in order to illegally receive money such as healthcare payments or a pension from the government. **About half as many** cases – fourteen per cent – are credit card fraud. In these instances, the identify thief usually uses stolen documents to obtain a credit card in someone else's name. The theft is usually caught when the first bill arrives, but the money is already spent and, usually, the thief simply disappears. Phone or utilities fraud occurs at **about the same** rate **as** credit card fraud – thirteen per cent. Employment fraud accounts for about nine per cent of identity theft. The rate is **similar** for bank fraud. **A small minority of** instances involve loan fraud – taking a bank loan in another person's name and then vanishing. Finally, **a sizeable portion of** ID thefts – 26 per cent – are in the 'other' category. This includes social media identity theft, sending email from another person's address, and pretending to be someone else on the phone.

1 Which two quantifiers in bold are used with fractions and percentages?
2 Which expression refers to an especially large amount and which to an especially small amount?
3 Which two expressions are used when there is very little difference between two amounts?
4 Are a *minority of, half of,* and *a sizeable portion of* used with singular or plural verbs?

Check your answers on page 142 and do Exercises 1–5.

4 Choose the correct options to complete each sentence.

1 There was twice as *much / many* credit card fraud this year as last year.
2 These figures are about the same *than / as* last week's.
3 We had half the *portion / number* of stolen credit cards in 2015 as in 2014.
4 Only a *handful / vast majority* of the stolen passports were recovered – less than five per cent.
5 Virtually *half / none* of the police officers had any special training in dealing with fraud.
6 A great *per cent / deal of* our work is done behind the scenes.

5 Look at bar graph B. Complete the sentences with the age group.

1 Only a small minority of identity theft victims are _70 and over_ .
2 Nearly a quarter of identity theft victims are _20 – 29%_ .
3 Exactly twice as many identity theft victims are _40 – 49_ -year-olds as _60 – 69_ -year-olds.

4 The figure for those _9 and under_ is similar to that of 60–69-year-olds.
5 At fifteen per cent, a relatively small portion of identity theft victims are _50 – 59_ -year-olds.

6 Look at bar graph C. Complete the sentences explaining the data using these expressions.

Nearly half	Nearly twice the number
About a quarter	The vast majority
The number	

1 _The vast majority_ of those 65 and over haven't experienced phone loss or theft.
2 _Nearly twice_ of 25–34-year-olds compared with over 65s have had a lost or stolen phone.
3 _The number_ of 35–44-year-olds who've lost a phone or had one stolen is the same as the number of 45–54-year-olds.
4 _Nearly half_ of all 18–24-year-olds have lost a phone or had one stolen.
5 _About a quar_ of 55–64-year-olds have had a lost or stolen phone.

Pronunciation Weak *of*

7a 🎧 **11** Listen and note how *of* is pronounced in these phrases.

1 About half of our employees have a company credit card.
2 The vast majority of criminal behaviour isn't detected.
3 A small portion of missing cards turn out to be lost, not stolen.
4 This month, we had three times the number of ID theft cases as last month.
5 A considerable amount of money is stolen every day.

7b Work in pairs. Practise saying the sentences with the weak form of *of*.

SPEAKING Evaluating data

8 **21st CENTURY OUTCOMES**

Work in pairs. Discuss the questions.

1 Why do you think 18–25-year-olds have the highest number of lost phones and over 65s the lowest?
2 If you ran a campaign promoting responsible mobile phone use, how would you do it? Who would you aim it at?

9 Work in groups. Research your classmates' attitudes about identity theft.

- Think of five questions about attitudes.
  How worried are you about using your credit card online? – Very worried? – Only a little worried? – Not worried
  How likely do you think it is that you'll be the victim of bank fraud? – Very likely? – A little likely? – Not at all likely?
- Circulate around the room asking and answering questions.
- Rejoin your group and analyse the results.
- Present your findings to the class.

2.3 You are what you wear

READING Image, identity and clothing

1 Work in pairs. Before you read the article look at the photos. Discuss these questions.

   1 Which person do you think probably has more money? What makes you think that?

   2 Which person do you think is younger? Why?

   3 Which person do you think is the most likely to get good service in an expensive department store? Why?

2 Read the article. Does the article agree with your answers to Exercise 1? Then match each heading (a–c) with a section (1–3).

   a You are what you wear

   b Dangerous prejudices

   c Reverse psychology

3 Answer the questions.

   1 Which section of the article do the photographs illustrate?

   2 Do the first two experiments in the article contradict one another? Why? / Why not?

   3 What message did the business suit send in the second experiment? What about the old, scruffy clothes?

   4 What does the third experiment imply about people's view of themselves, painters and doctors?

4 Which of the following statements could be supported by the experiment results described in the text? Underline the specific parts of the text that either provide the support or contradict each statement.

   1 There is some disagreement about the message sent by wearing certain types of clothing.

   2 In most situations, people simply don't pay attention to what other people are wearing.

   3 The clothing people wear is probably not a reliable way of judging them.

   4 Someone will almost always come to the aid of a person who is obviously in need.

   5 Clothing is interesting, but ultimately not of huge importance in society.

   6 It seems likely that if a person wants to feel better about him or herself, choosing some nice-looking clothes could be a good starting point.

5 Work in small groups. Discuss the questions.

   1 How do you usually dress for work? What sort of clothing do office workers in your country usually wear?

   2 What do you think Mark Zuckerburg's casual dress says about him?

   3 Do you think the experiment described in paragraph 1 would have the same result in the place where you live?

   4 What about the experiment described in paragraph 2?

   5 Can you think of other ways of dressing that might have similar results to the experiments described in paragraph 3? For example, what might happen if someone put on a soldier's uniform?

   6 What do all three experiments say about the power of personal appearance?

VOCABULARY Describing dress

6 Choose the best options to complete the sentences.

   1 His outfit – a T-shirt and jeans – was *inappropriate / clashing*, considering it was his brother's wedding.

   2 The media praised the *tasteful / unconventional* dress she wore for the film opening, describing it as 'classic'.

   3 The designer was known for wearing *trendy / imaginative* clothes – jeans cut up and re-made as dresses, for example.

   4 His business suits were *well cut / glamorous*, and always fit extremely well.

   5 I would describe his sense of dress as *scruffy / eccentric*, because he would often wear a heavy fur coat in hot weather, and sandals when it was snowing.

7 Put the words from Exercise 6 in the correct list.

   1 generally negative: *clashing*

   2 basically neutral: _____

   3 generally positive: _____

8 Work in pairs. Describe the clothes worn by someone you know or a well-known person. Use the adjectives from Exercise 6.

SPEAKING Talking about image

9 **21st CENTURY OUTCOMES**

Work in small groups. Discuss these questions.

   1 Why do you think the appropriateness of clothing is so important to people?

   2 In some work situations, a business suit would make the wearer seem responsible and serious. In what situations could a business suit send a different message?

   3 Do you think the world would be a better place if people weren't so concerned about clothing, or is it important for us to have clear rules about what's appropriate and what's not? Explain your answer.

IMAGE, IDENTITY AND CLOTHING
Science reveals the power of personal appearance

1 Facebook founder Mark Zuckerberg was once a hoodie-jeans-and-trainers-wearing university student with a good idea for a social network. Now he's a billionaire businessman – who wears a hoodie, jeans and trainers to work, including to important meetings. Not everyone approves. When he wore casual clothes to meet with Wall Street investors, some critics claimed that it showed he was uncommitted and immature.

Harvard Business School researcher Francesca Gino has a different idea. She says that while most people seem to think that dressing differently from those around you generally has a negative effect, her belief is that it can actually have a very positive effect. And she's done experiments to prove it. When her researchers, wearing sportswear, visited speciality shops selling luxury brands in Milan, they found that shop assistants usually assumed they were wealthier and more important than those who visited the shops 'properly' dressed in furs and designer clothes.

Reporter Randi Newton of the *New York Observer* newspaper ran her own version of the experiment at one of New York's major department stores. When she visited the store dressed in hiking books, track suit bottoms, a T-shirt, casual jacket and woolly hat – with messy hair underneath – one assistant asked her if she was an actress and showed her the most expensive cosmetics. She repeated the experiment with her hair carefully styled, wearing glamorous clothes and even carried a small dog – and was largely ignored. According to the Harvard Business School research, if the relatively strange style of dress looks as though it's intentional, or trendy, many people will believe you're wealthy or important.

2 But is it always the case that people judge less formal clothing more positively? Is the effect on others of the clothing we wear the same everywhere we go?

Researchers in France used a similar approach to Gino's and Newton's, but rather than testing the perceptions of assistants in high-end boutiques, they took their research out into the street, to the general public. The video they made of the experiment shows an actor dressed in a smart, well-cut suit with a tasteful tie and polished shoes walking along the road. He begins to cough, stops and bends over to catch his breath, then falls down. Before he even calls for help, people rush to his aid.

In a second video, the actor comes back to the same crowded location and repeats the actions in exactly the same way. But this time, not one person comes to help him, even when he repeatedly calls out for help. The difference? In the second version of the experiment, he's wearing scruffy clothes and old trainers and looks like a poor or homeless person. In a situation such as this, the clothes you're wearing could mean the difference between life and death.

3 It seems that our clothing doesn't only alter the way others view us, but also the way we see ourselves – and apparently it affects our intelligence as well. Researchers at the Kellogg School of Management at Northwestern University in the USA did some simple experiments with students.

One experiment tested subjects' ability to pay attention to details. One group wore their usual, everyday clothes while a second group wore a white lab coat. A second experiment tested the group's ability to concentrate for several minutes in a task that involved spotting minor differences between two very similar images. For this one, there were three groups: one wearing their normal clothes, one wearing a white coat that had been described to them as a painter's coat, and the third wearing a white coat they were told was a doctor's coat. Amazingly, the test subjects wearing the so-called doctor's coat performed better in both tests. The researchers believe that the test subjects' 'basic abilities' were improved as a direct result of the clothing they wore.

What the experiment didn't show was whether there were any longer-term effects. If people always wore a doctor's coat, would they be permanently more intelligent? More experiments are needed before we decide to make the white coat the fashion accessory of choice.

2.4 I need to work on my image

Do   **Don't**   **Do**   **Don't**

LISTENING Preparing for a job interview

1 Imagine a friend has asked you for advice about what to wear for a job interview. How would you respond?

2 🎧 **12** Listen to two friends talking about job interviews. Choose the best words to complete each sentence.

  1 The man says he stands out more *on his CV / face-to-face*.
  2 At a recent interview, he didn't fit in because his clothes were *inappropriate / unconventional*.
  3 The woman says office dress rules are usually *unspoken / unimportant*.
  4 She suggests that he asks interviewers for *advice / feedback*.
  5 She thinks the man should *get training and practice / apply for a job at the library*.
  6 She urges the man not to feel *angry / discouraged*.

3 🎧 **12** Listen again. Match the two parts of the sentences.

  1 Have you considered asking about
  2 I would seriously consider asking about
  3 You might want to pay for
  4 If you don't want to spend the money on a coach, why not try
  5 You mustn't
  6 Remember, it's all

  a how people usually dress.
  b getting a book?
  c the 'unspoken dress code'?
  d an interview coach, too.
  e practice for the one that finally works out!
  f lose heart.

Pronunciation Sounding encouraging

4a 🎧 **13** Listen to three versions of the same sentence. In each case, does it have a rising (↑), a falling (↓) or a flat (–) intonation? Then underline the words, if any, that are stressed.

  1 You might want to try doing some practice interviews. *Flat*
  2 You might want to try doing some practice interviews. *Rising*
  3 You might want to try doing some practice interviews. *Falling*

4b 🎧 **13** Listen again. Which one sounds:

  a uncertain?
  b bored?
  c encouraging?

4c 🎧 **14** Listen to five pieces of advice. Which version of each sentence (A or B) sounds more encouraging? Why?

4d 🎧 **14** Listen again and repeat the sentences, trying to sound encouraging.

SPEAKING Making suggestions

5 **21st** **CENTURY OUTCOMES**

Work in pairs. Read this request for advice from Nadia on a chat forum and brainstorm suggestions that you could make to her. Take notes. Think about:

- different approaches she could take to her job search.
- ways she could become more specialized.
- ways she could develop her skills and abilities.
- types of employer that might need her skills.
- possible courses of study that might make her more marketable.

I graduated from Warsaw University in Poland nine months ago with a good degree in English language studies. I had expected to find that my language abilities (I'm virtually bilingual – Polish and English) would open many job possibilities. I would be happy to move almost anywhere and try any type of work, but it appears that my ability in English just isn't enough to make me interesting to any employers. I've filled in dozens of online applications and sent nearly a hundred letters and emails, but I can't even get an interview. I'm very open to suggestions and would even consider returning to my studies if I thought it would help.

NADIA   Join Date: 2015   Posts: 5   QUOTE

6 Roleplay a conversation between Nadia and a friend. Use your notes from Exercise 5 and the expressions in the Useful expressions box.

Begin: *How's the job search going?*

MAKING SUGGESTIONS

Questions

Have you considered / thought about / tried (+ noun or gerund)?
If … , why not try (+ gerund or infinitive)?

Statements with modals

You might want to (+ infinitive without *to*)
(Noun *or* gerund +) might be a good idea.
I would seriously consider (+ gerund)
You mustn't (+ infinitive without *to*)

Imperatives

Keep trying. / Don't give up. / Don't lose heart.

Signalling expressions

One other thing to consider:
Remember, …

WRITING Giving feedback

7 Read the letter. What's its main purpose?

Dear Mr Johnson,

Thank you for your interest in BCC Technology Group, Ltd. We appreciate the time you took to apply for the job and attend the interview.

We were impressed with your skills and qualifications, in particular the work experience you undertook in your final year of university. However, we're looking for a candidate who has a somewhat higher level of Spanish ability – CEF C1, at a minimum. Additionally, we're looking for someone who exhibits a real passion for sales.

We will keep your application on file for six months and contact you if another suitable role within the company opens up. Please feel free to apply for any other job openings at BCC that you see advertised.

I wish you well with your continuing job search.

Yours sincerely,

Inge Krum

Writing skill Being diplomatic

8a Answer the questions.

1 What two things does the letter do before getting to the main purpose?
2 What two reasons are given for rejecting Mr Johnson?
3 How does Ms. Krum diplomatically explain what she's looking for that Mr Johnson hasn't got?
4 What other things does she mention to make the letter positive and supportive?

8b Rewrite these negative remarks diplomatically.

1 Your restaurant is too small for our meeting.
2 Your hotel is too far away from the town centre.
3 We didn't expect the rooms to be so expensive.
4 The sound system is very old fashioned.
5 There isn't a wide enough selection of food on your menu.

9 You have been trying to find a venue for a large family gathering. Write an email to the hotel you visited explaining why you don't want to use their hotel. Use the notes below and remember to:

- say thank you.
- say something positive.
- deliver the rejection diplomatically.
- end on a positive note.

– great location

– very friendly staff

– the view from the 'party patio' is awful – a busy city street

– the indoor party area is very open and not at all private

– possible location for a future business meeting?

READING

1 Read the article about The Real Junk Food Project and answer the questions.

1 What does 'junk food' mean in the context of the Real Junk Food Project?

2 What two social problems does the Real Junk Food Project address?

3 What happened when government officials inspected the Real Junk Food Project?

4 What evidence does Adam Smith offer for the safety of the food he prepares?

5 Based on what you've read in the article, what do you think the motto 'No chuckin' our chicken' means? (Hint: You may want to look up the verb *chuck*.)

GRAMMAR

2 Choose the correct options to complete the news article.

New Bristol café serves food found in bins

A café serving food taken from supermarket rubbish bins ¹ *opened / has opened* in Bristol, as part of the growing Real Junk Food Project. The organization ² *worked / has been working* to reduce food waste, fight hunger, and strengthen communities. Before starting the project, founder Adam Smith ³ *lived / has lived* in Australia, working on farms. He ⁴ *hadn't / hasn't* thought much about food waste previously, but during that time, he ⁵ *has become / became* obsessed with it and began thinking about practical solutions. Upon returning to the UK, he started the Real Junk Food Project, which ⁶ *was / will have been* running for a year next month.

THE **Real Junk Food PROJECT**

The Real Junk Food Project is showing the world how to radically re-think food and food waste. The café in Leeds, in the north of England, where the movement started, has fed more than 10,000 people using 20,000 kilograms of food that had either been, or was going to be, thrown away. The pricing model for the establishment is PAYF – 'pay as you feel' – which means customers hand over the amount of money that they think the meal was worth, or what they can afford. The idea behind the project is two-fold; first, to reduce food waste, and second, to feed people who can't afford to feed themselves.

By law, UK food retailers aren't allowed to sell food that is past the 'best before' date stamped on the packaging. As a result, supermarkets, independent grocery stores and even food banks discard food that is perfectly edible, because they want to play it safe, and avoid accidently selling food that has passed its 'sell-by' date. Real Junk Food Project founder and chef Adam Smith would like to see the law changed, but in the meantime, the café takes food donations from restaurants that have surplus, and from supermarkets that are discarding food. Many food retailers are happy to give this food to the café rather than throw it away. But in an interview with the UK's *The Independent* newspaper, Smith described how they

regularly take food from supermarket bins if they have to. He said, 'We watch them throw it away, then we go and take it back out again ten minutes later. Over 90 per cent of the goods are perfectly fine.'

The Independent asked Smith if he was concerned that The Real Junk Food Project might itself be prosecuted, but he said that the authorities know what Real Junk Food are doing and have passed the café as safe. 'Environmental Health came to inspect us,' Smith said, 'and gave us three out of five stars.' That translates as 'generally satisfactory'. And while still hoping the law will change, the café has a perfect record. Smith says, 'We have fed 10,000 with this food and not one has got ill.'

With both hunger and food-waste levels unacceptably high in the developed world, the idea has spread quickly, with nearly 50 new PAYF cafés opening in the UK alone, and others, inspired by Real Junk Food, starting up in the USA, Brazil, Poland and Switzerland.

At least one restaurant chain that has donated food is positively proud to be involved. Nando's restaurant gives as much as 150 kg of frozen chicken per week and promotes itself with the motto 'No chuckin' our chicken.'

3 Complete the text with these words.

> half   deal   majority   much   per cent   twice

About ¹ _half_ of the food produced in the world is thrown away, according to a recent report. The report, entitled 'Global Food: Waste Not, Want Not' says that thirty to fifty ² _per cent_ of the four billion tonnes of food produced around the world globally never reaches the table. In some countries, a great ³ _deal_ of edible produce is discarded simply because it doesn't look perfect. There is also a worrying level of waste associated with water, according to the report. By 2050, the demand for fresh water is likely to increase to more than ⁴ _twice_ as ⁵ _much_ as today. The solution, according to the report, lies in improving agriculture, storage and infrastructure, and in convincing the vast ⁶ _majority_ of consumers to stop demanding cosmetically perfect food.

VOCABULARY

4 Complete the words with *over* or *under*.

1 Experts say that industrial agriculture _over_ uses chemicals and that their use should be reduced.
2 Large-scale farming _under_ values diversity, favouring huge areas of single crops.
3 During the 20th century, the benefits of small-scale farming were _under_ rated, though people are now beginning to appreciate them again.
4 As the world's biggest cities become more and more _over_ crowded, the food supply infrastructure will come under more strain.
5 Until recently, the importance of small, diverse farms has been _under_ estimated, but some experts now think they may help solve the world's future food problems.
6 Many consumers consider food to be _____ priced, but when you consider the resources required to grow and transport food, it's amazing it doesn't cost a lot more.

5 Complete the text with the correct options.

Jillian Owens: Refashionista

Jillian Owens is loved for the ¹ *imaginative / appropriate* clothing she designs, but you won't find her name on any labels. No two of Jillian's ² *clashing / eccentric* designs are alike because they all begin with an unexpected raw material: old clothes that other people have given away. She calls herself a 'refashionista' because she turns second-hand, discarded, sometimes ³ *refined / scruffy* clothing into ⁴ *tasteful / conventional* outfits, often by cutting garments up and sewing them back together again to create a totally new style. Because of the unusual way in which the clothes are produced, the result is usually ⁵ *tasteful / unconventional* but that doesn't mean her creations are strange or unattractive. In fact, her 'refashions' are generally seen as very ⁶ *formal / trendy* – and in some cases, positively ⁷ *glamorous / casual*.

DISCUSSION

6 Work in pairs. Discuss these questions.

1 Can you think of other ways in which things that people no longer need are reused rather than thrown away?
2 Would you be willing to eat in a Real Junk Food Project restaurant? Why? / Why not?
3 Would you consider wearing one of Jillian Owens's designs? Why? / Why not?

SPEAKING

7 Mr Khan is due at Ada and Dan's catering company, where he is going to present his proposal for a management training day. Rewrite Dan's words as hedges or suggestions using the words in brackets.

Ada: It's nine o'clock, so we're supposed to start the meeting.
Dan: The traffic's terrible today. Mr Khan is going to be late.
(think / reasonable / assume)
¹ *I think it's reasonable to assume* Mr Khan is going to be late.
Ada: How long should we wait for him? We've got an awful lot to do.
Dan: We can't start without him.
(seems / me)
² _____ without him.
Ada: I guess you're right.
Dan: Phone him.
(you / tried phoning)
³ _____ him?
Ada: No, but that's a good idea. Has anyone got his mobile number?
Dan: Ask Stef for it.
(might want)
⁴ _____ Stef for it.
Ada: Good thinking.
Dan: You should check with reception first.
(might not / bad idea)
⁵ _____ with reception first.
Ada: You're right. He may already be in the building.
Dan: Reschedule the meeting if he isn't here if five minutes.
(I / just suggest)
⁶ _____ if he isn't here in five minutes?
Ah, here he is now!

8 Act out the conversation with your partner.

3 Harmony

The Voca People, international vocal theatre group, combine a capella singing with the art of beat box

TEDTALKS

MAY EL-KHALIL was a marathon* runner and local sports official in Beirut, Lebanon. In 2003, she was inspired to found the Beirut Marathon after she nearly died in a running accident. Beirut had been the scene of a long-running civil war in Lebanon. Over the past decade, the Beirut Marathon has become not only the largest running event in the Middle East but also a powerful force for peace. May El-Khalil's idea worth spreading is that political turmoil can be overcome if opponents can put aside their differences for a day and join together to complete something challenging and rewarding – like a marathon.

marathon (n) a 42-kilometre running race

BACKGROUND

1 You are going to watch a TED Talk by May El-Khalil called *Making peace is a marathon.* Read the text about the speaker and the talk, then work in pairs and answer the questions.

   1 Why do you think people in a war-torn country would be interested in a sporting event?

   2 What skills and qualities do you think are necessary to prepare for and run a marathon?

   3 Do you know other stories of people who created something good out of something that seemed very bad?

KEY WORDS

2 Read the sentences (1–6). The words in bold are used in the TED Talk. First guess the meaning of the words. Then match the words with their definitions (a–f).

   1 The country was torn apart by a **civil war** that lasted six years.

   2 The leaders of the opposing parties are **civil** when they meet.

   3 Something happened one **fateful** day that changed everything for me.

   4 The country is **unstable** and likely to fall into chaos.

   5 The peace agreement is new and still **vulnerable to** being destroyed.

   6 Doing good is **contagious** because when people see the result, they want to join in.

   a life-changing

   b easily spread to other people

   c conflict between different groups of people from the same country

   d weak and easily hurt by

   e likely to change suddenly

   f polite in a formal way

AUTHENTIC LISTENING SKILLS
Discourse markers

> Discourse markers are words and expressions such as *anyway, right, as I say, to begin with* that show the connections between ideas and to engage listeners. Others, such as *frankly, as a matter of fact*, and *by the way* show a speaker's attitude. Recognising discourse markers will help you understand how ideas are connected.

3a 🎧 **15** Look at the Authentic listening skills box. Then listen to extracts 1–3 from the TED Talk. Underline one discourse marker in each extract. Check your answers. Then match your underlined words with functions a–c.

   1 You know, Lebanon as a country has been once destroyed by a long and bloody civil war.

   2 Honestly, I don't know why they call it civil war when there is nothing civil about it.

   3 For years, the country has been divided between politics and religion. However, for one day a year, we truly stand united, and that's when the marathon takes place.

   a showing contrasting ideas

   b engaging the listener by identifying shared knowledge

   c showing the strength of the speaker's feeling

3b 🎧 **16** Read sentence 4. What are the missing discourse markers? Listen and check.

   4 The marathon grew. _____ did our political problems. _____ for every disaster we had, the marathon found ways to bring people together.

3.1 Making peace is a marathon

TEDTALKS

1 ▶ **3.1** Watch the TED Talk. Number the sections of the talk in order. Then check your answers with a partner.

2 **a** El-Khalil is struck by personal tragedy

1 **b** Lebanon, a country ripped apart by war

5 **c** Peace is possible and other lessons from the Beirut Marathon.

3 **d** El-Khalil comes up with the idea of the Beirut marathon.

6 **e** Hope for the future

4 **f** The dream becomes a reality

2 ▶ **3.1** Find and correct five errors in the summary of the first part of the talk. Then watch the first part (0.00–3.43) of the talk again and check your answers.

The idea of starting a marathon came to May El-Khalil while she was recovering from a terrible rail crash. As a result, she spent two years in hospital and had six surgical operations. During this difficult time, she needed an objective to look forward to, and wanted to give something back to her doctors. After she got out of hospital, she visited and spoke with lots of people in different parts of the city. They shared their stories and together they built trust. They all agreed that together, they would show the politicians that Lebanon wanted to live in peace and harmony.

▶ I stayed in **the** hospital. **N AM ENG**
▶ I stayed in hospital. **BR ENG**

▶ center **N AM ENG**
▶ centre **BR ENG**

3 ▶ **3.1** Watch the second part (4.44–7.24) of the talk again. Answer the questions.

1 What year was the first Beirut Marathon held?
2 What national tragedy occurred in 2005?
3 How was the 2005 Marathon a turning point?
4 Between 2006 and 2009, what three things did Lebanon lose?
5 In those same years, what did the country *not* lose?
6 How many countries were represented in the 2012 Marathon?

4 ▶ **3.1** Watch the third part (7.25 to the end) of the talk again. Are these sentences true (T) or false (F)?

1 As the BMA has grown larger, the organizers have included more professional runners and not allowed as many inexperienced runners to join in.
2 More than four thousand runners joined a separate race, just for women.
3 The BMA has helped raise money to promote peace and cooperation in Lebanon.
4 Neighbouring countries such as Iraq and Syria have said they think the event should be stopped.
5 El-Khalil's main message is that realistically, peace is probably an impossible goal.

5 Do you think sport always encourages harmony?

VOCABULARY IN CONTEXT

6 ▶ **3.2** Watch the clips from the TED Talk. Choose the correct meaning of the words.

7 Work in pairs. Discuss the questions.

1 When in your life have you started something from scratch, for example learning a new skill or making something?
2 What stereotypes exist about teenagers? About mothers-in-law? About politicians?
3 What kind of event or activity would allow your country to show its true colours?

CRITICAL THINKING Distinguishing between fact and opinion

8 When you hear about someone's life and achievements, it's important to distinguish between facts and opinions. Are the following sentences fact (F) or opinion (O)? Give reasons.

1 May El-Khalil is a successful sporting event organizer. F
2 Lebanon has a long history of conflict. F
3 Sporting events are the most effective solution to civil conflict. O
4 Running a marathon is one of the best ways to learn about yourself. O
5 Runners from all over the world participate in the race. F
6 Runners in some countries dislike the idea of the Beirut Marathon. F

9 Read the comments* about the TED Talk. Decide if they are fact (F) or opinion (O).

Viewers' comments
I **Ismail** – El-Khalil is the best TED speaker ever. ○
Y **Yuka** – I agree, Ismail. I believe that running can truly bring peace to the world. ○
J **Joey** – I like the talk, too. But it doesn't go into detail about the causes of Lebanon's civil war.
L **Liz** – But is that necessary? The talk explains the history of the Beirut Marathon.

*These comments were created for this activity.

10 Write two additional facts and two opinions about the talk, May El-Khalil, or the Beirut Marathon.

PRESENTATION SKILLS Being personal and relatable

Be personal and relatable so that people identify with you and your ideas.
• Include relevant stories about yourself or people you know.
• Give examples that show the idea in action.
• Make sure the talk isn't too abstract.

11 ▶ **3.3** Look at the Presentation tips box. Then watch how El-Khalil includes her personal stories in the TED Talk. Answer the questions.

1 Watch the clips from the talk. What effect do El-Khalil's personal stories have on you? How do they make you feel?
2 Why do you think El-Khalil chooses to tell her personal stories rather than just explaining the history and benefits of the marathon?
3 El-Khalil talks about the importance of 'walking the talk'. What examples in her personal stories can you find of this?

12 Prepare a presentation on one of these topics. What stories could you tell from your own experience? Think about breakthroughs, difficult times, and misunderstandings, etc. Be personal and relatable!

• learning English or some other skill
• preparing and participating in a performance or competition
• your own idea

13 Work in pairs. Take turns to give your presentation. Use the ideas from the Presentation tips box. Was your partner's talk personal and relatable?

▶ moms **N AM ENG**
▶ mums **BR ENG**

▶ colors **N AM ENG**
▶ colours **BR ENG**

TWO'S COMPANY

Tech blogger Chan Chaiyochlarb looked at 22 successful, big-name companies such as Microsoft, Apple and eBay and counted the **number of founders** each company had.

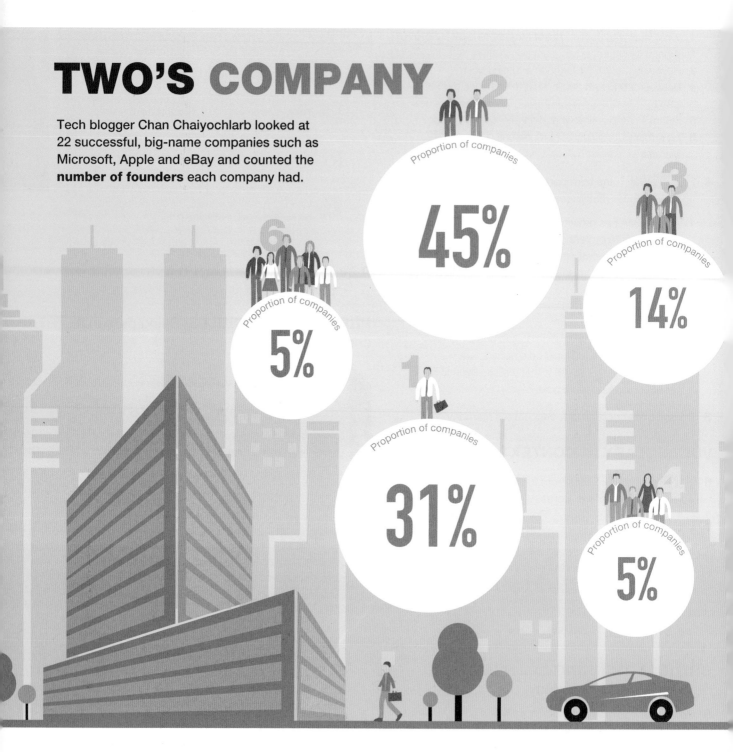

Proportion of companies

45%

Proportion of companies

14%

Proportion of companies

5%

Proportion of companies

31%

Proportion of companies

5%

GRAMMAR Cleft sentences

1 Work in pairs. Imagine you're starting your own company. Discuss the questions.

1 What would be the advantages and disadvantages of working alone?

2 What would be the advantages and disadvantages of working with one or two partners? What about with three, four or six partners?

3 What do you think are the most common reasons that start-ups (newly established businesses) fail?

2 Look at the infographic. Answer the questions.

1 How many founders did the greatest number of successful companies have?

2 What number of founders was the least common?

3 What percentage of successful companies had just one founder?

3 Read the text in the Grammar box. Answer the questions (1 and 2).

CLEFT SENTENCES

According to business blogger Jeremie Berrebi, the biggest problem that start-ups face isn't a bad product or a lack of money, but rather arguments between co-founders. And <u>**it's** often the small disagreements that can grow into the biggest problems</u>. Co-founders allow minor disagreements to turn into big conflicts because of poor communication. Berrebi recommends co-founders take the time early in the life of the company to sign a founders' agreement that sets out exactly how the company should be run, how profits will be divided, and how founders can leave – or be removed from – the organization. This isn't just a key issue for start-ups. <u>**What** makes established companies successful is their day-to-day conflict management</u>. Not surprisingly then, having only one co-founder to resolve issues with appears to make this easier.

1 Which information is emphasized by the way the underlined sentences are constructed?

2 Rewrite the two underlined sentences in a simpler way, without using the word in bold.

Check your answers on page 144 and do Exercises 1–6.

4 Rewrite the sentences as cleft sentences.

This graph tells us that sales are increasing. (*Wh-*)
What this graph tells us is that sales are increasing.

1 Start-up founders need good communication skills. (*It*)

It is good communication skills what start-up founders need.

2 Poor communication causes problems. (*Wh-*)

What causes problems is poor communication.

3 Co-founders need to have a clear legal agreement. (*The thing that*)

The thing that cofounders need to have, it's a clear agreement.

4 Personal conflict causes businesses to fail. (*It*)

It's personal conflict what causes business to fail

5 It's important to find a solution when communication breaks down. (*Wh-*)

what is important to find when communication breaks down it's find a solution.

6 You need to be honest with your business partner. (*The person*)

The person you need to be honest with, it's your business partner.

Pronunciation Sentence stress in cleft sentences

5a 🎧 **17** Listen and check your answers to Exercise 4. Underline the information that is stressed.

5b Practise saying the sentences with natural stress.

6 Work in pairs. Take turns turning these sentences into cleft sentences.

On the whole I love Sao Paolo, but I can't stand the traffic.

I love Sao Paolo but what I can't stand is the traffic.

1 My older brother has helped me a lot.
2 Dave really wants to try surfing.
3 I need a long holiday.
4 When people drive too fast, it really annoys me.
5 I have trouble waking up early for work.
6 People need to learn to relax!

7 Write about yourself using cleft sentences. Share with a partner.

- Something you really enjoy

  What I really enjoy is playing the guitar.

- A person you admire
- Somewhere you feel comfortable and relaxed
- Something you have to do that you don't really enjoy
- Something you'd like to do in the near future

SPEAKING Evaluating teamwork

8 **21st CENTURY OUTCOMES**

Read the statements about teamwork. Which ones describe teamwork positively? Which ones describe it negatively? Can any of them be either positive or negative?

Teamwork is two or more people doing something that one person could have done better alone. — anonymous

Eagles fly alone. Sheep flock together. — Polish proverb

None of us is as smart as all of us. — Ken Blanchard

Alone we can do so little, together we can do so much. — Helen Keller

There's no 'I' in teamwork. — anonymous

Teamwork is having plenty of other people to take the blame for your mistakes. — anonymous

9 Think of an example of a genius working alone who came up with a great idea. What might have been the result if that person had been forced to work in a team?

10 Think of an example of something that was accomplished only by team effort. What would have been the result if the team hadn't worked together towards the goal?

3.3 Dare to be different

READING How groupthink closed the 'flying bank'

1 Work in pairs. Discuss the questions.

1 Conformity is the act of behaving in a way that is generally acceptable in society. How many ways can you name in which people generally conform?
2 In what different ways are non-conformists usually viewed by society?
3 Do you think conformity is a good thing or a bad thing? Why?

2 Read the article. Then answer the questions.

1 Read the introductory paragraph. What are the pros and cons of conformity?
2 Read 'The Symptoms'. How can groups suffering from groupthink be identified?
3 Read 'Groupthink Case Study: Swissair'. What happened in the case study? What does this show?
4 Read 'Know the Difference'. What do groups need to do to avoid disaster?

3 Certain phrases are used to point to key information. Find the following phrases in the article and then paraphrase the key information they refer to.

1 The fact is … (line 12)
2 There are three main … (line 20)
3 at the heart of … (line 57)
4 The key … (line 70)

VOCABULARY Conformity and non-conformity

4 For each expression in bold, write C (conformity) or N (non-conformity).

N 1 Paul doesn't mind **swimming against the tide** when he believes in an idea.
C 2 It's important to hire people who **fit in** with the team.
N 3 I didn't raise my concerns in the meeting because I didn't want to **rock the boat.**
C 4 I think when you're new to a team, the best approach is to **go with the flow.**
C 5 When I was at secondary school, all I wanted to do was to **blend in.** → be part of
N 6 You shouldn't be afraid to **stand out** sometimes, even if it's a bit painful.
N 7 Louise was **sticking her neck out** when she said she'd like to double the budget.
C 8 When it comes to investment, I prefer to **play it safe** and put my money in established companies.
9 You have to **stand up to** Ollie if you think he's making a mistake. speak out
N 10 I think it's better to **toe the line** than to make trouble at this point.

5 Choose the correct expression to complete each sentence.

1 Fiona is terrified of heights, so she couldn't just *swim against the tide / go with the flow* when everyone opted to go rock climbing.
2 I'm not afraid to *rock the boat / play it safe* if I think the group is making a truly bad decision.
3 If you want to *stand out / fit in* at the office, it's a good idea not to dress too differently from your co-workers.
4 When everybody was angry with Claire, I *stuck my neck out / blended in* and said that I could see Claire's point of view.
5 Joe is very good at his job, but you really have to *stand up to him / toe the line* if you want him to change his mind about anything.

6 Work in pairs. Think of an example of a person – you, or someone you know of – who has stuck their neck out or rocked the boat. Why didn't they just go with the flow?

SPEAKING Dealing with groupthink

7 Work in small groups. Discuss these questions.

1 A small company that has been successful is beginning to show signs of failure. The four co-founders believe the company still has the potential to make great products, but one of them – Beata – suspects that the team of co-founders is suffering from groupthink and isn't making good decisions. However, when Beata suggested that this may be the case, the others accused her of being disloyal to the company. What are Beata's options? Should she continue to rock the boat, or just toe the line?

2 You enjoy walking in the hills with your friends Ellen, Peter and Otto. It's a good way to keep fit, and you enjoy one another's company. Increasingly, however, the others often insist on going off the path and more than once this has put the group in a dangerous situation. You have made your opinion clear, but your friends have begun accusing you of being no fun. However, you're a more experienced hill walker, and you understand that the danger is real. What's the best solution?

3 A group of friends often go out in the evening after work. Several members of the group often say very negative – and basically untrue – things about another friend who rarely joins the evenings out. One of the group, Bob, has challenged them a couple of times, but they've accused him of having no sense of humour. Bob thinks the behaviour is creating a lot of unnecessary negative feeling for everyone, but he's also aware that he's sticking his neck out and is in danger of making himself unpopular. What should he do?

Imagine the ideal team. Everyone sees the world in the same way, is focused and working together, and everyone knows exactly the direction that the group is going, all in complete harmony.

With no time wasted arguing or trying to manage conflict, the potential to do great work is huge, right? Well, maybe. But then again, maybe not. Sometimes when a group of people focuses too much on harmony or conformity, their ability to make good decisions vanishes. What happens is that the desire to fit in with the group results in a failure to think critically or argue enough about ideas. The fact is that disagreement and discussion can have a profoundly beneficial effect on our thinking, provided the conflict remains constructive. Too little conflict, meanwhile, can mean that the group's ideas simply aren't being tested enough, which in turn can lead to bad performance. The name psychologists give this phenomenon is 'groupthink.'

THE SYMPTOMS

There are three main ways to identify cases of groupthink. First, members of the group overestimate the group's power and often its moral right to do what it does. They have the feeling that they can do no wrong. Groups suffering from these symptoms often fail to understand that their actions will have negative consequences and, as a result, they take risks.

The second characteristic of groupthink is close-mindedness. Groups suffering from groupthink tend to take the view that anyone who expresses doubts or has questions is weak, evil or stupid – even when critics make valid, well-informed points. The group knows what's right and doesn't want to discuss it any further.

Third, when groupthink occurs, the group's complete agreement becomes all-important. Group members who disagree with the group have to stop themselves from saying anything and just go with the flow. Any member who openly disagrees or appears to be rocking the boat is usually labelled disloyal. If the behaviour continues, they will soon find themselves no longer part of the group – an outsider.

GROUPTHINK CASE STUDY: SWISSAIR

Swissair, founded in 1931, flew passenger routes in Europe through the 1930s and 40s and was soon well established. From 1947, when it began flying to New York, South Africa and South America, the airline quickly became a hugely successful company – so much so that by the early 1970s, it was known as 'the flying bank' and was considered so stable and reliable that it came to be regarded as a national symbol of Switzerland.

By the late 1970s, however, the airline business had become more competitive and in the early 80s, Swissair began to lose its edge. In an article entitled, 'The

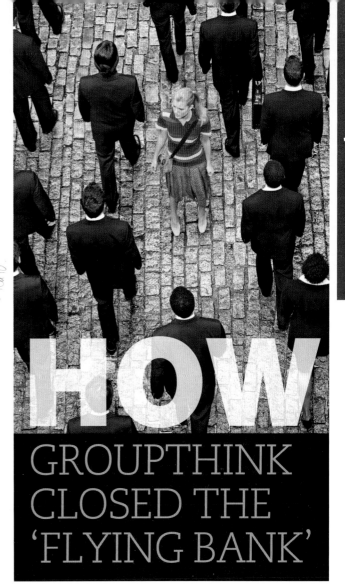

HOW GROUPTHINK CLOSED THE 'FLYING BANK'

grounding of the "flying bank"', management experts Aaron Hermann and Hussain G. Rammal suggest that groupthink took over at Swissair in the late 1980s, when the size of the company's board was reduced. They believe that at the heart of the problem was the fact that the directors who remained not only all came from similar backgrounds but also lacked any airline industry experience. There were two clear signs of groupthink: firstly, they believed that Swissair was too powerful to fail, and secondly, they thought their decisions were morally right. In the 1990s, no one on the board had the knowledge or experience to disagree when the company made a series of bad business decisions that finally led to the failure of 'the flying bank' on 31 March, 2002, after 71 years of service.

KNOW THE DIFFERENCE

Of course not all conflict is constructive, nor is harmony always a problem. The key is to understand the difference between harmful conflict that damages people and organizations and constructive conflict that leads to better ideas. Next time your team seems to be working in peace and harmony, before you sit back to enjoy it, ask yourself: Is 'groupthink' taking over? If it is, watch out: you may be headed for disaster.

3.4 Which one gets your vote?

LISTENING Choosing a logo

1 Work in pairs. Think of one or two company logos you really like. Why do you think they're effective?

2 A medium-sized city plumbing company is designing a new logo for the sides of its vans. Look at the three options. Discuss the questions.

   1 Which design do you think is the least appropriate? Why?
   2 Which design do you think is the most appropriate? Why?

     Option A   **Option B**   **Option C**

3 🎧 **18** Listen to a discussion about logo options between colleagues at the plumbing company. Make notes about what is said about each option. What is their decision?

	Option A	Option B	Option C
Pros			
Cons			
Decision			

4 🎧 **18** Listen again and complete the sentences from the conversation. Then match the sentences with the correct heading in the Useful expressions box.

   1 Do you have any _____ on any of them?
   2 I don't _____ about you, but Option C really stands out for me.
   3 Hmmm. I'm not so _____.
   4 _____ you want that guy to come to your door?
   5 I'd _____ that style so long as it doesn't show a person.
   6 I _____ with Cath that Option C looks a bit too serious.
   7 I think one way of _____ at that is to say that none of the options really works.
   8 Can we _____ this by agreeing that we don't need to show a plumber at all?

DEALING WITH DISAGREEMENT AND REACHING CONSENSUS

Asking for opinions

What's your take on this?
What's your view?

Disagreeing by expressing uncertainty

I can't say for certain that …
I may be wrong, but …

Disagreeing by asking a question

Do you really want … ?
Can you seriously picture … ?

Hedging (softening your own opinion)

… I guess you could say.
Maybe it's just me, but …

Reframing the disagreement

So here's the real question: … ?
We could look at this from a different perspective.

Setting conditions

I'll agree to your … , so long as …
I'd accept … on the condition that …

Proposing a resolution

So why don't we … ?
I'd like to suggest that we …

Signalling agreement

Right.
I'm with Bob.

Pronunciation Stress in expressions of disagreement

5a 🎧 **19** Listen to the expressions of disagreement. Underline the words that are stressed.

   1 Are you sure about that?
   2 I think you're wrong there.
   3 That's one way of looking at it.
   4 Sorry, but I'm really not sure that's correct.
   5 I can't agree with you on this.
   6 I totally disagree.
   7 No, I can't agree.
   8 I don't think we quite see eye-to-eye on this one.

5b 🎧 **19** Listen again. Which expressions sound more polite (P)? Which sound more direct (D)?

SPEAKING Choosing a logo

6 Work in groups of three. You're going to choose a logo for an English club you're setting up. First, as a group, agree on answers to these three questions.

1 The most important part of our image is … .
a English   b communication   c excellence

2 We want people to think of us as … .
a fun   b skilled   c professional

3 When we speak English, we're … .
a sophisticated   b friendly   c intelligent

7 **21st** CENTURY OUTCOMES

In your groups, discuss the three logos. Choose one design or decide on changes that need to be made to one to make it appropriate. Use the language in the Useful expressions box.

WRITING Emails dealing with disagreement

8 Read two versions of the same email message. What does Anna want?

Writing skill Encouraging cooperation

9a Answer the questions.

1 Which message do you think is more appropriate? Why?
2 In the second version of the message, why do you think Anna apologizes for emailing?
3 Which message has a more combative tone? Which has a more cooperative tone?

9b Match each combative sentence (1–5) with the best cooperative replacement (a–e).

1 I've changed my mind about replacing your computer.
2 Replacing your computer would be a waste of money.
3 Don't you understand what I said about replacing your computer?
4 Explain to me why we need to replace your computer.
5 I'm too busy to talk about replacing your computer.

a I'm afraid I may not have explained myself very clearly.
b I wonder if you could tell me a bit more about what's going wrong?
c I've had second thoughts about replacing your computer.
d Could we possibly find another time to discuss replacing your computer?
e A replacement computer may not be cost effective.

FROM:

TO: CC:

SUBJECT:

Bob,

I've been thinking about our logo conversation. I'd like to go back to Option B, and I think it's a complete waste of time to rethink the logo or go back to the designer. There's really nothing wrong with Option B. Can't we two just resolve this without involving Cath in the discussion and go with Option B and dump the other two options?

Anna

FROM:

TO: CC:

SUBJECT:

Bob,

Sorry to email about this, but you're on the road and out of contact until later today, when I'll be in meetings. If we can have a phone call later this evening, let me know.

I've had second thoughts about the logo discussion and I wonder if we could reconsider the style question? As I mentioned in the meeting, Option B was my idea, and I don't think I explained very well why I feel it's appropriate. Could we discuss our options again before you go back to the designer?

Thanks.

Anna

---

10 Write a reply from Bob to Anna responding to the polite version of her message, suggesting an appropriate way to deal with the conflict.

- Acknowledge that email isn't the best way to communicate, and explain why you're sending an email.
- Be extra sensitive to tone. Make the email positive rather than combative. Stress that you hope to resolve the conflict by working together.
- State clearly that you still believe that Option B isn't appropriate and you think it's important to go back to the designer for some fresh input.
- Invite Anna to continue the discussion by email or by phone or in person, if possible.

11 Exchange emails with a partner and check that the points in Exercise 10 were followed.

4 Challenges

BACKGROUND

1 You are going to watch a TED Talk by Joe Kowan called *How I beat stage fright*. Read the text about the speaker and the talk. Then work in pairs and answer the questions.

   1 What situations usually make you feel nervous?

2 Have you heard about or learned any techniques for controlling your nerves? What are they?

3 Stage fright is the fear of performing in front of an audience. Have you ever felt stage fright? If so, when?

TEDTALKS

JOE KOWAN is a Boston-based graphic designer by day, but by night he's a musician who has been struggling with stage fright since he first started writing songs aged 27. Despite his fears, he charms audiences with his own style of quirky folk and acoustic hip-hop. In 2009 he released the video for his original song 'Crafty', and in 2011 he was a finalist in the USA Songwriting Competition. In this talk, he uses his own stage fright as a subject for his art. Joe Kowan's idea worth spreading is that you can overcome fear by using it as a tool and turning it to your own advantage.

Men on wooden stilts fish using traditional methods, on the south coast of Sri Lanka.

KEY WORDS

2 Read the sentences (1–6). The words in bold are used in the TED Talk. First guess the meaning of the words. Then match the words with their definitions (a–f).

1 **Physiologically**, the body does not know the difference between excitement and fear.
2 I'm not really a performer, but I told some jokes at an **open mic**, once.
3 The body's **sympathetic nervous system** is what stimulates our 'fight or flight' response.
4 As I waited to go onstage, the **adrenaline** made it difficult to keep my body relaxed.
5 When you're nervous, your **extremities** often feel cold.
6 When I realized that the audience was understanding – and actually enjoying – my speech, it was a bit of an **epiphany**!

a a moment when you suddenly understand something important
b a chemical produced by your body when you feel very excited or afraid
c one of the functions in the body that controls our unconscious actions.
d relating to the body and its functions
e hands and feet
f a relatively informal performance where anyone can stand up and do an act

AUTHENTIC LISTENING SKILLS
Collaborative listening

Often when you listen, you aren't alone. People naturally discuss what they've just heard because it's common for different members of an audience to hear and remember different things. This allows you to compare notes and reactions, and also to find that as a group, you've understood something better than any one individual. In this way, collaborative listening can be a skill worth developing.

3a 🎧 **20** Look at the Authentic listening skills box. Then listen to Joe Kowan describing what happened to his body before a public performance. Note down the verb that he uses with each noun.

- body
- wave of anxiety
- fear
- sympathetic nervous system
- rush of adrenaline
- heart rate
- breathing
- non essential systems

3b Work in groups of three. Compare notes. Did you get all of them between you?

3c 🎧 **21** Listen to the next part of the talk. Write down all the physiological responses that you hear. In your groups, compare what you heard. You can check the audioscript on page 165.

41

4.1 How I beat stage fright

TEDTALKS

1 ▶ **4.1** Watch the TED Talk. Use collaborative listening and answer the questions in pairs.

1 When did Kowan decide to confront his stage fright?
2 What was his initial plan for beating stage fright?
3 Did it work? Why? / Why not?
4 What was his second plan for beating stage fright?
5 Did it work? Why? / Why not?
6 What words or images can you remember from the stage fright song? Did you and your partner remember different things?

2 ▶ **4.1** Watch the first part (0.00–3.12) of the talk again. Write the adjectives that Joe Kowan uses to describe his situation.

Kowan's first impression of the audience was that they looked [1] _____, and Kowan himself felt [2] _____ before the performance. When he finally got to the stage, his voice had a [3] _____ vibrato that made him feel very [4] _____, which in turn made the audience feel very [5] _____. But he'd felt a connection with the audience so he decided to go back until he no longer felt [6] _____. However, even with time, it didn't improve.

▶ focused **N AM ENG**
▶ focussed **BR ENG**

▶ route /raut/ **N AM ENG**
▶ route /ruːt/ **BR ENG**

3 ▶ 4.1 Watch the second part (3.13–5.05) of the talk again. Answer the questions.

1 Kowan had an epiphany. What was it?
2 'Exploit' can mean 'use well' or 'use unfairly.' When Kowan says he wanted to exploit his stage fright, which meaning do you think he was using?
3 Kowan thought about how his listeners might feel. What effect does stage fright often have on his listeners?
4 Does Kowan still use the stage fright song in his musical performances?

4 ▶ 4.1 Watch the third part (5.06 to the end) of the talk again. The song has four main themes. Number them in the order that Kowan sings about them.

a If I try to imagine the whole audience naked (a technique sometimes advised to make the situation seem less serious), it makes me feel more embarrassed, not less.
b You can tell from the sound of my voice that I'm very nervous.
c I'm not making fun of stage fright, I'm facing it and eventually I'll get over it.
d Don't tell me not to be nervous – it doesn't help.

VOCABULARY IN CONTEXT

5 ▶ 4.2 Watch the clips from the TED Talk. Choose the correct meaning of the words.

6 Complete the sentences in your own words. Then discuss with a partner.

1 It always helps me feel relaxed and comfortable if …
2 When I want to shake feelings of unhappiness or worry, I usually …
3 For me, a feeling of relief kicks in when …

CRITICAL THINKING Emotive language

7 A speaker may use strong or emotive language to help listeners feel the emotions being described. Can you remember what emotive words Kowan used instead of the more neutral words in bold? What effect does his choice of words have on his story?

1 My whole body **reacted badly.**
2 **A feeling** of anxiety **came** over me.
3 I have never been more **nervous** – until now.
4 This is my whole body just convulsing with fear. I mean, it's a **bad feeling**.
5 And that's when I had a **sudden realization**.

8 Look at the comments*. What emotive language do they use?

Viewers' comments	
B	**Bernice –** I can really relate to Kowan's fear. I completely freeze up every time I have to give a talk at work. Maybe I can use some of his tricks!
F	**Freddie –** It's amazing that Kowan says he's so nervous, because he seems at home on stage. I feel totally sick and miserable every time I have to talk to more than four or five people. Maybe there's hope for me?
H	**Helsie –** I'm so pleased to know that Kowan battled his stage-fright monster and turned the story into a song to help himself and other people. Good work!

*These comments were created for this activity.

PRESENTATION SKILLS Controlling nerves

TIPS

Almost everyone feels nervous before a presentation. These tips can help overcome the effects of feeling nervous.

Before the talk

- Rehearse your talk a lot. If possible, practise in front of more than one audience.
- Visit the room you'll be presenting in. Check out the stage area and also try sitting in the worst seat in the room. Imagine how you will look onstage.
- Memorize the first few and last few sentences of your talk.

During the talk

- Wear clothes you feel comfortable in.
- Don't rush, and don't forget to breathe.
- Have water onstage and don't be afraid to use it.
- Make eye contact.
- Engage directly with the audience.
- Remember, the audience rarely sees that you are as nervous as you feel. You may think you look and sound terrible, but the audience would often be surprised to hear this.

9 ▶ 4.3 Read the Presentation tips box then watch the clips from the TED Talk. Which of the tips in the box can you see Kowan using?

10 Work in pairs. Prepare a two-minute mini-presentation. Make some brief notes on ways of addressing stage fright when you perform in front of an audience. Use the ideas in the Presentation tips box and your own.

11 Work with a new partner. Take turns to give your presentation. Did you come up with similar ideas?

▶ patronizing /ˈpeɪtrəˌnaɪzɪŋ/ **N AM ENG**
▶ patronizing /ˈpætrəˌnaɪzɪŋ/ **BR ENG**

▶ feel bad for **N AM ENG**
▶ feel sorry for **BR ENG**

4.2 Information overload

WE ARE CONNECTED 12 HOURS A DAY

INFORMATION OVERLOAD

People see more than
34 BILLION BITS

of information per day – an equivalent of
TWO BOOKS A DAY

HUMAN ABSORPTION RATE	128
MACHINE TRANSFER RATE	2,000,000

BITS PER SECOND

MORE INFORMATION WILL BE GENERATED IN THE NEXT FOUR YEARS THAN IN THE HISTORY OF THE WORLD

THE GROWTH OF DATA

WORLDWIDE MOBILE SUBSCRIBERS

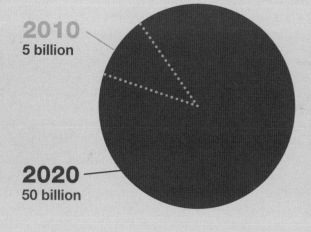

2010
5 billion

2020
50 billion

AMOUNT OF DATA

2010
1.2 zettabytes

01010010101110100

2020
35 zettabytes

0101001010111010101010100101001010111010101010
1001010010101110101010101001010010101110101010
1010010100010101110101010101001010010101110101 0
1010100101001010111010101010100101001010111010
1010100100101001010111010101010100101001010 11
1010101010100101001010111010101010100101001 01
0111010101010100101001010111010101010100101001
0101110101010101001011010101010010100101 01110
1010101010010100101011101010101010010100101011
1010100101111

GRAMMAR Approximation

1 Work in pairs. Discuss the questions.

1 What devices – smartphone, tablet, computer, e-reader, etc. – do you use regularly?

2 About how many electronic messages (texts, emails, social media messages) do you send and receive each day for work or connected to your studies?

3 How many for non-work, social reasons?

2 Look at the infographic. Answer the questions.

1 According to the infographic, what do people spend half of the day doing?

2 What fact about the human mind and body makes dealing with information a big challenge?

3 How many mobile phone users will there be in 2020?

3 Read the text in the Grammar box. Answer the questions (1 and 2).

APPROXIMATION

Dealing with electronic communication and incoming information is time-consuming for most workers. A typical manager spends approximately 20 hours each week reading email and the average company employee receives in the order of 200 emails per day, in addition to sending and receiving as many as 35 text messages. By 2020, the amount of digital data in the world will increase to about 35 zettabytes. For comparison, consider that one expert calculated that every human word ever spoken in the history of the world would take roughly 42 zettabytes of storage if recorded on a computer.

1 What words and expressions in the text express approximation?

2 What expressions do you know that mean 'slightly above' or 'slightly below' a given number?

Check your answers on page 146 and do Exercises 1–5.

4 Look at the data. Write sentences using the approximations in brackets below.

Worldwide mobile email users (smartphones, tablets) in billions

	2013	2014	2015	2016	2017
	0.897	1.152	1.422	1.632	1.779
Annual growth:		28%	23%	15%	9%

1 (about) *There are about 1.6 billion users in 2016.*
2 (just under)
3 (nearly)
4 (just over)
5 (roughly)
6 (or so)

5 🎧 **22** Complete the conversation with these words and phrases. Then listen and check your answers.

about	at least	elevenish	hundreds
kind of	more or less	or so	some

A: ¹ _More or less_ how many hours a day are you away from a device – your phone or tablet or computer?

B: You mean when I'm awake? Zero. I'm on or near a device ² _about_ all day long – communicating.

A: That sounds ³ _Kind of_ extreme. Is it absolutely necessary, or is it your choice?

B: Good question! To do my job, I have respond to ⁴ _hundreds_ of emails every week. And I'm responsible for my company's social media presence, so I re-tweet ⁵ _some_ interesting link or other, or write a new tweet every hour ⁶ _or so_ and I update our Facebook status ⁷ _at least_ twice a day.

A: What time do you switch off?

B: Usually ⁸ _elevenish_, but sometimes later, if I'm catching up on my personal messages.

Pronunciation Approximations

6a 🎧 **23** Listen to the sentences from the conversation. Underline the stressed words in the bold parts of the sentences.

1 **About how many hours a day** are you away from a device?
2 I'm on or near a device **more or less all day long**.
3 That sounds **kind of extreme**.
4 I have to respond to **hundreds of emails every week**.
5 I retweet **some interesting link or other** or write a new tweet **every hour or so**.
6 I update our Facebook status **at least twice a day**.
7 **Usually elevenish**, but **sometimes later**.

6b 🎧 **23** Listen again. Answer the questions.

1 In which sentences is the approximation itself the most important information?
2 In which sentences is the approximation less important?

SPEAKING Using approximations

7 **21st CENTURY OUTCOMES**

Work in small groups. Take turns to answer the questions. Use approximations.

- How old were you when you first started communicating with text messages, emails or social media? *twelvish*
- About how many hours a day are you *away* from a device – your phone or tablet or computer?
- Do you suffer from information overload, or is the amount of information you deal with manageable?
- Do you have any techniques for dealing with information overload?

8 Turn the information from the discussion in Exercise 7 – and any other ideas you have – into data for your group. Group the data under these topics or create your own.

- the average age that you began using technology
- the time you have away from devices
- attitudes – positive, negative or neutral – about constant communication

9 Present your findings. Explain whether or not your group suffers from information overload and support your position with you data. Use approximations.

4.3 Get the name right

READING One man's meat ...

1 Work in pairs. Discuss the questions.

  1 What foods, drinks, styles of clothing, etc. do you think are found in your country, but not all over the world?

  2 What products do you use that are originally from other countries?

2 Read the article. What do all of the companies mentioned have in common?

3 Write the names of companies from the article for 1–5.

  1 The company that sells different versions of products in different regions.

  2 Two companies that have successfully avoided language-related difficulties.

  3 The company that accidentally sent completely the wrong message. HSBC

  4 The company that originally had different logos and brands in countries around the world. Unilever

  5 The three companies that use the same product name in all of their markets.

4 Read the text again. Are these statements true (T) or false (F)?

  1 Coca-Cola is the exception among the four companies because its product is the same everywhere.

  2 Doritos began as a Mexican brand that relocated to the USA. F

  3 Before 1998, Unilever had no global ice cream brand.

  4 HSBC used different advertising slogans in different markets. F

  5 Coca-Cola has been a global brand for over 100 years.

  6 It is against the rules to transport durian in some places.

  7 Durian is sold in some countries under a different, local-friendly name. F

  8 Coca-Cola was made illegal in France for a brief time.

5 The text title and section headings contain four common English expressions. The title + the fourth section heading make one expression. Match each expression with its meaning (1–4).

  1 Everyone is entitled to their own tastes and preferences – we don't all like the same things. *Ten men, ten tastes* is a similar expression in Japanese.

  2 People and things are important, but what we call them doesn't matter.

  3 The ending of this expression is ... *try, try again.* It is often used to encourage someone who's struggling to overcome a challenge or accomplish a difficult task.

  4 This expression has a similar meaning to *To each his own.* The idea is that something we like may be completely disliked by someone else.

6 Work in pairs. Discuss the questions.

  1 Which of the Doritos flavours mentioned would be successful in your country? Which would not?

  2 Is there a Heartbrand ice cream available in your country? What's it called?

  3 When we assume something, we suppose that it's true, without proof. What do you think the slogan 'Assume nothing' was intended to mean?

VOCABULARY Obstacles and opportunities

7 Complete the expressions that describe imagined reactions to something. Use these words.

| a brick wall | concern | hotcakes | issue |
| an obstacle | opposition | reception | a splash |

  1 I think importing durian to New York on a large scale would be met with _____.

  2 I'm sure my country's traditional music would make _____ at some music festivals abroad.

  3 My grandmother's hand-made clothes would sell like _____ in Tokyo.

  4 I think if I tried to sell traditional dress from my country, I'd get a cool _____ abroad, because people in other countries are not used to wearing this type of clothing.

  5 I think the strong smell of some of our traditional cheeses would be _____ to selling them abroad.

  6 You'd probably come up against _____ trying to get people to use chopsticks in my country.

  7 For my country's best TV shows to be popular abroad, we'd have to address the _____ of translation.

  8 People in my country have voiced their _____ about having too many goods – and new ideas – imported from abroad.

8 Answer the questions.

  1 Which two expressions in Exercise 7 describe a product or idea being readily accepted?

  2 Which four expressions describe the challenge of trying to sell a product or idea?

  3 Which expression describes people raising a worry?

  4 Which expression describes trying to overcome a challenge?

SPEAKING Talking about sales potential

9 **21st CENTURY OUTCOMES**

Work in pairs. Student A turn to page 172, Student B turn to page 183.

One man's meat ...

One of the real pleasures of international travel is discovering unfamiliar foods, different styles of clothing, and unexpected versions of familiar products in shops. From chocolate toothpaste in the Philippines to salt and vinegar potato crisps in the UK, products popular in one place often receive a cool reception elsewhere. There are of course some notable exceptions. Good luck finding a place
10 where you can't buy Coca-Cola in its familiar red-and-white bottles and cans. According to the manufacturer, the world's favourite soft drink is sold in more than 200 countries. But very few products enjoy that sort of global success.

15 What challenges do companies seeking to export their brands come up against? What do they have to understand about the world in order to win customers over?

To each his own (4)

Taste – the flavours people love and the ones they hate –
20 varies greatly from culture to culture. So how does the snack-food company Frito-Lay, maker of the globally popular Doritos tortilla chip, address the issue? Their success is discovering the best-loved flavours in each of their markets. So while cheese, spicy chilli and barbecue are popular flavours in the
25 USA, Canada goes for intense pickle, Turkey prefers yogurt and mint, the French like olive and Japan has sushi, seaweed and corn soup flavours. But all of them are sold under the globally familiar Doritos brand. Frito-Lay's understanding of local tastes around the world – and the successful
30 adaptation of their product – has made Doritos one of the world's most popular snack foods.

What's in a name? (2)

Everyone, everywhere loves ice cream, it seems. The Anglo-Dutch food giant Unilever sells it in over 40 countries. The
35 company used to sell their ice cream under a lot of different brands, which created the sense that the companies were local. In 1998, the company launched the 'Heartbrand' logo to increase international brand awareness, but kept the familiar local names for the ice cream products. This
40 transformation helped avoid the problem of some names not sounding good in other languages. So in Bulgaria, the Czech Republic, Cyprus and Greece, you buy Algida but in China, Malaysia, Singapore, Thailand and the UK, it's Wall's. The Heartbrand logo, however, is used throughout the world.

If at first you don't succeed ... (3)
45
In 2009, global banking giant HSBC changed its slogan from 'Assume nothing', which it had used for five years, to 'The world's private bank'. One reason for the change was that in some countries, the slogan 'Assume nothing' was mis-translated as 'Do nothing' – not exactly a good image for a
50 global bank. After the problem was identified, HSBC changed their advertising.

When you're working in a foreign language, it's important to acknowledge that some words and expressions in your own language may not translate easily. Of course it's also
55 important to work with translators you trust!

... is another man's poison (1)

There are some products that will always remain at home. Known as the 'the king of fruits' in its homeland of Southeast Asia, the durian is probably one such commodity. The fruit's most notable feature is its strong odour, described by some
60 as that of rotten onions and by others as old gym socks, though it is said to taste delicious by its fans. Try taking it on a train in Singapore, and you'll be met with opposition: the smell is so intense, durians are forbidden on Singapore's local transport system. Though some durians are grown outside of
65 Southeast Asia – small amounts in the USA and Australia, for example – the only place the fruit enjoys any wide popularity at all is in Southeast Asia – and even there, some people can't stand it! So don't expect to see durian – by any name, or in any package – in your local supermarket any time soon.
70

The same the world over?

Coca-Cola is famously the same the world over. As of 2015, there are only two countries where the beverage is not officially sold: North Korea and Cuba. Established in 1886 in Atlanta, Georgia, the fizzy drinks company set out on worldwide expansion early
75 in its existence, setting up bottling operations in Europe and Asia in the early 1900s. But not everyone has been happy about Coke's global invasion. In the 1950s, some French people started speaking of 'coca-colonization' and protested against the imported drink as a threat to their society.
80

4.4 I thought it would be easy

LISTENING Asking how something works

1 Work in pairs. Discuss the questions.

1 Think of a product you've used that had features you didn't completely understand. Did you learn how to use the features or just ignore them?

2 When you encounter something you don't completely understand on your computer or other device, where do you usually turn for help?

2 🎧 **24** Listen to three conversations asking for help. Answer the questions.

1 What three things does Oscar learn to do with his new phone?

2 What does Lydia want to do with her watch? What two buttons does she need to use?

3 What does Dave have to press and in what sequence to operate the electronic door lock?

3 🎧 **24** Listen again. Which expressions in the Useful expressions box are used for the following?

1 To ask for repetition of how to dial the phone.

2 To clarify the reason for using 'contacts'.

3 To ask for repetition of how to set the date on the watch.

4 To ask for clarification of how to use the 'mode' button.

5 To ask for repetition of how to use the electronic door lock.

6 To ask for clarification on when the 'lock' key is pressed.

ASKING FOR CLARIFICATION AND REPETITION

Asking for repetition

I'm not with you. Could you just go over that last bit again, please?

You've lost me. Would you mind giving that to me one more time?

Sorry, I didn't quite catch that. Could you run it by me again?

Would you mind backing up for a second? I missed that last bit.

Asking for clarification

Can you explain why I would need to … ?

I'm probably just being a bit slow, but am I supposed to … ?

Sorry, I didn't get that last bit. Do you mean … ? / Are you saying …?

Sorry, I'm a bit confused. Did you say … or … ?

PRONUNCIATION Intonation in questions

4a 🎧 **25** Listen to the questions. Notice the intonation rises at the end of some questions and falls at the end of others.

1 Which one is that?

2 So are you saying I can enter my friends' numbers in the phone?

3 The home key?

4 Carla, what's the trick to unlocking this door?

5 And then I click it to change the year, right?

6 Would you like me to give you a hand with that?

4b Look at the questions in 4a again. Find:

a two *wh*-questions

b two *yes-no* questions

c two statements that have been turned into questions

4c 🎧 **25** Listen again. Do the same types of questions have the same intonation in each case? If not, why do you think they might be different?

SPEAKING Giving and receiving instructions

5 Work in pairs. Student A turn to page 172. Student B, turn to page 183. Use the language in the Useful expressions box.

6 Work in groups of three. Take turns explaining what you do on a typical weekday. Ask the person who's speaking to clarify and repeat. Use the words in the Useful expressions box.

WRITING Information for a house guest

7 **21st** CENTURY OUTCOMES + Remember.

Kelly occasionally rents her house out to guests when she's travelling for work. Read the information she leaves. Which four of the following does she mention?

☑ the shower   ☑ the kitchen   ☐ the burglar alarm

☐ the neighbours   ☐ the pet fish   ☑ the spare key

☐ the TV   ☑ the post

Writing skill Instructions

8a Underline the instructions in the letter. Circle the reasons given for why they're important.

8b Complete the sentences with words from the text.

1 Bear in _____ that the walls are very thin and the neighbours can hear any noise you make.

2 Be _____ to turn the water heater on half an hour before you want to shower.

3 Just to be _____, please don't leave the dishwasher running when you're not at home. We've the occasional leak.

4 _____ of opening the sitting room window on a windy day – the wind can grab it.

5 I have one _____ : please listen to any phone messages and let me know if there's anything important.

6 I'd be _____ if you'd let the neighbours know if you're going away overnight.

9 Write instructions for a guest who is coming to stay where you usually stay, while you're away for a few days. Use Kelly's letter as a model.

10 Exchange instructions with a partner. Did they give clear instructions and say why they're important? Did they give useful advice?

Dear Guest,

Welcome to my flat. I hope you enjoy your stay in London! Please make yourself at home! Here are a few things you should bear in mind to make your stay comfortable and enjoyable:

After you've showered, make sure you turn the water off tightly. Otherwise it tends to drip and that might keep you awake. You need to turn it harder than you might imagine!

When cooking, please be sure not to make too much smoke. It can make the fire alarm for the whole building go off, and everyone has to leave. A ringing smoke alarm can be especially annoying at mealtimes! Just to be on the safe side, every time you're cooking, you might want to turn on the extractor fan.

Beware of letting the front door shut behind you and locking yourself out. (It's easier than you think!) In the event that you do get locked out, there's a spare key hidden underneath the plant outside the door. If you use it, please be sure you put it back so that when I return, I can use it to get in if I need to.

If you have any problems, text message me and I will try to get back to you within 24 hours.

And one final request: Please keep an eye out for my post and any other deliveries. The key to the letter box is on a hook by the front door. If the letter box gets too full, the postman will stop delivering. I'd be grateful if you'd just bring the post into the flat every few days.

All the best,

Kelly

LISTENING

1 🎧 **26** Read the introduction and listen to the podcast about One Earth Designs. Answer the questions.

1 What was Catlin Powers researching in 2007?
2 What problem did a local person bring to her attention?
3 What had Scot Frank been doing before he met Powers?
4 What power source did Powers and Frank decide to use for their stove?
5 What was the main problem with existing models?
6 What shape makes the stove effective?
7 What successes have the SolSource stove and One Earth Designs enjoyed?

2 🎧 **26** Listen again. Complete the sentences.

1 Indoor air was _____ten_____ times more polluted than the outdoor air in Beijing.
2 _____4 million_____ people die globally because of cooking smoke indoors.
3 The main fuel sources are _____animal poop_____ and wood.
4 As well as indoor pollution, _____fuel scarcity_____ is a big problem.
5 _____students_____ helped Frank, Powers and Qian collect feedback on stove designs. Engineers'
6 SolSource can boil _____a litre of_____ of water in about ten minutes. water
7 One Earth Designs raised US $ _____1_____ to expand their business. one million 1 hundred thour

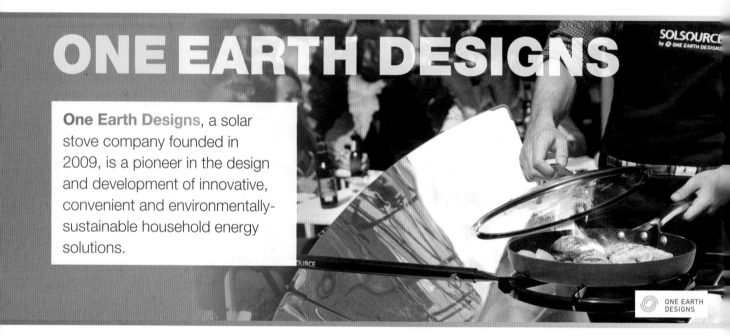

One Earth Designs, a solar stove company founded in 2009, is a pioneer in the design and development of innovative, convenient and environmentally-sustainable household energy solutions.

SOLSOURCE
by ONE EARTH DESIGNS

ONE EARTH DESIGNS

GRAMMAR

3 Complete the cleft sentences in the blog post with these words.

> it's   that   the thing about   what   what's   where

¹ _____ we often forget is that companies such as One Earth Designs aren't always started by people who were planning to go into business. ² _____ great start-up ideas is that sometimes they present themselves even when no one is looking for them. ³ _____ a desire to solve a specific problem ⁴ _____ leads to the development of a new product or service rather than a wish to run a business. ⁵ _____ Powers and Frank found their inspiration was in their day-to-day work, not in a quest to be CEOs. ⁶ _____ important for would-be entrepreneurs to remember is that a compassionate awareness of the world around us can be a great starting point for a successful business idea.

4 Look at the bar chart. Choose the correct options to complete the presentation.

In 1997, ¹*at least / as few as* 1,500 megawatts of new wind energy capacity was installed globally. According to the Global Wind Energy Council, new installations in 2014 accounted for ²*nearly / just over* 50,000 megawatts. With the exception of a decrease of ³*sort of / roughly* 10,000 MW in 2013, the number has increased each year since 1997. Travis Burns, head of a local pro-wind group says, 'With all the ⁴*stuff in the / hundreds* of daily news about climate change, people are ready for wind power.' The GWEC predicts a growth rate of ⁵*around ten per cent / ten percentish* in the coming years.

Global Annual Installed Wind Capacity 1997–2014 (Megawatts)

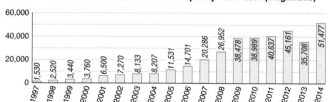

Year	MW
1997	1,530
1998	2,520
1999	3,440
2000	3,760
2001	6,500
2002	7,270
2003	8,133
2004	8,207
2005	11,531
2006	14,701
2007	20,286
2008	26,952
2009	38,478
2010	38,989
2011	40,637
2012	45,161
2013	35,708
2014	51,477

VOCABULARY

5 Complete the idiomatic expressions in the text. Use these words and phrases.

> a brick wall   concerns   a cool reception   hotcakes
> the issue   their necks   an obstacle   safe
> a splash   the tide

In 1991, inventor Trevor Baylis saw a TV documentary showing how the lack of a telecommunications infrastructure in rural Africa was ¹ _____ to the promotion of healthcare and disease prevention there. Healthcare workers were coming up against ² _____ in their efforts to use education to stop the spread of deadly illnesses. Baylis immediately saw a way to address ³ _____ : provide low-cost radios to rural populations. The problem would be powering them. Taking up the challenge, Baylis headed to his workshop and soon developed a radio powered not by batteries or electricity, but by hand, simply by turning a small handle. Bayliss expected his invention to sell like ⁴ _____ ; however when he tried to get funding for his new business, he always got ⁵ _____ . Companies with the cash to fund his project voiced ⁶ _____ about its marketability, playing it ⁷ _____ and saying no rather than risking investment. For a few years, Baylis felt he was swimming against ⁸ _____ . Then, in 1994, Baylis appeared on TV's *Tomorrow's World* with his wind-up radio, and finally reached some investors who were willing to stick ⁹ _____ out and back the project. Baylis's Freeplay radio made ¹⁰ _____ , winning several awards and becoming a popular product worldwide. A later, smaller model allowed the radio to be played for longer with less effort and a more recent updated version also includes a solar panel, making it even easier to use.

6 Match the two parts of the sentence.

1 The plan to build a wind farm was met   c
2 Often, inventors have big new ideas that don't fit in   b
3 Sometimes, to get people to change their thinking, you need to rock   e
4 When our block of flats wanted to install solar panels, I wasn't too sure, but I went   a
5 After you get used to wind farms, they begin to blend   f
6 Our house stands   d
7 It's important to stand   h
8 Sometimes it's better to toe   g

a with the flow and voted yes.
b with people's expectations or ways of thinking.
c with opposition.
d out, because we're the only one with solar panels.
e the boat.
f in to the landscape, I think.
g the line than to make trouble.
h up to companies that waste energy and create pollution.

DISCUSSION

7 Work in pairs. Discuss the questions

1 Do you think people in your country would use a solar oven like SolSource? Why? / Why not?
2 Is wind energy used where you live? Why? / Why not? What about other alternative power sources?
3 What appliances, apps, or anything else do you use regularly that are an entrepreneur's great idea? Which ones would you find it hard to live without?

SPEAKING

8 Luke, Rosa and Sylvie are talking about managing the temperature control system in their office. Complete the conversation using the prompts to make hedging phrases.

Luke: Sylvie suggests we could reduce our carbon footprint by lowering the office temperature in winter by a few degrees. (what / take / that) ¹ *What's your take on that*, Rosa?

Rosa: You've lost me already. (mind / giving / that / me) ² _____ one more time?

Sylvie: We currently heat the office to 23 degrees Celsius in the winter. If we lowered that to 20, we'd use less energy – and save some money.

Rosa: (maybe / just / me) ³ _____ the office is already pretty cold, isn't it?

Luke: I think the idea is that some people may choose to dress more warmly for work.

Rosa: (seriously / picture / everyone) ⁴ _____ sitting around in coats and jumpers? I don't think people will like that.

Sylvie: (can't / say / certain) ⁵ _____ people won't mind, but (guess / could / say) ⁶ _____ we should do what we can to reduce our carbon footprint.

Rosa: Yes, but (could / look / different perspective) ⁷ _____ . People have the right to a comfortable working environment, so, (here / real question) ⁸ _____ : What are the health and safety recommendations for minimum workplace temperature?

Luke: Twenty degrees.

Rosa: Twenty, huh? OK, (accept / that / on / condition) ⁹ _____ no one complains if I start exercising at my desk to keep warm!

Rosa: [Later] (probably / just / be / slow / but) ¹⁰ _____ I supposed to use this button to adjust the target temperature?

Luke: I'm not sure. The instructions say 'the setpoint can be adjusted from 5 °C to 35 °C with a fixed setpoint throughout the day'. And then it says we need to push the green button to confirm the setting.

Rosa: (Sorry / not / get / last bit) ¹¹ _____ . Do you mean I need to select the temperature first?

5 Inspiration

A man climbs the mast of a sailing boat during the round-Barbados yacht race.

TEDTALKS

STELLA YOUNG was a comedian, supporter of people with disability and the editor of *Ramp Up*, an online space for news, discussion and opinion about disability in Australia. She advised the government in Australia on disability and was twice a finalist in the Melbourne International Comedy Festival's Raw Comedy competition. In this talk, she describes her 'normal' upbringing and explores the way disabled people are viewed by society. Stella Young died on 8th December 2014, aged 32. Stella Young's idea worth spreading is that disability doesn't make you special, but that questioning your assumptions about it does.

BACKGROUND

1 You are going to watch a TED Talk by Stella Young called *I'm not your inspiration, thank you very much.* Read the text about the speaker and the talk. Then work in pairs and answer the questions.

    1 What would you define as a 'normal' upbringing? What do you think Stella Young means by a 'normal' upbringing?

    2 What assumptions about disabled people do you think Young wants us to question?

    3 How well are people with disabilities integrated into the workplace in your country?

KEY WORDS

2 Read the sentences (1–6). The words in bold are used in the TED Talk. First guess the meaning of the words. Then match the words with their definitions (a–f).

    1 My cousin **is an inspiration** to me because he's a great athlete, not because he's disabled. c

    2 It seemed a **contradiction** when the doctor said she'd be 'as good as new' but unable to return to her job. f

    3 After climbing Everest, they gave **motivational** talks a about the challenges they'd overcome.

    4 Some people **propagate** the lie that disabled people are completely different from everyone else. d

    5 Some TV shows are guilty of the **objectification** of people with certain body types. b

    6 I read about an **exceptional** child who'd mastered four instruments by the age of six. e

    a causing people to take action, often for self-improvement 3

    b the treatment of people as though they were something less than or other than human 5

    c does something or deals with a situation so well that others want to be like that 1

    d spread or promote (an idea) 4

    e impressive in a way that is unusual or not typical 6

    f a combination of ideas that oppose one another 2

AUTHENTIC LISTENING SKILLS Elision

Native speakers of English don't pronounce every letter of every word, especially at word boundaries, where words come together. When two consonants come together at word boundaries, one of them often disappears. Being aware that this happens and of which sounds it affects may help you follow the message when words sound different in fast speech.

- The most common elisions are /t/ and /d/ when they appear in a consonant cluster: *next door* → /neksdɔː/
- Complex consonant clusters are simplified: *acts like* → /ækslaɪk/
- The /v/ in *of* can disappear before consonants: *a lot of time* → *a lot uh time*

3a 🎧 **27** Look at the Authentic listening skills box. Then listen to extracts 1–3 from the TED Talk. Underline the consonants that you don't hear.

    1 ... when I was fifteen, a member of my local community approached my parents and wanted to nominate me for a community achievement award.

    2 This kid had only ever experienced disabled people as objects of inspiration.

    3 I wasn't doing anything that was out of the ordinary at all.

3b 🎧 **28** Read sentences 4 and 5. Then listen and write the words you hear.

    4 I am here to tell you that we have been _____ about disability.

    5 I've lost count of the number of times that I've been _____ strangers wanting to tell me that they think I'm brave or inspirational.

5.1 I'm not your inspiration, thank you very much

TEDTALKS

1 ▶ [____] Watch the edited version of the TED Talk. Are these sentences true (T) or false (F) for Stella Young's talk?

1 Stella Young was unable to attend school as a child. F
2 Her first job was giving inspirational talks at schools. F
3 Young feels that people with disability could be better integrated into Australian society. T
4 She feels that Internet images of disabled people are good because they help the world understand disability. F
5 She feels that the biggest challenges disabled people face are related to their bodies. F
6 She feels inspired by practical ideas that she learns from disabled people. T
7 She thinks that one of the keys to overcoming disability is to maintain a positive attitude. F
8 She feels that too many people have unrealistically high expectations for people with disability. F

2 ▶ [5.1] Watch the first part (0.11–3.09) of the talk again. Answer the questions.

1 What did a member of Young's community want to nominate her for? *Achievement award*
2 What was the response of Young's mother?

3 What did Young realize about her student's experience of disabled people?
4 In the talk Young says that we have been lied to. What lie is she referring to? *disability was a bad thing.*

3 ▶ [5.1] Complete the summary of the second part of the talk. Then watch the second part (3.10–7.19) of the talk again and check your answers.

disabled people	images	life
nondisabled people	people	perspective
that person	the problem	

Some ¹_____ on social media objectify
²_____ for the benefit of ³_____, to help them put their worries in ⁴_____. They make nondisabled people think, 'My ⁵_____ could be worse. I could be that person.' But Stella Young is ⁶_____, and she doesn't think her life is bad. For Young, her body and her diagnosis aren't ⁷_the problem_. She looks at the pictures and sees ⁸_____ who aren't doing anything out of the ordinary. For Young, the problem is that society objectifies disabled people and views them as exceptional.

4 ▶ **5.1** Match the three parts of the sentences that summarise Young's argument in the final section of the talk. Then watch the third part (7.20 to the end) of the talk and check your answers.

1	'The only disability in life is a bad attitude'	won't make	the books to Braille*.
2	Smiling at stairs	isn't	an achievement.
3	Smiling at a TV	is	a lie.
4	Radiating a positive attitude in a bookshop	won't turn them	closed captions** appear.
5	Being disabled	won't turn	into a ramp.

*__Braille__ (n) letters that blind people can feel with their fingers
**__closed captions__ (n) written words on a screen for deaf people

5 Does Stella Young inspire you? Why? / Why not?

VOCABULARY IN CONTEXT

6 ▶ **5.2** Watch the clips from the TED Talk. Choose the correct meaning of the words.

7 Work in pairs. Discuss the questions.

1 Do you prefer big parties or more low-key celebrations?
2 Who can you think of who has achieved something out of the ordinary?
3 What have people said to you so often you've lost count?

CRITICAL THINKING Understanding examples

8 Arguments are often supported with examples. Match each argument (1–3) with the example (a–c) that Stella Young uses in her TED Talk to support it.

Arguments

1 The disabled aren't seen as real people. They're there to inspire, not to do 'real' jobs. b
2 The disabled are objectified to make non-disabled people feel better about themselves. c
3 Society has low expectations for disabled people. a

Examples

a People who don't know Stella Young often tell her she's brave or inspirational just for living her normal life.
b A student asked when she was going to do her motivational speech, assuming that she couldn't possibly just be a 'normal' teacher.
c Pictures on the Internet show disabled people doing normal things, with 'inspirational' captions.

9 Read the comments* about the TED Talk. Do you think the commenters understood the purpose of Young's talk? Why? / Why not?

Viewers' comments

E **Elise** – Stella Young is an incredible speaker. It's amazing to think that a disabled person could do everything that she has done.

D **Des38** – I hadn't thought about how much society objectifies the disabled. It's easy to see the disability, but not the person.

B **Ben000** – This talk gives us a lot to think about. Sooooo inspirational! It makes me think my little problems aren't so bad!

*The comments were created for this activity

PRESENTATION SKILLS Repeating key ideas

TIPS

You may want to introduce a theme and keep returning to it, so that the audience stays focused on your point. Repetition of a particular phrase or idea can help in these ways.

- It can help the audience identify and remember what's most important in your talk.
- It can give the talk a powerful, almost musical quality, like the structure of a song.
- It can create a more emotional impact by, for example, returning to a shared problem or goal.

But be careful! If you say the same thing over and over again, it can simply make the talk seem boring. Getting the balance right requires preparation and practice.

10 ▶ **5.3** Look at the Presentation tips box. Then watch the clips from Young's TED Talk. Answer the questions.

1 What is the key idea that Stella Young wants to impress upon the audience?
2 What word does she repeat, and how many times?
3 What effect does her repetition have – does it serve a purpose, or is it simply repetitive?
4 Does Young's talk convince you to agree with her?

11 Explain your ideas to someone from another pair. Did you come up with similar answers? Can you remember any other words Stella Young repeated several times?

12 You are going to give a two-minute mini-presentation about a commonly held belief that you want to disagree with. Choose one of these topics or your own idea.

- People become lawyers to make money.
- A university education is the best way to succeed.
- Watching TV is a waste of time.

13 Prepare your presentation.

14 Work in pairs. Take turns to give your presentation. Follow the tips in the box and use repetition.

▶ bag out **AUS**
▶ criticize **N AM ENG / BR ENG**

▶ quit **AUS / N AM ENG**
▶ give up **BR ENG**

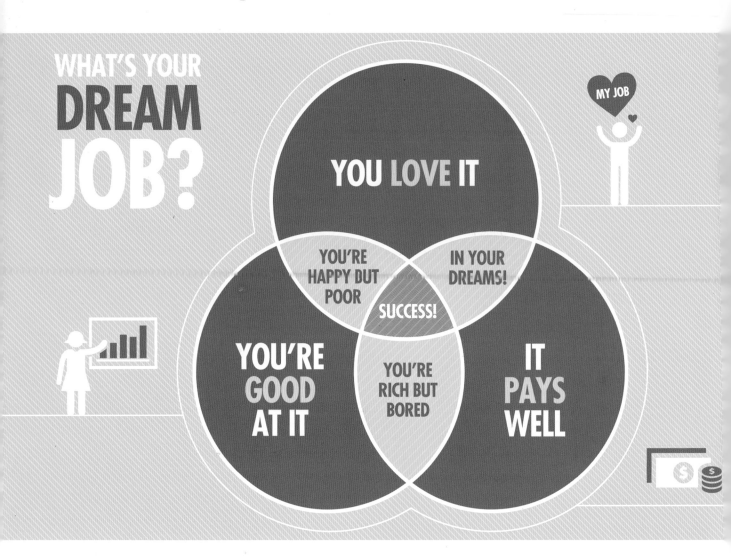

WHAT'S YOUR **DREAM JOB?**

MY JOB

YOU LOVE IT

YOU'RE HAPPY BUT POOR

IN YOUR DREAMS!

SUCCESS!

YOU'RE GOOD AT IT

YOU'RE RICH BUT BORED

IT PAYS WELL

GRAMMAR Unreal past

1 Work in pairs. Discuss the questions.

> **1** Why did you go into the job or course of study you're doing now, or that you've done in the past?
> **2** What would your dream job be?
> **3** What would inspire you to leave your current job for different work?

2 Look at the Dream job diagram. What three factors combine to make the perfect job? Are there any other important factors that are missing from the list, in your view?

3 Read the sentences in the Grammar box. Match each of the statements (1–3) with an orange section of the diagram. Then match the bold words and phrases with the best description (a–d).

UNREAL PAST

B/C **1** 'All I ever wanted to be was a painter. Everyone says I have real talent, and most importantly each day feels like a great adventure, although it isn't always easy to pay the bills. **Supposing someone offered me real money to do a different job?** I could never say yes to that. My life is good.'

A **2** '**I wish I hadn't worried so much about money when I was at university,** I wouldn't be stuck working at this bank. **It's high time I gave up the money to do something that's more interesting,** so I plan to start looking for a job soon.'

D

B **3** 'Science was always my favourite subject, but I didn't get very good marks. Still, **if only I was able to somehow earn a lot of money doing science.**'

a a regret
b a wish for something that is unlikely to happen
c a question about the consequences of a situation
d a statement that action needs to be taken soon

Check your answers on page 148 and do Exercises 1 and 2.

[handwritten top margin: I rather / I prefer]

4 Complete the conversation with one word in each space.

A: If only I [1] _____ *(had)* a different job, I'd be a lot happier.

B: What if you [2] _____ made redundant tomorrow. Would that make you happy?

A: Well, not really. I'd [3] _____ I had some idea of what to do next before I lost my job. But it's high [4] _____ I made a change.

B: [5] _____ you were able choose any job in the world – what would you choose?

A: That's the problem – I have no idea! I'd [6] _____ someone told me what I should do!

GRAMMAR Inversion in conditionals

5 Read the text in the Grammar box. Underline three conditional sentences in the text. Answer the questions (a–c).

INVERSION IN CONDITIONALS

When asked to complete a questionnaire on whether or not they're happy at work, a lot of people admit that they're not working in their dream job. Some express regrets about the past: 'Had I studied something different at university, I wouldn't be stuck here now.' Others focus more on what they don't have: 'Were I in a higher-paid job, I'd be a lot happier.' And quite a few simply wish for a change of scene.

But should you not know what career you could – realistically – change to, you may choose to see a careers counsellor. Or simply live with the idea that the dream job is just that – a dream.

There are three conditional sentences in the text. Which one is used:

a to explain a possible but currently untrue situation?

b to make a suggestion or talk about a possible outcome?

c to express a regret about the present that was caused by an action in the past?

Check your answers on page 148 and do Exercises 3–6.

6 Rewrite the sentences using inversion.

1 If you need to use a car this week, you can borrow mine. Should *you need to use a car* _____ .

2 If I'd been late for the plane, it would have ruined my holiday.

_____ .

3 If you applied for the job, I'm sure you wouldn't be sorry.

_____ .

4 You wouldn't have met Olga if you hadn't joined the book club.

Had you joined the book club, you would _____ .

5 If you need help with the application, please ask.

_____ .

6 My job would be a lot easier if people arrived on time for appointments.

_____ .

7 Complete the text using the words in brackets. Use unreal past forms and inversions.

As a careers counsellor, I often work with people who *wish* [1] *they were* (wish / be) in a different field altogether, but don't know how to make a change. The initial questions I ask them are basic: '[2] *Supposing you could* (supposing / can) have any job – what would it be?' '[3] *What if you didn't* (What / you / not) have to work at all – what would you do?' Some feel that life would be better now [4] *If only they had known* (if only / know) about more options as a young person. So I ask, '[5] *were you able* (be able) to speak to your youngor self, what advice would you give?'

A surprising number of people feel a lot of fear about making a big life change, especially from a relatively secure job, but I [6] *would rather people considered* (rather / people / consider) the options, even if they end up staying where they are. Interestingly, the statement '[7] *If only I had* (if only / have) a different job', when closely examined, often leads to people sticking with their career but, instead, making changes to find more fulfilment in their free time.

8 Complete the sentences so they're true for you.

1 If only ... *I had a degree.*

2 I'd sooner ... *we went to the beach.*

3 It's high time ... *I slept.*

4 Had I known ... *I would be very* (?)

5 Were it not for the fact that ... *I*

6 Had I not ...

7 Were I able to do so, I'd ...

8 Had it not been for ...

SPEAKING Talking about life experience

9 21st CENTURY OUTCOMES

Complete the Dream job diagram about yourself. Then discuss the questions.

- How has your life experience helped you to be good at what you're good at? *Had I not ...*
- When and how did you begin to love what you love? (If you haven't yet found something you love, think about something you've at least enjoyed.) *Were it not for the fact that ...*

10 Work in pairs. Explain your diagram and ask questions about your partner's. Can you think of jobs that might fill the 'Success!' position, and how you might get there?

5.3 I've got it!

READING Eureka moments?

1 Work in pairs. Discuss the questions.

  1 Can you think of someone who came up with a brilliant idea that is part of daily life today? Netflix

  2 Do you know whether the idea came all at once in a moment of inspiration, or was developed slowly over time? Slowly over time

2 Read the book review. Are these sentences true (T) or false (F)?

  1 King Hieron II believed that Archimedes might be cheating him. F

  2 It's unlikely that Archimedes actually existed. T

  3 Most big discoveries or developments occur over a long time – often years T

  4 The 'adjacent possible' is basically the next logical step. T

  5 It's extremely rare for more than one person to come up with the same idea for a new invention. F

  6 Johnson believes that sharing ideas is one of the best sources of inspiration. T

3 Work in pairs. Discuss the questions.

  1 Why do you think a 'eureka' story is often more appealing than the truth?

  2 Is an untrue 'eureka' story the same as a lie? Why? / Why not?

  3 How can stories be important or useful or 'true' even if we aren't sure of the facts?

4 Choose the correct meaning (a, b or c) for each of these words or expressions from the review.

  1 **innovation** a machine (b) new idea c question

  2 **incubation** a education b practice (c) development

  3 **hunch** (a) an idea based on feeling b an unoriginal idea c an incorrect idea

  4 **adjacent** a imagined b unexpected (c) next to

  5 **without exception** (a) in every case b in unusual circumstances c with no disagreements

  6 **in solitude** (a) alone b actively c secretly

5 What are each of the following expressions meant to make us think or feel about the topic?

  1 (line 1) 'The story goes …' and (line 47) 'so-called eureka moments'

  2 (line 67) 'They want to say … . But in fact …'

  3 (line 71) 'while there may even be … , in fact, …'

VOCABULARY Having ideas

6 Complete the suggestions for reducing a budget. Tick the expressions that mean 'I haven't thought of an idea'.

can't come up with	coming	dawning	drawing ✓
haven't	'm	occurs	strikes

  1 Looking at our research costs, I'm _drawing_ a blank.

  2 It _occurs_ to me that we spend too much on training.

  3 I checked through our warehousing costs, and I _can't come up_ anything there.

  4 I have one part-time assistant, so I _haven't_ the faintest idea how we can cut any staff costs.

  5 It's _dawning_ on me that we could reduce our office space.

  6 Checking the IT budget, I'm _coming_ to the realization that we can't afford a computer upgrade.

  7 I _am_ stuck for ideas.

  8 Going through our meeting costs, it _strikes_ me that we could save some money by reducing travel.

7 Discuss the following puzzles. Can you work any of them out? Use the expressions from Exercise 6. Then check your answers on page 172.

  1 What's special about the number 8,549,176,320?

  2 What's special about the words *assess*, *banana*, *dresser*, *grammar* and *potato*?

  3 A man is on one side of a river and his son is on the other side. He calls his son to come over, which he does – without using a bridge or a boat, and without getting wet. How did the son do it?

SPEAKING Where my ideas come from

8 **21st CENTURY OUTCOMES**

Work in small groups. Discuss the questions.

  • Is there a time that good ideas tend to occur to you? When you're not thinking about anything special? Some particular time or place?

  • Can you describe a time when an idea hit you about how to solve a problem, organize your life, make an education or career move, or something else?

  • Do you have a childhood memory of coming to the realization that something you had always believed was incorrect or incomplete?

  • When you're working on something and you feel stuck, is there something you do to try to encourage a moment of inspiration to come?

Eureka moments?

The story goes that 2,200 years ago, King Hieron II of Syracuse in Sicily ordered a jeweller to make him a crown from a bar of the king's gold. However, the king suspected the jeweller of keeping some of the gold and mixing in a cheaper metal like silver to make up the difference. The weight would be the same, and the king wouldn't know the difference. The king asked Archimedes – a Greek inventor and great thinker – to figure out a way to check the purity of the gold in the crown.

Archimedes already knew that gold was denser than silver, so the same weight of gold would take up less space than silver. But how could he measure the volume of an irregular object?

History tells us that Archimedes was lying in the bath when he had a sudden realization about how to solve the problem: he had noticed that when he himself got into the bath, the level of the water increased. The same would be true of the crown. He knew if it were made of pure gold, it would raise the water level by exactly the same amount as a standard, solid gold bar. But if some of the gold in the crown had been replaced with less dense silver, the crown would have slightly greater volume than solid gold, and would raise the water level a little more. It's said that at the moment of this realization, Archimedes jumped out of the bath and ran around shouting 'Eureka!' – Greek for 'I've found it!'. It's the classic story of sudden inspiration that gives us the term 'eureka moment' – but it probably isn't true.

STEVEN JOHNSON

"A FIRST-RATE STORYTELLER." –*THE NEW YORK TIMES*

WHERE GOOD IDEAS COME FROM

A *NEW YORK TIMES* BESTSELLER

THE NATURAL HISTORY OF INNOVATION

ENTERTAINING AND SMART
–LOS ANGELES TIMES

FROM THE BESTSELLING
AUTHOR OF *EVERYTHING
BAD IS GOOD FOR YOU*
AND *THE INVENTION
OF AIR*

In his book *Where Good Ideas Come From*, author Steven Johnson discusses many cases of so-called eureka moments, but says that the most interesting thing about them is that they're actually fairly rare. Most big innovations – in science, in technology, in the arts – don't arise out of nowhere as sudden realizations, but rather, dawn on people slowly. And they come to people who have been thinking about a topic or trying to solve a problem usually for years. In a 2010 TED talk, Johnson explained that people like to make their stories of innovation sound more dramatic. As he says, 'So they want to tell the story of the eureka moment. They want to say, "There I was, I was standing there and I had it all suddenly clear in my head". But in fact, if you go back and look at the historical record, it turns out that a lot of important ideas have very long incubation periods' – something Johnson calls the 'slow hunch'. So while there may even be the feeling of sudden inspiration, in fact, the ideas have been in the person's mind for some time and are simply the next logical step, both for the individual and within the field they work in. Johnson's term for this is the 'adjacent possible'.

'The history of cultural progress,' Johnson writes, 'is, almost without exception, a story of one door leading to another door, exploring the palace one room at a time'. In practical terms, this means that certain ideas will only be great ideas at the right time. If someone had come up with the idea for YouTube in 1995, before everyone had broadband and a cheap video camera, it would have been a failure – a bad idea. It wasn't yet the 'adjacent possible'. However, in 2005, it followed on naturally from the technology already in existence – it was the next logical step. This may explain why some great ideas occur to more than one person at about the same time; electrical batteries, early steam engines and the telephone were all developed around the same time by multiple people who didn't know about the others' work, but all were familiar with the existing technology of the day.

Where does this all lead? If you think you might just have an idea for the next big thing, Johnson's advice isn't to work in solitude in the hope of making a major breakthrough that will change the world. Not at all. Fortunately for you innovators, his recommendation is instead that you read a lot, spend a lot of time talking with people who share your interest, and so discover first where we are now, and second, what the next step – the 'adjacent possible' – might be.

5.4 Anyone got a bright idea?

LISTENING Planning a party

1 Work in pairs. Discuss the questions.

1 Think of an enjoyable party that you've been to. What was the occasion? Who planned it?
2 What made the event special? The food? The people? The venue? The entertainment?

2 ∩ 29 Listen to three colleagues planning a party. Make notes on as many of their ideas as you can.

The occasion: *Gustawy* *it*
The food: *Sushi or the ___*
The entertainment: *Band ___ dress like music*
The venue: *Park*

3 ∩ 29 Match the two parts of the sentences. Then listen again and check your answers.

1 We need to come up *i*
2 I really fancy *h*
3 Any votes *c*
4 Sure, I'd go *g*
5 That would be *j*
6 We could think about asking *d*
7 What about entertainment? Any *f*
8 That's *a*
9 Maybe it's a bit *e*
10 We should probably opt *b*

a an original idea!
b for the barbecue instead of sushi.
c for sushi?
d everyone to bring something to cook.
e too original?
f bright ideas?
g along with that.
h the idea of Japanese food.
i with a great idea.
j good fun.

Pronunciation Softening negative statements

4a ∩ 30 Listen to these two statements where the speaker softens the impact of a negative statement. Underline the most strongly stressed words in each sentence.

1 Sushi isn't especially cheap.
2 Live music wouldn't be so easy to get on a budget.

4b ∩ 31 Work in pairs. Practise saying these sentences so that you are softening the negative statements. Then listen and compare your pronunciation.

1 A barbecue in winter may not be very practical.
2 It wouldn't be that easy to organize a party in a museum.
3 A fancy dress party may be a bit too original?

Rachiade
me gusta

SPEAKING Brainstorming and choosing the best ideas

5 Work in groups of three. Imagine you're planning a party for your English class. Brainstorm ideas using the language in the Useful expressions box. Then select the best ideas for the party.

BRAINSTORMING AND CHOOSING THE BEST IDEAS

Stating objectives

We need to come up with a great idea.
Let's try to put together a good plan for a send-off.
What we need to do is get some good entertainment.

Encouraging contributions

Any thoughts on food?
Anyone got a bright idea?
Don't hold back!

Making suggestions

I really fancy the idea of a barbecue.
Any votes for karaoke?
Anyone got any objections to burgers?

Showing enthusiasm and agreeing

That's an original/inspired idea!
Yes, I'd go along with that.
That would be good fun!

Comparing ideas

The same goes for a band.
That's also true of live music.

Getting rid of ideas

Which ideas can we reject?
A barbecue may not be a very practical idea.
It wouldn't be that easy to live music on our budget.

Choosing ideas

We should probably opt for a disco instead of a live band.
Let's go with a fancy dress party.
That sounds like a plan!

WRITING A to-do list

6 Look at the to-do list for the leaving party. Answer the questions.

1 Has the date of the party been set yet?
2 How many people are expected to come?
3 What gift will Hilary receive?
4 What will some of the speakers talk about?

THINGS TO DO

Hilary's leaving party

1 Email Westside Country Park to check dates (17 or 24 Aug) and reserve picnic/BBQ area from 7 p.m. (approx. 35 people) – check re: picnic tables, grills, rubbish bins – party permit required?

2 Organize disposables (i.e. plates, cups, table cloths, plastic cutlery)

3 Email invitation to all staff, incl. map, directions and info re: food (BYO burgers, chicken, etc. for grill & drinks) – incl. invitation for family members – ask for RSVP

4 Decide on speeches (i.e. how many, how long, who, etc.)

5 Send sep. email to all staff re: ideas for gift & also ask for people to share good (funny?) 'Hilary stories' (e.g. Jim's coffee machine story)

6 Buy card and circulate for everyone to sign (incl. cleaning and maintenance staff)

Writing skill Abbreviations

7a Find abbreviations in the to-do list with each meaning (1–13).

1 including
2 barbecue
3 bring your own
4 about; approximately
5 regarding
6 and so on
7 and
8 that is; specifically
9 for example
10 separate
11 August
12 afternoon/evening
13 let us know if you can attend

7b Rewrite these sentences in note form.

1 We need to talk to Kevin regarding his trip to New York schedule and other matters.
2 People will bring their own food to the party, but we will supply drinks for approximately 50 people.
3 We need to ask people to tell us if they're coming in the morning or the afternoon.
4 Let's confirm the date of 12 December for the barbecue.
5 Everyone will have to buy a ticket, which will include food and entertainment.

8 **21st CENTURY OUTCOMES**

Make a to-do list for the class party you brainstormed in Exercise 5. Use the to-do list in Exercise 6 as a guide and use abbreviations.

9 Exchange lists with a partner. Did you come up with similar ideas?

6 Solutions

BACKGROUND

1 You are going to watch a TED Talk by Michael Pritchard called *How to make filthy water drinkable*. Read the text about the speaker and the talk. Then work in pairs and answer the questions.

    1 Why is it so important for people to have clean water?
    2 How do natural disasters cause problems with drinking water?
    3 When assisting victims of a natural disaster, how do you think aid agencies usually try to provide clean water?

TEDTALKS

MICHAEL PRITCHARD is a water-treatment expert. During the 2004 Asian tsunami and 2005 Hurricane Katrina, he watched helplessly as televised coverage showed thousands of refugees waiting for days for a simple drink of clean water. Pained by the continued failure of aid agencies to solve this basic problem, Pritchard decided to do something about it. In this talk, he demonstrates the portable Lifesaver filter, which can make the dirtiest water drinkable in seconds. Michael Pritchard's idea worth spreading is that thinking differently about a problem that seems impossible to solve just might bring forth an ingenious solution.

The Self Employed Women's Association helps women learn to build and repair solar lanterns in India

KEY WORDS

2 Read the sentences (1–6). The words in bold are used in the TED Talk. First guess the meaning of the words. Then match the words with their definitions (a–f).

1 The lake was **contaminated** with waste from the nearby factory.

2 I fitted a **filter** to the tap to remove some of the chemicals.

3 If drinking water isn't **sterile**, it can cause stomach problems.

4 The dangerous chemicals were absorbed through tiny **pores**.

5 When you have **diarrhoea**, it's important to drink plenty of water.

6 Viruses are typically 20 to 400 **nanometres** when measured around the middle.

a completely clean and free of germs

b a medical condition that causes stomach pain and frequent production of liquid rather than solid waste

c one thousand-millionth of a metre

d a device that can clean things that pass through it, for example air or water

e holes

f made unclean, containing chemicals, poison, or other harmful substances

AUTHENTIC LISTENING SKILLS
Signposts

Signposts are words and phrases that speakers use to explain the structure of their talk to the audience. Signposts guide the audience through the talk by calling attention to what is going to happen next, or to what has just happened. For example, *I'd like to start today by talking about … . Now that I've explained … , I'd like to tell you a little more about … .*

3a 🎧 **32** Look at the Authentic listening skills box. Then listen to extracts 1 and 2 from the TED Talk. Underline the signposting expressions.

1 Good morning everybody. I'd like to talk about a couple of things today. The first thing is water.

2 However, after a few failed prototypes, I finally came up with this, the Lifesaver bottle. … OK, now for the science bit. Before Lifesaver, the best hand filters were only capable of filtering down to about 200 nanometres.

3b 🎧 **33** Listen to sentences 3, 4 and 5. Write down the signposting expressions the speaker uses to introduce what he's going to talk about.

6.1 How to make filthy water drinkable

TEDTALKS

1 ▶ 6.1 Watch the TED Talk. What is Michael Pritchard's main message?

1 Relief operations after natural disasters need to be greatly improved.
2 By providing the Lifesaver bottle, the UK government could save a lot of foreign-aid money.
3 Providing safe, affordable drinking water for everyone on Earth could save millions of lives.

2 ▶ 6.1 Watch the first part (0.00–3.22) of the talk again. Answer the questions.

1 What medical condition, caused by drinking contaminated water, does Pritchard talk about?
2 Why do we (and governments and aid agencies) 'switch off' in discussions about the global need for clean water around the world?
3 In the Asian tsunami, what was the alternative to drinking contaminated water?
4 After Hurricane Katrina in the USA, how many days passed before clean water arrived?
5 What does Lifesaver filter out that other filter systems can't?

▶ got /gɒt/ **BR ENG**
▶ gotten /ˈgɑt(ə)n/ **N AM ENG**
▶ nought /nɔːt/ **BR ENG**
▶ zero /ˈzɪroʊ/ **N AM ENG**

3 **6.1** Complete the description of Pritchard's demonstration. Then watch the second part (3.23–5.56) of the talk again and check your answers.

audience	demonstration	filter	leaves
pond	poo	pump	water

For his ¹_____, Pritchard takes water from two rivers, his garden ²_____ and a sewage plant. He then adds some ³_____ and soil and also some rabbit ⁴_____ . At this point, the contaminated ⁵_____ looks filthy and the ⁶_____ clearly thinks it's disgusting. He then puts the filthy water in the Lifesaver, pushes the ⁷_____ a couple times to push the water through the ⁸_____, and produces sterile water.

4 **6.1** Watch the third part (5.57 to the end) of the talk again. Complete the sentences with the missing facts.

1 One Lifesaver filter cartridge purifies _____ litres of water.

2 After a disaster, people usually have to go to _____ to get clean water.

3 The traditional way of transporting water is _____ .

4 When people use Lifesaver, the water is transported by _____ .

5 The Lifesaver jerry can purifies _____ litres of water.

6 By providing clean water, we could save the lives of _____ million kids each year.

VOCABULARY IN CONTEXT

5 **6.2** Watch the clips from the TED Talk. Choose the correct meaning of the words.

6 Work in pairs. Discuss the questions.

1 Can you think of something you did as a child to the dismay of your parents or teachers?

2 In your town or city, where do people congregate when they want to relax and socialize?

3 What problems in the world are self-perpetuating? Think of issues associated with poverty and wealth, crime and punishment, and disease.

CRITICAL THINKING Using supporting evidence

7 Match each piece of evidence Michael Pritchard uses (1–4) in his TED Talk to the point it supports (a–d).

1 the pictures of natural disasters
2 the scientific explanation
3 the demonstration
4 the explanation that the operating cost of the bottle is only one half of one cent per day

a The Lifesaver is incredibly easy to operate.
b The Lifesaver filters out everything that could make you ill.
c The Lifesaver is inexpensive.
d The problem of not having clean drinking water is terrible.

8 What evidence from the talk do you find particularly effective?

9 Read the comment* about the TED Talk. Do you think Mikhail makes a valid point? Why? / Why not?

Viewers' comments

M **Mikhail** – I'm not convinced that the problem is as serious as Pritchard says it is. I think he's just trying to create a market for his product.

*The comment was created for this activity.

PRESENTATION SKILLS Demonstration

Audiences understand and remember demonstrations better than descriptions. Try to show your audience what you're talking about.

• When possible, make the demonstration interactive.
• Make sure the demonstration set-up is big enough for everyone to see.
• If your demonstration involves movement, make your movements large and expressive enough to engage the audience.

10 **6.3** Look at the Presentation tips box. Then watch Michael Pritchard's demonstration. Find examples of each of the three tips. Then answer the questions.

1 Why did Pritchard add the pond water, sewage, poo and plants as the audience watched instead of putting them in before?

2 Why did Pritchard ask the cameraman to smell the water?

3 Why did Pritchard ask the man named Chris to drink the water?

11 Work in pairs. Think of a simple process you can demonstrate: operating an app on your phone or tablet, using a cash card in a banking machine, or another idea. Prepare how you will demonstrate it.

12 Work with another partner. Take turns to present your demonstration following the tips in the Presentation tips box. Did you come up with similar ideas?

▶ source / pour /sɔː(r)s/ /pɔː(r)/ **BR ENG**
▶ source / pour /sɔrs/ /pɔr/ **N AM ENG**

▶ been /biːn/ **BR ENG**
▶ been /bɪn/ **N AM ENG**

6.2 What a waste of time!

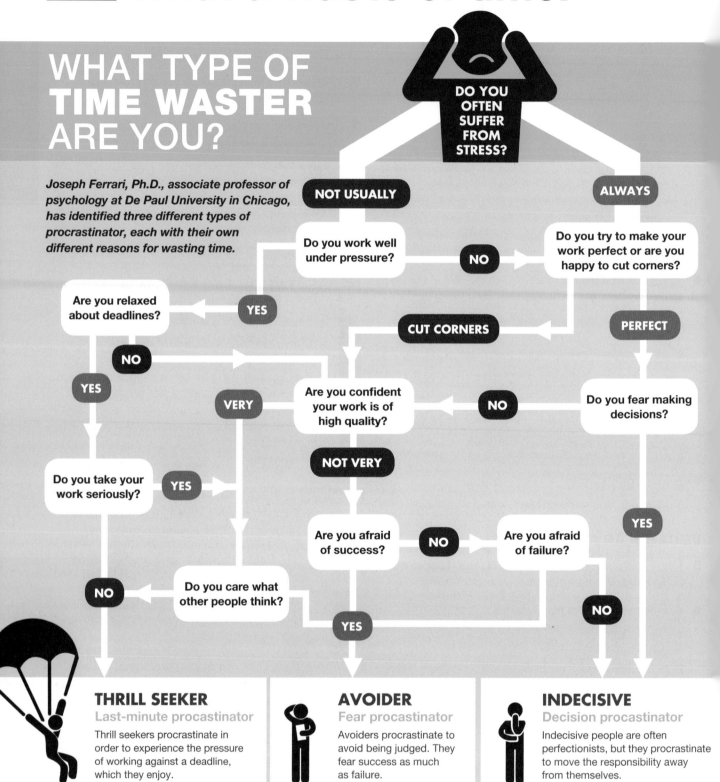

WHAT TYPE OF TIME WASTER ARE YOU?

Joseph Ferrari, Ph.D., associate professor of psychology at De Paul University in Chicago, has identified three different types of procrastinator, each with their own different reasons for wasting time.

DO YOU OFTEN SUFFER FROM STRESS?

NOT USUALLY

Do you work well under pressure?

ALWAYS

Do you try to make your work perfect or are you happy to cut corners?

Are you relaxed about deadlines?

YES

NO

CUT CORNERS

PERFECT

YES

NO

VERY

Are you confident your work is of high quality?

NO

Do you fear making decisions?

Do you take your work seriously?

YES

NOT VERY

Are you afraid of success?

NO

Are you afraid of failure?

YES

NO

Do you care what other people think?

YES

NO

THRILL SEEKER
Last-minute procrastinator

Thrill seekers procrastinate in order to experience the pressure of working against a deadline, which they enjoy.

AVOIDER
Fear procrastinator

Avoiders procrastinate to avoid being judged. They fear success as much as failure.

INDECISIVE
Decision procrastinator

Indecisive people are often perfectionists, but they procrastinate to move the responsibility away from themselves.

GRAMMAR Purpose

1 Work in pairs. Everyone wastes time sometimes. When you waste time, what do you think is the reason? Stress? Boredom? Something else?

2 Look at the flow chart. Answer the questions.

1 What's the purpose of the flow chart?
2 Work your way through the questions on the chart. What does it tell you about yourself?
3 Do you agree with the chart's description of you? Why? / Why not?

3 Read the text in the Grammar box. Answer the questions (1–5).

PURPOSE

Solutions for time-wasters

Thrill seeker: Constantly set and adjust deadlines **so that** you still get the adrenaline rush, but are using your time more effectively than procrastinating.

Success story: 'I used to leave work until the last minute **so that** I would feel the pressure to get it done – I thought I needed that. I talked to my boss, and for my next big project she's set me a series of smaller deadlines **in order that** I feel a bit of pressure, but still have enough time to get the work done.'

Avoider: Success is a good thing and nothing to be ashamed of. Failure is a way to learn and improve. **To** work efficiently, focus on doing the best job you can do and not on what others think.

Success story: 'It's all about the process. I used to think that the final product was all that mattered, but I've come to realize that it's important to learn from your mistakes **so as not to** repeat them in the next project.'

Indecisive: Not everything has to be perfect so try to take small risks and use your intuition. Mistakes may mean you learn something new. **To avoid** getting stuck or stressed, split up the task into more manageable parts.

Success story: 'In the past, starting projects was difficult, because it always seemed the job was just so big. I've learned to break up projects into a set of smaller projects **in order to** make things feel more achievable.'

Which expression in **bold**:

1 is followed by a present tense to refer to the future?
2 introduces something that happened in the past?
3 can be followed by a new subject?
4 is followed by the infinitive? (x3)
5 is being used to refer to something you *don't* want to happen? (x2)

Check your answers on page 150 and do Exercises 1–6.

4 🎧 **34** Listen to the conversation. Complete the statements with the expressions they use.

1 They should leave in about ten minutes _____ be late to the meeting.
2 They'll go via East Street _____ the road works in the town centre.
3 Part of East Street is closed _____ traffic building up in the area.
4 They may not have left for the meeting early enough _____ be on time.
5 One of them will text Raymond _____ he knows they may be delayed.

5 Rewrite the words in italics using the word in brackets.

1 Sally starts projects at the last possible minute *because she wants to feel the adrenaline rush*. (to) *to feel the adrenaline rush*
2 Liam started on his presentation weeks before the conference *because he didn't want to work under pressure*. (avoid)
3 I often break tasks into smaller parts *because it makes work seem more manageable*. (order)
4 Piet is trying to work more quickly *because he doesn't want to miss his deadline*. (so that)
5 Rafa started the work earlier than necessary *because he wanted to avoid a last-minute rush*. (to)
6 Helena switches off her phone when she's writing *because she needs to concentrate*. (in order that)
7 I'd like to change some of my work habits *because I want to work more efficiently*. (so that)
8 I used to avoid responsibility *because I didn't want to make mistakes*. (so as)

6 Answer the questions. Use the expressions in brackets.

1 Why do you avoid doing certain activities? (so as not to)
   I avoid drinking too much coffee so as not to be awake half the night!
2 Think of one piece of clothing that you have. What is its purpose? (for)
3 Why are you studying English? (in order to)
4 What is the purpose of a piece of safety equipment in your home, in your car, on your bicycle, etc.? (to prevent)
5 What is the purpose of an action that you take or an activity you do? (to avoid)
6 Why do you carry a certain thing with you most of the time, for example your keys or your phone? (so that)

SPEAKING Talking about why things are useful

7 **21st CENTURY OUTCOMES**

Work in pairs.

1 Think of something you use regularly that simplifies your life, helps you be more efficient, or makes a job easier. It might be an app on one of your devices, a gadget in your kitchen, or a service you use.
2 Think of as many reasons as possible why your partner should start using the same app, gadget or service.
3 Try to convince your partner to try it. Your partner should say why they would or wouldn't like to try it.

6.3 Thinking outside the box

READING The parable of the stones

1 Read the short text. Do the puzzle.

> The expression 'thinking outside the box' comes from the nine-dots puzzle, often used in management training in the 1970s and 80s. To solve the puzzle, draw four straight lines that connect all nine dots without lifting your pen or pencil off of the paper.

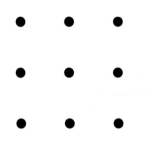

2 Check your answer to Exercise 1 on page 172. Then work in pairs and discuss the questions.

    1 Were you able to solve the puzzle?

    2 What is the connection between the puzzle and the expression 'think outside the box'?

    3 The puzzle is said to require 'lateral thinking'. What do you think this term means?

3 Read the story. Then find and underline phrases that contradict these statements.

    1 The farmer was in debt because he hadn't managed his farm well.

    2 The landowner wanted the farmer and his daughter to find happiness, because he loved the daughter.

    3 The old man planned to leave the decision to chance.

4 Work in small groups. Discuss what you think the girl did. Then turn to page 183 and read the conclusion of the story.

5 A parable is a story that teaches a lesson. Which sentence is the best statement of the parable's lesson?

    1 Some people lie and cheat to get what they want, so you must be prepared to lie and cheat yourself in some situations.

    2 Debt can force people into terrible situations, so when possible, you should avoid owing anyone a lot of money.

    3 Complex problems often have a simple solution, but we may have to change our thinking about the problem to find it.

6 In your groups, discuss what the nine-dots puzzle and the parable of the stones have in common.

VOCABULARY Solution collocations

7 Choose the correct options to complete these phrases about finding solutions.

    1 I *solved / got to the bottom* of the dilemma of which university to go to by flipping a coin!

    2 It took me six months to *overcome / sort out* the mess caused by having my credit card stolen.

    3 Yusuf and Zehra finally *cleared up / cracked* the misunderstanding with their neighbour.

    4 There are still some obstacles to *figure out / overcome* before we can sign the contract.

    5 Were you able to *solve / clear up* the riddle of Sal's missing shoes?

    6 I've been trying to solve this puzzle all day, and I've finally *interpreted / cracked* it.

    7 I never *got to the bottom of / got round* the mystery of why Jessie stopped calling me.

8 Match the two parts of the sentences.

    1 I phoned her to clear up the misunderstanding

    2 In Spain, I had to overcome several obstacles,

    3 I never did solve the riddle

    4 It took me a couple of years to crack the problem

    5 It wasn't easy to solve the dilemma

    a including my lack of ability to speak Spanish.

    b of how to avoid rush hour traffic and get to work on time.

    c of the missing television remote control.

    d about our plans for the weekend.

    e of whether to buy the Porsche or the BMW – so I bought a Mini.

SPEAKING Describing a solution

9 **21st CENTURY OUTCOMES**

Think of a time when you had some kind of problem. Choose one or two of the following and explain the problem, but not the solution.

- a difficult-to-solve problem that you needed to crack
- a mystery that you wanted to get to the bottom of
- a misunderstanding with a friend, colleague, neighbour or family member that needed to be cleared up
- an obstacle that was blocking your progress in some way, that you needed to overcome
- some other puzzle that you needed to solve.

10 Work in pairs. Listen to one another's problems and offer suggestions.

11 Reveal to your partner the real solution that you found to your problem.

The parable of the stones

A LONG TIME AGO, there was a poor but honest farmer who managed, through long days of labour and with the help of his two
5 strong sons and his hardworking wife and daughter, to lead a happy, if simple, life. But during one hard winter, his wife and sons became terribly ill and then died.

This tragedy was followed by several
10 seasons of hot, dry weather with little rain. As a consequence of his great misfortune, the poor farmer had to borrow money from a rich landowner, just to feed himself and the one remaining member of his once-happy family – his daughter.

The landowner, who was old and not very good-looking, had fallen in love with the
15 farmer's daughter and wanted to marry her. He didn't care about the money itself, but he saw the situation as an opportunity to demand from the farmer something of great value. He said, 'Give me your daughter in marriage and I will forget about the debt.' This put the farmer and his daughter in a very awkward position, with no idea what to do, knowing that they had no way to repay the debt. One thing was certain: they were both horrified at
20 the thought of the marriage, and the old man could see this.

However, the hard-hearted old landowner wasn't going to let the unhappiness of the poor farmer and the obvious dislike his gentle daughter clearly felt towards him be an obstacle. He was used to getting his way, and he was not opposed to cheating when necessary, so he immediately came up with a plan. As the three were standing in the road
25 talking, a small crowd had gathered. The old man said, 'Why don't we let chance decide? I will put two pebbles in this bag – a black one and a white one.' The curious bystanders looked on as he picked up several stones from the path. 'If you reach into the bag and pull out the black pebble, you do not have to marry me, and I will forgive your father's debt. If you choose the white pebble, you must marry me and I will forgive your father's debt. If
30 you refuse to pick a pebble, I will have your father thrown into prison.'

The poor farmer knew that the landowner would probably cheat, but realized sadly that there was nothing he could do about it, and so he quietly agreed to the arrangement. The girl watched carefully as the old man put two stones into the bag, and to her horror, she saw that he put in two white pebbles – though she was the only one
35 who had noticed. Now the girl had a serious dilemma. Logical thinking would seem to lead to the conclusion that there were three possible ways to respond: 1) Show everyone who had gathered round that the rich, old landowner was a cheat – and probably get thrown in prison as a result; 2) refuse to draw out a stone and allow her father to be thrown into prison; 3) reach in and take a stone, knowing that it could only result in her
40 having to marry the old man. The old man stared impatiently at the girl, as the farmer looked away, too nervous to watch. But the girl looked confident. She knew the solution to her problem.

What do you think the girl did?

6.4 What are our options?

LISTENING Discussing options for solving a problem

1 Have you ever been lost – in the city, in a shopping centre, in the countryside? What happened?

2 Look at the photo of the lost walkers. Work in pairs. Discuss the questions.

1 What problems will they face if they don't find their way?
2 What options do you think they're discussing?
3 What advice would you give them?

3 🎧 35 Listen to a conversation between three walkers and answer the questions.

1 What are they looking for?
2 What time of day is it?
3 What options do they consider?
4 What solution do they find?

4 🎧 35 Listen again. Match the sentences (1–6) with their responses (a–f).

1 What are our options?
2 We could split up. Maybe one of us would find the path?
3 Let's just take stock of what we have first. Did anyone bring a torch?
4 If we have to stay out all night, we'll have enough water.
5 How about if we just call out?
6 Let's try it.

a I'm not too sure about that. I'd rather stick together.
b It's worth a try.
c We could go back the way we came.
d OK, sure. What have we got to lose?
e Good. We may not have any choice.
f Not me. I didn't expect to be out at night.

Pronunciation Stress in content and function words

5a 🎧 36 Underline the word or words in each sentence that you think will be stressed. Listen and check your answers.

1 What are our options?
2 We could split up.
3 I'd rather stick together.
4 Did anyone bring a torch?
5 There's one on my phone.
6 Do you two have any matches?
7 It's worth a try.
8 What have we got to lose?

5b Practise saying the sentences with natural stress patterns.

SPEAKING Finding solutions

6 Work in groups of three. Imagine you are in very remote countryside and your car has got stuck in the mud. What would you do? Discuss options and decide the best way to solve the problem. Use the expressions in the Useful expressions box.

FINDING SOLUTIONS

Considering options

What are our options?
We could go back the way we came.
Why don't we try looking at the map?
Maybe we should consider phoning the police.
Let's just take stock.
I'd rather stay together.

Talking about possible outcomes

It's worth a try.
What have we got to lose?

Raising doubts

I'm not too sure about that.
Are you sure that will work?

Deciding to take action

Let's try it.
Let's give that a try.

7 Compare solutions with another group. Did you come up with similar ideas?

WRITING Online advice forum

8 Read the online advice. Answer the questions.

1 What do colleagues' interruptions prevent the writer doing?
2 What solutions are offered?
3 Do you think the advice would be useful in most cases? Why? / Why not?

Writing skill Softening advice or recommendations

9a Rather than 'You need to communicate more clearly,' the writer says 'It sounds as though you may need to learn to communicate more clearly.' What effect do the extra words have? What similar expressions does the writer use?

9b Complete the sentences with these words.

consider	find it	include
may have to	might	the possibility of
think	will probably	

1 _____ working from home some days.
2 You _____ want to talk to your boss about the problem.
3 _____ about sending an email round to your colleagues.
4 Some people _____ beneficial to schedule a coffee break.
5 This could _____ making time for small talk.
6 There's always _____ wearing headphones at your desk.
7 You _____ accept that you can't completely control the situation.
8 You _____ be doing yourself a favour if you don't get too angry with anyone.

10 **21st** **CENTURY OUTCOMES**

Imagine you are giving advice in an online forum. Choose one of the following to offer help with.

- I'm buried under piles of disorganized paperwork. I constantly lose important information and I can't find documents when I need to refer to them.
- I need to save money, but I can't. I earn a pretty good salary but I always seem to spend it. I'm worried now about not having enough money when I need it in the future.
- I have no time for my family or myself. All of my time is spent either at work, or sorting out household jobs like food shopping, cooking and cleaning.

11 Exchange texts with a partner. Do you think your partner's solutions would be effective? Can you add any ideas?

 ASK DAVE Sticky problem?

Dear Dave,

I like my colleagues and we get on well, but I find they're always interrupting me. I'm getting increasingly frustrated by it, because I can never fully concentrate on my work. What can I do?

Signed,

LM, Harrogate

Dear LM,

'Friendly' interruptions are an all-too-common problem at work. While an office chat is important, too much can seriously damage your productivity.

It sounds as though you may need to learn to communicate more clearly with interrupting colleagues. Consider putting a 'Do not disturb' sign on your (closed) office door. If you work in an open-plan office, you might put the sign on your desk. If someone interrupts you anyway, think about firmly but politely saying, 'Can we talk about this in about an hour? I'm in the middle of something right now.'

When electronic interruptions are part of the problem, some workers find it beneficial to remove all distractions for certain periods of time during the day. This could include turning off your email notifications and switching your phone to voicemail, thereby creating periods for clear concentration.

Additionally, there's always the possibility of finding a hiding place. If you are able to work away from your desk, you could try to find an available meeting room, empty office, or other place to work where people won't find you. If necessary, clear this with your manager first.

Finally, you may have to accept that some interruption is part of having good working relationships. If you do hide for part of the day, you will probably be doing yourself a favour if you can remain clearly available some of the time as well.

Good luck!

Dave

READING

1 Read the article about Sonidos de la Tierra. Answer the questions.

   1 What does the Sonidos de la Tierra motto suggest about the effect on young people's lives of playing music?

   2 What's unusual about the instruments played by the H2O Orchestra?

3 What negative effect of the political situation in Paraguay from the 1960s to the 1980s does Sonidos de la Tierra seek to address?

4 What was Luis Szarán's childhood like, and what did he go on to accomplish as an adult?

5 What evidence is there of Sonidos's positive effect?

Sonidos de la tierra

'The young person who plays Mozart by day does not break shop windows at night.'

—Motto of Sonidos de la Tierra

With instruments made from recycled junk such as old bottles, pipes, funnels and hoses, the H2O Orchestra uses music to educate the world about water conservation. It's just one of many projects set up by Sonidos de la Tierra – (Sounds of the Earth), a music education programme that started in Paraguay, South America. In addition to teaching young people to make music and furthering people's understanding of water use, the group also holds the Guinness World Record for the largest group of harp players ever to play together – 420 in all.

Founded in 2002, Sonidos has used music to transform the lives of young people in more than 180 towns, cities and rural areas by putting musical instruments into their hands. In addition to the usual classical music instruments, students can also learn the traditional instruments of Paraguay, including the Paraguayan harp. The project aims to keep kids out of trouble and also to support and strengthen a sense of national and cultural identity, which was widely seen as having been badly damaged by a 35-year dictatorship that ended in 1989. And they don't only play instruments, they make them as well. More than 400, including recycled musical instruments made out of junk, have been produced in Sonidos's musical instrument workshops.

The organization's founder, Luis Szarán, understands the power of music to change lives. Born in 1953 in Paraguay, Luis was the eighth child of farmers who struggled to make a living. When he was a young man, his musical talent was noticed by a prominent Paraguayan musician, who made it possible for him to study music in Europe with some of the world's greatest teachers. After several years of study, he dedicated himself to musical research, and began publishing his findings on Native American music and the popular music of Paraguay, among other topics. He also composes music and works as the director of the Asunción City Symphony Orchestra and has won more than twenty prestigious awards.

More than half of the Sonidos teachers were themselves Sonidos students, and about a third of the professional players in Paraguay's orchestras are former Sonidos students who won their orchestra places by audition.

The project has been so successful in Paraguay that it's expanded to Argentina, Bolivia, Brazil and Uruguay and as far away as Germany, where in 2006, an international orchestra Welweite Klänge (Sounds of the World) brought together young people from the Americas, Europe, China and Africa. Globally, more than 14,000 young people participate. Meanwhile, the H2O Orchestra has released an album of songs promoting water conservation, and continues to tour extensively, spreading the word one song at a time.

GRAMMAR

2 Choose the correct options to complete the interview.

A: Sonidos de la Tierra exists partly to [1]*prevent / avoid* kids from getting into trouble – and it seems to work well. Why is it so effective?

B: [2]*So that / In order* to keep kids out of trouble, you need to give them something interesting to do, some structure.

A: What do you mean by 'structure'?

B: It's easy to think that kids – especially 'bad' kids – hate rules. In fact, most kids would [3]*suppose / rather* they had some boundaries and limits. [4]*What if / If only* no one ever gave *you* any clear guidance or direction?

A: But every school has rules. Surely there's more to it than that?

B: Definitely. Playing orchestral music, the rules aren't there [5]*to / for* stop you doing things. It's all about working together [6]*for / so that* you can produce something great.

3 Put the words in the correct order to make sentences.

1 got / Had / have / I / I'd / into / music, / not / played / trouble

_____

2 advice, / any / ask / need / please / Should / you

_____

3 a / able / buy / do / I / I'd / so, / to / violin / Were / you

_____

4 a / decision / high / It's / made / time / we

_____

5 cooperation / in / learn / music / order / play / to / together / We

_____

6 a / as / exam / fail / He / lot / music / not / practised / so / the / to

_____

VOCABULARY

4 Complete the texts about mysteries in the arts with these words.

the bottom	come	the faintest idea
figure	interpreting	it
obstacle	realization	riddle

What's the Stradivarius secret?

It's long been known that the best violins ever made came from the workshop of Italy's Stradivari family about 300 years ago. But no one has been able to [1]_____ out what makes their sound so rich and expressive – until now. After placing the violins in a medical scanner and [2]_____ the data, researchers came to the [3]_____ that the density of the wood used for the front and back body panels is extremely consistent – far more so than high-quality modern violins they used for comparison. This led to another [4]_____ that had to be solved: what was special about the wood in those violins?

It turns out that a combination of wood grown in spring and wood grown in summer was used in the violins, and that seems to have given them their special sound quality.

The Puzzle of Shakespeare

William Shakespeare is celebrated as one of the greatest writers in the history of the English language, but even after centuries of research, no one has got to [5]_____ of the mystery of how he did what he did. [6]_____ occurred even to early critics that the supposedly middle – class playwright had a surprisingly detailed understanding of how kings, queens and aristocrats lived – things that the average writer would be unlikely to have [7]_____ about. No one yet has [8]_____ up with an explanation. Does this mean someone else might have written 'Shakespeare's' plays? One [9]_____ facing anyone trying to find out more about these extraordinary works is the fact they were written over 400 years ago.

DISCUSSION

5 Read the quotations about music. Do you agree with them? Why? / Why not?

1 'Music produces a kind of pleasure which human nature cannot do without.' —Confucius, *The Book of Rites*

2 'Music is the universal language of mankind.' —Henry Wadsworth Longfellow

SPEAKING

6 Put these phrases in the correct place in the conversation. Then practise it with a partner.

- Any votes for
- Anyone got
- I really fancy
- I'd go along with
- I'm not too sure
- let's give that a try
- Maybe we should consider
- sounds like a plan
- The same goes for
- We could try
- What are our
- What we need to do is

A: [1]_____ come up with a great idea for the conference dinner. [2]_____ a bright idea?

B: [3]_____ the new Mexican restaurant in York Road.

C: [4]_____ about that. [5]_____ the idea of the Chinese buffet at Lucky House.

A: Yes, [6]_____ that. It would give everyone plenty of choice, and it's informal.

B: [7]_____ any kind of buffet, really. It wouldn't have to be Chinese.

A: [8]_____ options?

C: [9]_____ going to Antonio's. They have a buffet.

A: [10]_____ Italian food?

B: I've been to Antonio's loads of times, and it's always good.

A: OK, fine, then [11]_____.

C: That [12]_____!

7 Imagination

BACKGROUND

1 You are going to watch a TED Talk by Janet Echelman called *Taking imagination seriously.* Read the text about the speaker and the talk, then answer the questions.

1 The title of the talk is *Taking imagination seriously*. What do you think this means?

2 Echelman's sculptures are 'huge, flowing objects that respond to environmental forces'. What materials do you think she uses that behave this way?

3 Are there sculptures in public spaces in your city? Why do you think they are there? Do you have a favourite? If so, describe it.

TEDTALKS

JANET ECHELMAN is a North American artist who found her true voice as an artist when her paints went missing — forcing her to find a new medium for her projects. As a result, she turned from painting to sculpture, and now reshapes urban airspace with huge, flowing objects that respond to environmental forces — wind, water and light— and become inviting points of focus for city life. Janet Echelman's idea worth spreading is that by combining traditional art forms with high-tech materials, you can create public art that pays tribute to nature and brings people together.

A child's view of a sculpture by John Davies in the Museum of Fine Arts, Bilbao, Spain

KEY WORDS

2 Read the sentences (1–6). The words in bold are used in the TED Talk. First guess the meaning of the words. Then match the words with their definitions (a–f).

1 His work is **idiosyncratic** and striking but can be difficult to understand.
2 The sculptures are **ephemeral** because of the material they're made from.
3 The edges of the cloth were decorated with hand-made **lace**.
4 The ropes are tied together with a tight **knot**.
5 She uses only fabrics that are made from **natural fibres**.
6 Large pieces of fabric were **billowing** from the wires.

a lasting for a very short time
b long, thin pieces of natural material, such as wool or silk
c a fine cloth with patterns of small holes
d filled with air and blowing in the wind
e a fastening made by tying string or rope
f unusual, individual

AUTHENTIC LISTENING SKILLS Inferring meaning from context

When you hear a word you don't know, it can be useful to try to work out what sort of information it carries, to help you understand enough to keep listening. Often you can also gather information from the surrounding words. Sometimes you may also find clues inside words. You may not know the word *intensification*, but if you recognize the adjective *intense* in it, it may help you work out its meaning.

3a 🎧 **37** Look at the Authentic listening skills box. With a partner, try to work out what sort of word is missing. Then listen to the extract from the TED Talk.

1 I painted for ten years when I was offered a [1] _____ to India. Promising to give exhibitions of paintings, I shipped my paints and arrived in [2] _____ .
2 This fishing village was famous for sculpture. So, I tried bronze [3] _____ . But to make large forms was too heavy and expensive.

3b 🎧 **38** Listen to the next section of the talk. With a partner, use words or gestures to demonstrate what you think the meaning of these three words is.

bundle   mounds   volumetric

7.1 Taking imagination seriously

TEDTALKS

1 ▶ 7.1 Read the statements, then watch the TED Talk. Are these sentences true (T) or false (F)?

1 Janet Echelman became a sculptor by accident.
2 Her first giant net sculpture was made in India and displayed in Madrid.
3 It's impossible to design and make large nets using machines, so all of her sculptures are hand made.
4 Her net sculptures led her to work with other materials, too, including steel and water.
5 A piece that she created in Denver was inspired by scientific data about a natural disaster.
6 Echelman ends with a story about solving legal problems she had with one sculpture.

2 ▶ 7.1 Watch the first part (0.00–5.25) of the talk again. Answer the questions.

1 How did Echelman receive her training as an artist?
2 What two important features of the village of Mahabalipuram led Echelman to produce the work she made there?
3 Who worked with Echelman to make her first satisfying sculpture, and what was it an image of?
4 In addition to fishermen, what craftspeople did Echelman work with?
5 How was the work she was asked to do for the waterfront in Porto, Portugal, different from the work she had done before?
6 Who did Echelman work with to create the sculpture for Porto?

▶ fiber **N AM ENG**
▶ fibre **BR ENG**

▶ college **N AM ENG**
▶ university **BR ENG**

3 ▶ **7.1** Watch the second part (5.26–7.34) of the talk again. Then find and correct six errors in this text.

In Philadelphia, Janet Echelman sculpted with smoke that is shaped by the wind and through interaction with people. It represents the paths of trains that run above the city.

In Denver, Echelman represented the interconnectedness of the 35 nations of the Western hemisphere in a sculpture. She used photographs from NOAA (the National Oceanic and Atmospheric Administration) that showed the 2010 Pacific tsunami. The title '1.26' refers to the number of microseconds that the Earth's day was made longer as a result of the earthquake that started the tsunami.

Echelman couldn't use her usual steel ring to build this sculpture, so instead, she used a mesh fibre that was much more delicate than steel. This allowed the sculpture to be supported by nearby trees.

4 ▶ **7.1** Watch the third part (7.35 to the end) of the talk again. Answer the questions.

1 When she gave her TED Talk, how far along was Janet Echelman's project in New York?
2 What are the two different influences or methods that she combines in her artwork?
3 How did her work affect office workers in Phoenix, Arizona?

VOCABULARY IN CONTEXT

5 ▶ **7.2** Watch the clips from the TED Talk. Choose the correct meaning of the words.

6 Work in pairs. Discuss the questions.

1 Can you think of a time when you've been mesmerized by something?
2 What features do you often find on waterfronts? Can you think of an example you've visited?
3 Are there any places in your town or city that people think are very bland? And what about areas that aren't at all bland?

CRITICAL THINKING Reading between the lines

7 A speaker doesn't always have to say something directly for us to know that it's true. Which of the following can be read 'between the lines' of Janet Echelman's TED Talk? Say why.

1 Echelman is happy to adapt her art to the specifications of the person commissioning it.
2 Echelman is a well-respected artist internationally.
3 Echelman doesn't see firm divisions between art, craft and engineering.

8 Work in pairs. Compare answers. Do you agree?

9 Read these comments* about the TED Talk. Which ones do you think accurately 'read between the lines' of Echelman's talk? Match each comment with the best description (a–c).

a Definitely true **b** Likely to be true **c** Unlikely to be true

Viewers' comments

P **Pierre** – Echelman seems to think that her art is somehow more important than the craft of lace-makers or the calculations of engineers.

S **Sally** – Clearly Echelman loves working closely with other people – both learning from them, and teaching them.

L **L8R** – I love this work. Echelman obviously feels that art serves an important function in society.

*The comments were created for this activity.

PRESENTATION SKILLS Being authentic

10 What does it mean to be authentic? Tell a partner.

TIPS

There's no magic formula prescribing what a speaker should look like and do. Allow your personality to come through. Being human is an important part of being an excellent speaker.

- Where possible, include yourself in the talk as part of the story. The audience will be interested not only in the topic, but in your relationship to it.
- Use your own natural voice, and speak from the heart. Think of yourself as having a conversation with the audience and talking about something you really care about rather than being a presenter who is passing on information.
- Don't worry too much about being nervous. Even when you feel extremely nervous, the audience often won't even notice. And if they do, they'll usually be on your side because they want you to succeed.
- Stay physically relaxed. Move your body as you normally would. Don't move around so much that it's a distraction, but don't stand completely still, either.

11 ▶ **7.3** Look at the Presentation tips box. Then watch the clips from Janet Echelman's TED Talk. Answer the questions.

1 What examples of Echelman sharing her 'real self' do you notice?
2 How do you think she felt before and during the talk? How does she appear to feel while giving the talk?

12 Think of a something you've done in life that seemed unlikely to you or others at the time. Consider your studies, work, hobbies, or another area of life. Give a short presentation to a partner explaining your accomplishment. Relax and allow your personality to come through.

▶ art school **N AM ENG**
▶ art college **BR ENG**

▶ traffic circle **N AM ENG**
▶ roundabout **BR ENG**

7.2 I was miles away!

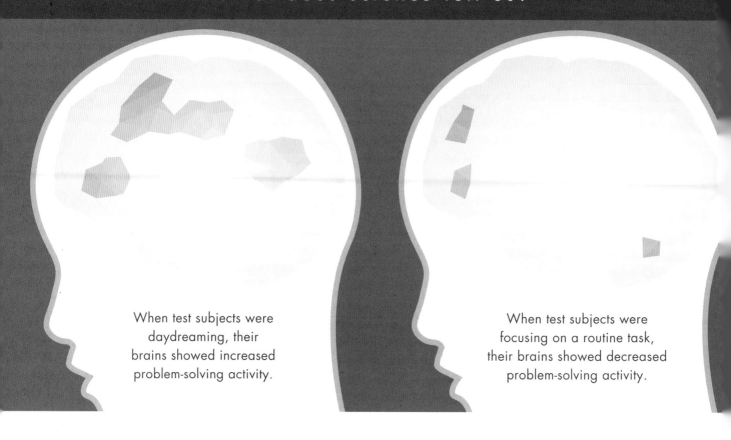

THE DAYDREAMING BRAIN
What does science tell us?

When test subjects were daydreaming, their brains showed increased problem-solving activity.

When test subjects were focusing on a routine task, their brains showed decreased problem-solving activity.

GRAMMAR The continuous aspect

1 Work in pairs. Discuss the questions.

  1 When, where and how often do you daydream?
  2 Do you find it a waste of time, or useful?

2 Look at the infographic. Answer the questions.

  1 What's happening in the 'colourful' parts of the brain?
  2 When does it happen?

3 Read the text in the Grammar box. Answer the questions (1–5).

THE CONTINUOUS ASPECT

Scientists in Canada **have been studying** the brain in the hope of understanding more about what happens when we daydream. In one recent experiment, researchers monitored the brain activity of test subjects while they **were performing** a simple routine task – pushing a button when numbers appeared on a screen. After the subjects **had been performing** the task for several minutes, they began daydreaming – and parts of their brain associated with problem-solving began lighting up on the brain scanner. The research **is altering** scientists' perception of daydreaming, because it shows that when we daydream, our brains are more active than when we focus on a routine task. One conclusion of the study is that when people are struggling to solve complex problems, it might be more productive to switch to a simpler task and let their mind wander. Psychologists interested in creativity and imagination **will be watching** developments in this area closely as our understanding of the mind and its workings deepens.

Look at the structures in **bold**. Can you find:

1 a changing situation in the present?
2 an action in progress from a point in the past to now?
3 an action in progress in the past?
4 an action in progress before an earlier point in the past?
5 an action in progress in the future?
Check your answers on page 152 and do Exercises 1–6.

1a Choose the correct forms to complete the text. In some cases, both options may be possible.

The power of daydreaming

When you ¹*suddenly realize / 're suddenly realizing* you've been daydreaming – especially when you ²*work / 're working* on a difficult problem – the usual response is to snap out of it and try to get back to work. But what scientists now ³*understand / are understanding* is that while we ⁴*daydream / 're daydreaming*, we are often solving problems at the same time. So daydreaming is actually one way the mind ⁵*has / is having* of getting work done.

Albert Einstein's story is a famous example. He ⁶*was thinking / had been thinking* about his special theory of relativity for about seven years when he finally had a breakthrough. In 1904, he ⁷*'d been / was* working for months on complex mathematical exercises when he ⁸*decided / was deciding* to take a break. As he rested, he ⁹*began / was beginning* to daydream. His mind ¹⁰*had been / was* wandering for several minutes when the image of a train formed in his brain – a train being struck by lightning. At that moment, it all ¹¹*fell / was falling* into place. Because he ¹²*hasn't / hadn't* been trying to think about it, Einstein ¹³*was / was being* able to produce a completely new description of the universe.

We probably ¹⁴*won't see / won't be seeing* teachers encouraging students to stare out the window instead of doing their lessons anytime soon. But we ¹⁵*'ll certainly see / 'll certainly be seeing* more research into the power and workings of the imagination.

4b Answer the questions. Which action(s):

1 were in progress when Einstein had his breakthrough?
2 had been in progress for the longest time. How long?
3 had been in progress for the shortest. How long?

5 Complete the article with the correct form of the verbs in brackets. In some cases, more than one form is correct.

'I'm not completely sure what went wrong,' says Mark Foyle. 'I ¹ _'ve been commuting_ (commute) by car every day for ten years and nothing like this has ever ² _____ (happen) to me.' On 30th November last year he got quite a shock. 'One minute, I ³ _____ (drive) to work, and the next I realized I ⁴ _____ (crash) into a parked car,' he explained. The police asked Foyle if he'd ⁵ _____ (text) at the time, but he hadn't. When I thought back, he says, 'I realized I ⁶ _____ (not pay attention).' A recent study in France found that of nearly 1,000 drivers injured in car accidents, 52 per cent reported that their mind ⁷ _____ (wander) at the time that it ⁸ _____ (happen). Not surprisingly, the study also confirmed that if you ⁹ _____ (daydream) while driving, you greatly increase the likelihood of being the person responsible for the crash. 'I ¹⁰ _____ (concentrate) on the road a lot more from now on,' said Foyle. 'I'm just glad no one was hurt.'

6 🎧 **39** Listen to Tom describing how his life changed. List the actions Tom talks about, in the order they happen.

7 Compare lists with a partner. Did you agree about the key events?

8 Which two activities mentioned are definitely still going on now?

Pronunciation /ŋ/ sound

9a 🎧 **40** Listen. Notice the /ŋ/ sound in the continuous verbs.

1 I'd been living here for four years when I met Ella for the first time.
2 We'd both been going to the same Spanish class for several weeks.
3 We've been going out together since then, and in about six months, we'll be getting married.

9b Practise saying the sentences in Exercise 9a with the /ŋ/ sound.

SPEAKING The benefits and drawbacks of daydreaming

10 **21st CENTURY OUTCOMES**

Work in small groups. Think of a time in the past when you have daydreamed. Explain what happened.

I was in a maths class at school. I had been paying attention, but then I started daydreaming and when the teacher called on me, I didn't hear my name until the third time he said it. It was really embarrassing.

11 Based on the stories that people shared, can you name any benefits of daydreaming? What about drawbacks of daydreaming?

7.3 In my mind's eye

READING The power of visualization

1 Work in pairs. Discuss the questions.

  1 Think of a place you would really love to be right now.

  2 Try to imagine the place in as much detail as possible. Also think about what you can hear and smell.

  3 Tell a partner some things about your experience. Was it easy or difficult? Were you able to imagine a lot of detail?

2 Read the article. Match the summaries (1–5) with the paragraphs (A–E).

  1 Visualizing the process rather than the success is probably the most effective approach.

  2 Imagining performing an athletic activity without ever doing it can affect the parts of the body you visualize using.

  3 Visualization can't create things that don't exist.

  4 For athletes, visualising both the process of competition and a successful outcome improves performance.

  5 Some people believe that visualization can be used to improve physical health.

3 Read the article again. Choose the correct options to complete the sentences.

  1 Researchers in the USA measured the response of weightlifters' *brains / muscles* to visualization.

  2 The research shows that visualization can strengthen your *mind / body*.

  3 Dr Shelley Taylor asked one group to focus on *emotions / memories* associated with success.

  4 Dr Taylor's more successful subjects visualized themselves *working / feeling* relaxed.

  5 Tiger Woods visualizes *the precise movements his hands will make* when *the golf club hits the ball / the path the ball needs to take*.

  6 Olympic athletes have found success visualizing themselves *competing / training*.

  7 Dr Marcia Angell believes that the mind *can't possibly help / can sometimes be effective in helping* to heal the body.

  8 Dr Bernie Siegel says that the mind can *convince / be convinced by* the body that something is happening.

4 Answer the questions.

  1 According to the weightlifting research, what is the most effective way to use visualization?

  2 What measurable benefit did experimental test subjects gain simply by visualizing themselves exercising?

  3 What was Dr Taylor's explanation for the results of her experiment?

  4 How does the golfers' use of visualization differ from what successful students do?

  5 Whose view is more supported by the information in the other parts of the article: Dr Angell's or Dr Siegel's?

VOCABULARY Expressions with *mind*

5 Complete the expressions from the text with these words.

  be bear put see

  1 When I visualize something, I try to _____ it in my mind's eye in as much detail as possible.

  2 To succeed at anything difficult, you really need to _____ your mind to it.

  3 While visualization might be helpful, you have to _____ in mind that there is no substitute for hard work.

  4 You seem to _____ in two minds about whether you want to do a master's degree or not.

6 Match the two parts of the sentences.

  1 When I try to concentrate for more than a few minutes,

  2 Knowing you'll be here to help me gives

  3 Sorry, I'm a bit distracted today because

  4 I know you're suspicious of these techniques, but try to

  5 Thinking about the hugeness of the universe

  6 Knowing that my brother is looking after my parents

  a I have something on my mind.

  b blows my mind.

  c my mind wanders.

  d me peace of mind.

  e keep an open mind.

  f eases my mind.

7 Think of:

  1 an amazing idea that blows your mind. What is it?

  2 a time when you put your mind to something challenging. What was it?

  3 a job in which it's important to keep an open mind. What is it? Why is it important to keep an open mind?

  4 a tough decision you are or have been in two minds about. What is or was it?

  5 something you do to feel better when you're worried or have a lot on your mind. What do you do?

SPEAKING Talking about visualization

8 **21st CENTURY OUTCOMES**

Work in small groups. Discuss the questions.

- Do you believe the scientific claim that muscle mass can be increased by 13.5 per cent simply by thinking of moving your muscles? Why? / Why not?

- The article discusses visualization in sport, academic work and medicine. Can you think (or have you heard) of other areas where it might be useful?

- Do you agree or disagree with the idea that the mind could be used to heal the body? Can you think of examples to support your position?

- Do you think there's any real difference between everyday planning about the future and visualization? Why? / Why not?

9 Present your ideas to another group.

The POWER of visualization

A Wouldn't it be great if you could lie in your bed and think about exercising and get some of the benefits of an actual workout? It sounds too good to be true, but researchers in the USA have discovered a stronger mind–body link than was previously realized: in experiments, the patterns of brain activity in weightlifters were the same when they lifted weights as when they only imagined lifting weights. According to the journal *Frontiers in Human Neuroscience*, other research shows that, in some cases, mental practice is almost as good for developing skills as physical practice, and that doing both together gives better results than doing either one alone. One experiment compared people who worked out at the gym and people who visualized workouts in their heads and found that people who put their mind to visualizing the repetition of certain muscle actions – without actually doing the physical actions – experienced a 13.5 per cent increase in muscle mass in the areas they'd imagined exercising. Your imagination may be more powerful than you thought.

B Psychologist Shelley Taylor, Ph.D., of the University of California conducted an experiment on a class of students who were preparing for an exam. She divided the group into two and got one group to use visualization to concentrate on the great feeling of getting a high mark on a test. The second group, by contrast, were instructed to picture themselves in the library, reviewing their notes and studying their textbooks to prepare for the test, keeping their minds focused on the process rather than on the eventual feelings of success. Who performed better? The second group, the one that imagined themselves doing the work necessary to succeed. Taylor's view is that visualization works as a 'mental rehearsal' of the actions needed to perform well when the time comes. (If you're a student, you should definitely bear this technique in mind!)

C This idea is supported by the typical use of visualization by athletes. Tiger Woods, one of the world's greatest golfers, has been using mental images to help him since he was a boy. He says that before each shot, he sees in his mind's eye exactly where he wants the ball to go. And judging by his game, the technique is highly effective. A generation before Woods, top golfer Jack Nicklaus used the same process to anticipate exactly how the shot would be played – also to great success. And it isn't just golf; more and more Olympic athletes from all over the world use the power of imagination in this way – often visualizing their competitions in great detail. 'The more an athlete can image the entire package, the better it's going to be', says sports psychologist Nicole Detling.

D Though many people have claimed to have cured themselves of serious diseases through the power of visualization and positive thinking, the medical profession appears to be in two minds about it. Dr Marcia Angell, a senior lecturer in social medicine at Harvard Medical School and a visualization sceptic says, 'There's tremendous arrogance to imagine that your mind is all that powerful.' On the other hand, Dr Bernie Siegel, a retired clinical assistant professor of surgery at Yale Medical School and author of a book called *Love, Medicine & Miracles* believes that visualization can improve the function of the human body in the same way that it has been shown to improve athletic performance. Siegel says, 'When you imagine something, your body really feels like it's happening.'

E Visualization is powerful, but it has its limits. As the comic actor Jim Carrey is supposed to have said, visualizing eating a sandwich when you're hungry isn't going to satisfy you. Our imagination may be an extremely useful tool, but it is most useful when used alongside genuine ability and actual effort and sometimes there's no substitute for the real thing.

7.4 That doesn't seem possible!

LISTENING Speculating about a mystery

1 Look at the photo. What do you think happened?

2 🎧 **41** Listen to this conversation about the photo. Tick which things are definitely true and which things are maybe true.

	Definitely true	Maybe true
1 The cars in the photo are in a forest in Belgium.		
2 There was a forest fire.		
3 There was an earthquake.		
4 The cars were abandoned suddenly.		
5 They were in the forest for about 70 years.		
6 The people were taken from their cars suddenly.		
7 The cars were added one by one.		
8 The cars were removed from the forest.		

3 🎧 **41** Listen again. Complete the sentences.

1 There _____ some natural disaster – a forest fire, maybe?

2 I _____ the cars were just abandoned.

3 And they _____ able to go back for them, right?

4 I _____ whatever happened, the cars couldn't be moved afterwards.

5 Or it _____ practical to move them.

6 That _____ why they could never go back!

Pronunciation Contraction with *have*

4a 🎧 **42** Listen. Underline *have* or *had* when it's contracted. Circle it when it isn't contracted.

1 Have you seen this picture?

2 There might have been some natural disaster.

3 It looks as though people had to run away quickly for some reason.

4 And they can't have been able to go back for them, right?

5 Or it mightn't have been practical to move them.

6 They had been there for about 70 years when this picture was taken.

4b Practise saying the sentences, using contractions where possible.

SPEAKING Speculating

5 Look at the illustration and read the text. Speculate about what the book might be about, who may have written it, and what it might show.

I imagine it was some kind of code.

THE WORLD'S MOST MYSTERIOUS MANUSCRIPT

Named after the bookseller Wilfrid M. Voynich, who acquired it in 1912, The Voynich Manuscript is a 240-page book written in a completely unknown language. It contains colourful drawings of unknown plants and strange diagrams. The original author is unknown, but it is estimated to have been written between 1404 and 1438. It has been called 'the world's most mysterious manuscript'.

SPECULATION

Speculating

I imagine
I expect   something happened suddenly.
I guess

They/He/She/It

… must/may/might/can't be right.
… must have / may have / can't have just disappeared.
… is / are likely to have left quickly.
… probably left quickly.

Could/Might there have been a fire?
What if there was an earthquake?
It/There was bound to have been some kind of sudden event.
Is it possible that the cars were put there?
It seems highly probable that there's a logical explanation.

Agreeing

That seems a likely explanation.
It certainly looks that way.
I think you're on to something there.

Disagreeing

That can't be right.
That doesn't seem at all that likely to me.
I'm not entirely convinced.
That doesn't seem possible.

WRITING A news story

6 Read the article. Answer the questions.

  1 What object has been found?
  2 What does the person who found it believe it is?
  3 What other explanation has been offered?

Writing skill Neutral reporting

7a The article carefully avoids commenting directly on whether or not McCoy's find is really an alien artefact. Underline the expressions that are used to say what is believed / has been said rather than to state what actually happened.

7b Rewrite the sentences using the expressions in brackets.

  1 Mr Price's car was stolen from in front of his house. (reportedly)
  2 My neighbour saw strange lights in the sky. (claim)
  3 The new metal sculpture in the park made strange noises. (is said to have)
  4 Local children avoided playing near the old tree. (apparently)
  5 Some people says the stones are magnetic. (speculation)
  6 The guitar made music even when no one was touching it. (allegedly)
  7 Hundreds of visitors have heard laughter coming from the empty room. (supposedly)
  8 The rocks move without being touched. (seemingly)
  9 A local police officer said it was a joke. (was quoted as saying)
  10 Pieter isn't the sort of person to make up stories. (by all accounts)

8 **21st CENTURY OUTCOMES**

Think of an object someone might find or an occurrence they might witness that would lead them to imagine that something very strange is going on. Write a news story about it similar to the one in Exercise 6. Use neutral reporting expressions.

9 Exchange stories with your partner. Read your partner's account. Did your partner use neutral reporting language?

Hiker claims to have found evidence of alien technology

Hill walker James McCoy has reportedly found what he believes may be evidence of past alien visits to planet Earth. While stopped for lunch on a riverbank, McCoy claims to have spotted a small piece of rusted metal in the soil. When he picked it up, he apparently realized that it was firmly attached to a rock weighing roughly five kilograms. On closer inspection, McCoy is said to have discovered that the metal ring appeared to be part of the stone itself, and that it was unlike anything he'd ever seen before.

Several locals I spoke to have claimed that McCoy told them about the find and its possible links to alien activity, but that he has reportedly refused to show them the rock itself. Despite our repeated attempts to contact him, McCoy couldn't be reached for comment and has allegedly returned to the area of the original find. There's speculation that he may try digging in the area in hopes of finding more supposedly alien artefacts. By all accounts McCoy has shown no previous interest in UFOs or

unexplained mysteries but is seemingly obsessed with his find, the exact location of which he has reportedly refused to reveal.

Local geologist Horst Lehman was quoted as saying that he believes the more likely explanation is that it's related to one of the many disused mines in the area, which were abandoned in the late 1800s.

8 Working together

BACKGROUND

1 You are going to watch a TED Talk by Tom Wujec called *Build a tower, build a team.* Read the text about the speaker and the talks. Then work in pairs and discuss the questions.

   1 Wujec studies how we communicate. What are your preferred ways to share and absorb information?

2 Wujec helps businesses present information visually – in a way that's easy to understand and apply. What types of business information might benefit from a visual treatment?

3 What's the connection between the photo above and Wujec's work?

TEDTALKS

TOM WUJEC, a North American writer, designer and business consultant, studies how we share and absorb information. He's an innovative practitioner of business visualization – using design and technology to help groups solve problems and understand ideas. Wujec is also interested in the individual qualities and team-working styles that lead to successful cooperation. In his talk, he describes how a simple design challenge using marshmallows can reveal surprising things about the ways we work together. Tom Wujec's idea worth spreading is that successful teamwork and problem-solving require not only specialized experience but also skillful facilitation.

Fishermen pulling a boat out of the sea in Kerala, India.

KEY WORDS

2 Read the sentences (1–6). The words in bold are used in the TED Talk. First guess the meaning of the words. Then match the words with their definitions (a–f).

D **1** I never work alone. **Collaboration** is important in my job.

A **2** The team leader doesn't tell us exactly what to do, but she provides **facilitation** and makes her own suggestions.

E **3** When I saw that her name was Giovanna Abbiati, I made the **assumption** that she was Italian.

B **4** The **executive admin** took detailed notes in the meeting.

F **5** We don't develop our finished product all at once. Instead, we follow an **iterative** process.

6 Joe is a **kindergartener**, but he's already a good reader.

a the process of making a task happen more easily, for example by helping assign roles or select priorities

b a person who works as an assistant to a top manager in a company

c a child in the first year of school

d the process of working together with other people

e an idea or belief that people have or a thing we imagine to be true without actually having seen any proof

f a way of developing an idea or products where things are continually changed and developed, and improved each time

AUTHENTIC LISTENING SKILLS
Understanding contrastive stress

Speakers often stress pairs of words when they are trying to emphasize the difference between them. The stress helps listeners focus on the contrast. For example, *I thought I was **late**, but actually I was **early***.

3a 🎧 **43** Look at the Authentic listening box. Then listen to the extracts from the TED Talk. Underline the words that are stressed. Which pairs of words are stressed to emphasize contrast between two things?

1 And though it seems really simple, it's actually pretty hard.

2 So CEOs: a little better than average, but here's where it gets interesting. If you put an executive admin on the team, they get significantly better.

3 So the same team went from being the very worst to being among the very best.

3b 🎧 **44** Listen to extracts 4 and 5.
Extract 4: which two ideas are being contrasted?
Extract 5: which two groups of people are being contrasted?

8.1 Build a tower, build a team

TED TALKS

1 ▶ **8.1** Watch the TED Talk. Are these sentences true (T) or false (F)?

F **1** Most teams build a successful tower on their first try.

F **2** Business people and kindergarteners approach the project similarly.

T **3** Teams that use prototypes and iterative processes are the most successful.

T **4** The addition of executive admins makes the CEO teams more successful.

F **5** When a cash prize is offered, teams perform very well.

T **6** The marshmallow challenge can help to identify hidden assumptions about tasks and teamwork.

2 ▶ **8.1** Watch the first part (0.00–1.00) of the talk again and complete these sentences.

1 The _____ has to be on top.

2 It's pretty hard because it forces people to _____ very quickly.

3 It reveals deep lessons about _____ .

3 ▶ **8.1** Number the steps in order. Then watch the second part (1.01–1.43) of the talk again and check your answers.

a They plan, organize, sketch, then lay out the spaghetti.

b They say ta-da and admire their work.

c Participants orient themselves to the task, talk about it, and jockey for power.

d Ta-da turns into uh-oh as the structure collapses.

e Someone carefully puts the marshmallow on the top.

f They assemble the structure.

4 ▶ **8.1** Watch the third part (1.44–3.11) of the talk again. Choose the correct word to complete each sentence.

1 *Business school graduates / Engineers* are the worst at completing that challenge successfully.

2 *CEOs / Kindergarteners* are the most successful.

3 Teams often *fail / succeed* because they make one plan and try to implement it.

4 Trial and error and 'playing in prototype' *waste time / are keys to success*.

▶ executive admin (executive administrative assistant) **N AM ENG**
▶ PA (personal assistant) **BR ENG**
▶ kindergarten **N AM ENG**
▶ reception (the first year of formal education) **BR ENG**

5 ▶ **8.1** Watch the fourth part (3.12 to the end) of the talk again and complete the summary with these words.

engineers and architects
hidden assumptions
questions
excecutive admins
prototyping
skills

Wujec says a winning team needs people with specialized skills – for example [1] _engineers and arch_ – and people with facilitation skills such as [2] _excecutive adm_. When Wujec first offered a prize of $10,000 for the tallest structure, no one even built a standing structure, because they didn't have the right [3] _skills_ on the team. However, when the same group tried a second time, they succeeded, because they had learned the importance of [4] _prototyping_. Wujec says every project has its own marshmallow, by which he means [5] _hidden assump_. In the case of the marshmallow challenge, everyone seems to assume that the marshmallow should go on last, for example. It seems so obvious that no one [6] _questions_ it.

VOCABULARY IN CONTEXT

6 ▶ **8.2** Watch the clips from the TED Talk. Choose the correct meaning of the words.

7 Work in pairs. Complete the sentences in your own words. Then discuss with a partner.

1 The last time I had a 'ta-da' moment was when I …
2 I saw people jockeying for power when …
3 A high-stakes decision you can make in life is …

CRITICAL THINKING Supporting the main idea

8 A talk usually has a main idea supported by other ideas. In a sentence of your own words, what would you say is the main idea of Tom Wujec's TED Talk?

9 Read these comments* about the TED Talk. Answer the questions.

1 Which of the ideas described in the comments does Tom Wujec present in his TED Talk?
2 Which comment describes the *main* idea of Wujec's talk?
3 Overall, do you think Wujec presents and supports his main idea well? Why? / Why not?

Viewers' comments

D **Dom** – Training and team-building exercises are essential and without training such as the marshmallow challenge, most companies will never reach their full potential.

A **Alicia** – Dom, it isn't just training. I think Wujec's idea is that teams need to have people with both specialized and facilitation skills – because it isn't only about what the team does, but how the team works together.

I **Ian** – You're right, Alicia. And business schools are producing graduates who don't understand 1) teamwork and 2) iterative processes.

B **Bert** – Right. What Wujec is saying is that identifying our hidden assumptions about team-work may help us avoid failure.

E **Elise** – I think it's so cool that kindergarteners perform well on the marshmallow challenge when they're just playing. We should make our work more like play!

* The comments were created for this activity

PRESENTATION SKILLS Using visuals

TIPS

Slides can be an extremely useful tool for presenters, but be careful: they also can be a distraction. Remember, slides should:

- present data clearly and simply.
- offer a few, powerful examples or illustrations of the main points.
- reinforce or amplify the speaker's words.
- not distract the audience or compete with the speaker.
- not require the audience to read a lot.

10 Work in pairs. List three slides you remember from Tom Wujec's TED Talk. Then answer the questions for each slide.

1 What type of image did it contain (graphic, photo, etc.)?
2 What information did it present?
3 How did it contribute to the presentation?
4 What made this slide especially memorable, in your opinion? What would have been a less memorable way to present it?

11 ▶ **8.3** Watch the clips from Wujec's talk. Match the clips (1–3) with the types of slide (a–c).

a a funny slide that surprises the audience
b a slide that helps clarify the significance of data
c a slide that repeats and reinforces the speaker's words

12 Work in pairs. Imagine you want to give a presentation about your English class.

1 Choose three pieces of information to present as graphics.
2 Choose three things to show photographs of.
3 Choose an image to support your main idea and also make people laugh.

13 Work with another partner. Take turns to give your presentation. Did you come up with similar ideas?

▶ execute on (a plan) **N AM ENG**
▶ execute (a plan) **BR ENG** / **N AM ENG**

▶ recognize / specialized **N AM ENG** / **BR ENG**
▶ recognise / specialised **BR ENG**

8.2 Having an off day?

THE REASONS WE MISS WORK

10%

6%

1%

2%

81%

MINOR ILLNESS (for example, colds/flu, stomach upsets, headaches and migraines)

INJURIES (for example, neck strains, repetitive strain injury, back pain)

STRESS AND MENTAL ILL-HEALTH (for example, clinical depression and anxiety)

HOME/FAMILY RESPONSIBILITY (for example, caring for sick children)

OTHER (for example, acute or recurring medical conditions, pulling a 'sickie')

GRAMMAR Cause and result

1 Work in pairs. Discuss the questions.

  1 What do you think is a valid reason to miss work?

  2 How would you solve the problem faced by some companies of employees regularly calling in 'sick'?

2 Look at the pie chart. Answer the questions.

  1 What are the two main causes of missed work days?

  2 What percentage of absences result from injuries?

3 Read the text in the Grammar box. Answer the questions (1–3).

CAUSE AND RESULT

Research carried out by a UK-based organization to find the common causes of absenteeism in the work place shows that over three quarters of working days missed **are the result of** minor illness. Unscheduled days off by some members of a team can force their already busy colleagues to take on more work, which can, in turn, **kill** motivation or **lead to** delays and missed deadlines.

The research found that another ten percent of missed days in manual jobs **result from** injury (but only three per cent in non-manual jobs which is presumably **due to** the lower physical risks at work). Stress and mental ill-health **cause** another six percent of missed work days; one per cent **arise from** home and family responsibilities such

as caring for a sick relative; and 'other' causes, including 'pulling a sickie' account for another two percent. Poor employee attendance sometimes **stems from** low morale. Many companies have found that a flexible working schedule can **foster** good will and **bring about** improved employee attendance.

1 In each sentence, say which part is the cause and which is the result.

2 Which of the cause verbs clearly implies a negative result?

3 Which clearly implies a positive result?

Check your answers on page 154 and do Exercises 1–7.

4 Complete the text with these words.

> bring   contributes   fosters   from   gives
> kills   lead   make   produce   result

Dos and don'ts of successful teamwork

An effective team divides work and multiplies success. However, serious problems are often the ¹ _result_ of the failure to apply some basic principles to teamwork. Here are three team-working dos and three don'ts that should ² _bring_ about success and reduce the possibility of failure.

DO

- have clear goals. They ³ _make_ work meaningful and ⁴ _lead_ to efficient use of time and energy.
- have well-defined roles and responsibilities. Good cooperation results ⁵ _from_ this.
- recognize contributions and strengths. This ⁶ _fosters_ collaboration.

DON'T

- force the group to agree. This ⁷ _kills_ creativity.
- let small conflicts grow. This ⁸ _gives_ rise to bigger conflicts for the whole team.
- assume everyone thinks like you. This ⁹ _contributes_ to misunderstanding and a failure to really listen.
- Following these simple rules will ¹⁰ _produce_ results – fast.

5 Look at the causes and results. For each pair, make a cause–result sentence using the phrase in brackets.

1 good reports about the local schools → more families moved into the area (because of)

More families moved into the area because of good reports about the local schools.

2 moving to a new house → people thinking about how many possessions they have (causes)

3 replacing our heating system → a reduction in our home energy costs (resulted from)

4 the failure to back up regularly → lost data (a consequence of)

5 effective driver education → safer roads (brings about)

6 being rude to customers → a local shop's popularity (kills)

6 Choose the most natural sentence (a or b) in each pair.

1 a Illness is often the consequence of bad diet.
  b Bad diet often fosters illness.

2 a The audience's lack of enthusiasm arose from the stormy weather.
  b Stormy weather killed the audience's enthusiasm for the outdoor theatre production.

3 a The success of the project was largely thanks to her hard work.
  b The failure of the project was largely thanks to her laziness.

Pronunciation Voicing in final consonants

7a 🎧 45 Listen. Is the bold final consonant sound in these words voiced or unvoiced?

1 foster**s**   **4** produ**c**e
2 brought abou**t**   **5** goo**d** will
3 cau**s**e   **6** ari**s**e from

7b The vowel sound before a voiced consonant tends to be longer than before an unvoiced consonant. Try saying the words in Exercise 7a with a longer vowel sound before the voiced consonants.

SPEAKING Cause-and-result relationships

8 **21st** CENTURY OUTCOMES

Look at the photos. Think of as many cause-and-result relationships as you can for each. Use expressions from the Grammar box.

Example (Photo 1)

Conflict at work kills creativity.
Poor organization gives rise to conflict at work.
Arguments are often the result of misunderstandings.
Overwork contributes to conflict in the office.
Office fighting often results in a negative atmosphere.

8.3 How *not* to motivate people

READING Bad team building

1 Work in pairs. Discuss the questions.

1 What teams are you in? At work? In sports? Clubs? Choirs?
2 What team-building activities have you heard about or participated in at work or elsewhere?
3 Were they effective? Why? / Why not?

2 Read the article. Which team-building activity:

1 wasn't taken seriously by the participants?
2 was an opportunity for revenge?
3 forced employees to perform in a way they didn't like?

3 Complete each sentence with the correct company name: A, B or C.

1 _____'s management chose a team-building exercise that forced people to perform.
2 _____'s team didn't have a lot of disagreement in the office before the training.
3 _____'s employees were happy about the team-building exercise for the 'wrong' reasons.
4 The main lesson from _____ is that for training to be effective, it needs to be suitable for the particular people it's being used with.
5 _____'s team-building exercise made angry people even angrier.
6 _____'s training was painful for one employee because of bad childhood memories.
7 When _____ announced plans for a team-building exercise, employees felt very negative about the idea.
8 _____'s employees treated the training as a joke and laughed about it together.

4 How would you feel about each of the team-building activities?

VOCABULARY Teams and teamwork

5 Complete the teamwork expressions with these verbs.

| be   bond   do   feel   go   have   pull   share |

1 It's good when new employees _bond_ as a group.
2 If you don't _feel_ a part of things, it can be hard to contribute to the team effort.
3 You have to _pull_ your weight if you expect to be promoted.
4 You always _do_ your fair share of the work.
5 I think it's important to _be_ a team player if you want to succeed in business.
6 I like to _have_ a sense of belonging, because it motivates me to work.
7 I hope my boss has noticed that I try to _go_ the extra mile when she asks me to do something.
8 If you and your colleagues can _share_ the load, everyone can work more productively.

6 Use the expressions from Exercise 5 to describe each of these situations (1–8).

1 I asked her to write some notes about the meeting by the end of the week. In fact, she wrote a full report by the end of the day. She _____.
2 Three of us seemed to be doing all the work, but one guy hardly contributed at all. That man _____.
3 There were 400 phone calls to make, so each of the three of us made about 130 calls. We _____.
4 She's very good at anticipating what her co-workers need. She's _____.
5 He feels that he has an important role in the office, and that other people appreciate and value his work. He has _____.
6 He had Friday off work because he was ill, but he came in on Saturday. He wanted to _____.
7 They didn't know each other when they started working together, but after several weeks of facing some big challenges, they learned to rely on each other. They _____ a team.
8 At first Jo's new job was difficult because she didn't know what to do. But after she got to know people and figured out her role, she _____.

SPEAKING Work issues

7 Complete the guidelines with these words.

| conflict   cooperation   employees   motivation
promote   tasks   team |

EFFECTIVE ACTIVITIES FOR TEAM BUILDING:

- guide trainees to accomplish [1]_____ that are in some way similar to tasks they do at work.

- provide [2]_____ for participants and engage [3]_____ members.

- enhance [4]_____ rather than encouraging too much competition.

- motivate [5]_____ to work well together when they return to work.

- [6]_____ harmony and give participants tools to resolve [7]_____.

8 *21st* CENTURY OUTCOMES

Work in small groups. What kind of work issues can be resolved by team building? Choose one and recommend some activities to help make the team stronger. Plan a team-building day following the guidelines in Exercise 7.

9 Explain your team-building day and how it follows the guidelines to another group.

BAD TEAM BUILDING

A good manager understands the benefit of teamwork and of making every employee feel a part of things in the workplace.

As a result, an industry has grown up around the provision of team-building exercises and events for businesses. However, talking to businesspeople in my network lately, I've come across many stories of team-building exercises that didn't have the effect that the organizers intended. So, managers, rather than my usual tips and advice on what works in management, this week I'm offering three case studies of situations that you should avoid at all costs. The stories are based on interviews with people who participated in the activities.

COMPANY A Paintball 'Fun' There were definitely problems with teamwork and cooperation in Company A. A number of people reported feeling anger and resentment about two junior colleagues who had been promoted over the heads of the rest of the team, and the negative feelings were affecting work badly. So when the manager announced a full day out of the office for a team-building activity, so that everyone could learn to cooperate better and maybe even bond as group, motivation was low and most people didn't feel good about it. But then the team found out what the training day was: paintballing. The mood lightened, because many of the workers saw it as a great opportunity. But it wasn't the prospect of improving teamwork that was appealing, it was rather that they were looking forward to having the chance to shoot paintballs at the colleagues they were angry with.

The exercise apparently didn't result in any immediate improvements at work – it just made most of the team members feel angrier. My advice to managers? Think carefully when planning a team-building exercise. Ask yourself: will it help employees to resolve conflict and have a sense of belonging, or could it possibly make things worse?

COMPANY B Office Sing-Along The Company B employee I interviewed told me that she is a team player and doesn't object to the idea of team-building exercises in principle. She also said that though she loves music, she can't sing. So when her company announced an awayday to enhance teamwork through singing, it brought up some very negative feelings for her – mostly childhood memories of being forced to sing at school. She participated in the training because she had to, but from start to finish, all she could think about was how to get out of there.

Many participants found the day somewhat stressful and in their reviews of the session, said that it didn't accomplish anything. Hey, managers: If you're planning a team-building day, choose an activity that people won't hate. If a team-building activity makes people feel bad, chances are it's not going to work.

COMPANY C Group Therapy The marketing team at Company C already knew how to cooperate pretty well. They were sharing the load with almost no conflict, and when there was work to be done, everyone was always willing to go the extra mile. So when the management announced a half-day of team-building exercises, no one thought too much about it and simply got on with their work. But on the day of the course, the 'corporate motivation specialist' in charge soon had everyone's attention. The first activity? Make a list of things you *don't* like about your colleagues. The second activity? Tell them. The Company C employee I spoke with said that, not surprisingly, the session was not at all effective.

Fortunately, the team that was being worked with get along well and many of them are friends outside of work. They all immediately understood that doing the exercise as instructed could only lead to problems. So they all just made up answers in order to complete the task, but many had difficulty keeping a straight face. After the session, the team were given a kind of computerized personality test to discover their 'teamwork style'. Lessons learnt? If you ever have to arrange any corporate team-building activities or teamwork training, try to choose something that's actually relevant to the team it's designed for. It seems kind of obvious, doesn't it?

8.4 If you'll just let me finish ...

LISTENING Reviewing a project

1 An advertising agency is working for a small smoothie maker to promote and sell their product in parks using small carts. Look at the photo. Answer the questions.

1 What team roles would be necessary to promote and sell smoothies in this way? Think about getting the carts, decorating them, getting permission to sell from them, supplying the product itself, and so on.

2 Who would need to work together closely to produce an effective product promotion?

3 Think of three ways the project could go wrong.

2 🎧 46 Listen to some people talking about a similar project. Choose the correct options to complete the sentences.

1 This meeting takes place at the *beginning / end* of a project.

2 There was no *administrator / project manager* on the team.

3 The team lacked *leadership / teamwork*.

4 Rudy thinks there should be better communication during *product analysis / development*.

5 Helen agrees that *shorter / longer* meetings encourage communication.

6 At the end of the meeting, everyone feels that the main points *have / haven't* been covered.

Pronunciation Emphasizing the main focus of the sentence

3a 🎧 47 Listen to four different versions of a sentence. Underline the main stress in each version.

1 I'd be interested in hearing your views.
2 I'd be interested in hearing your views.
3 I'd be interested in hearing your views.
4 I'd be interested in hearing your views.

3b Match each version 1–4 from Exercise 3a with the sense given by the stress (a–d).

a You may think I don't want to hear them but I would be interested in hearing your views.

b I've heard about your experience now I want to hear about your views.

c I've heard about everyone else's views, now I want to hear yours.

d The others heard your views, but I haven't heard them yet.

SPEAKING Taking part in a meeting

4 Which expression in each pair is more polite? In each, what makes it polite?

1 Let's begin.   Shall we begin?
2 If you'll allow me to finish … .   Be quiet. I'm talking.
3 What do you think?   I'd be interested in hearing your views.
4 Sorry for interrupting, but … .   I think …
5 That's all.   I think we can finish there.

5 Work in groups of three. Roleplay a meeting. Use structures from the Useful expressions box and the information below. Remember to be polite rather than abrupt.

Your team has recently hosted a conference for about 200 people. It wasn't seen as a big success because it wasn't very well organized.

↓

A: Introduce meeting topic: talking about issues with teamwork on the recent conference – coordination, administration, leadership. Invite views.

↓

B: Mention the conference organizer's role.

↓

C: Try to interrupt, to say that you think next time, the conference organizer needs to be a more active leader.

↓

A: Stop C's interruption.

↓

B: Suggest analysis of planning process – not enough time was allowed to plan the details.

↓

A: Invite C's views.

↓

C: Agree with B and add that people complained that the food was bad and it should be better next time.

↓

A: Close meeting.

TAKING PART IN A MEETING

Opening a discussion

Shall I go ahead / get us started / start the discussion?
I'd like to start the discussion by …

Stopping interruption

If you'll let me / allow me to finish …
I know you're dying to jump in, but …
Could I just finish what I was saying?

Inviting participation

I'd be interested in hearing your views.
Can you give me your thoughts?
What's your take on … ?
Any thoughts on … ?

Interrupting

Before you continue, can I just say … ?
Can I just say something here?
I hate to interrupt, but …
Sorry for interrupting, but …

Wrapping up

If no one has anything else, I think we can stop there.
I think we can finish there.
I guess we've covered everything.
All right, I think that's everything.

WRITING Debriefing questionnaire

6 Use these words to complete the questionnaire.

delivered	designed	featured	finished	led
looked	lost	started	took	went

Writing skill Linking devices

7a The writer uses linking words and phrases to connect ideas. In the debriefing questionnaire, find the following.

1 four cause-and-result expressions
2 two adverbials of time, one referring to the past and one referring to the future
3 an adverb that signals additional information
4 an adverb that contrasts two pieces of information
5 an adverb that signals summary

7b Complete the sentences with the expressions from Exercise 7a.

1 The project was delivered on time; _____ , we were way over budget.
2 We didn't spend the entire budget _____ that the materials were cheaper than expected.
3 _____ finished the project, everyone was ready for a break.

PROJECT DEBRIEFING
QUESTIONNAIRE

1 Briefly (up to 60 words) summarise the project.

We had six weeks from start to finish to create a mobile product-promotion cart for a small organic drinks company. We [1]_____ and built the cart which [2]_____ the name of the company, an attractive logo, and a cooler to store the drinks. It also included a sunshade for hot, sunny weather.

2 What went well and why?

The design phase [3]_____ very well owing to the fact that we [4]_____ the time to have several meetings with the drinks company owners and to develop a look and feel for the cart that they were completely happy with. As a result, we had a very clear vision for the project before we [5]_____ building it.

3 What was the project's biggest challenge?

Because of the lack of coordination, we [6]_____ the cart about ten days late. This wasn't a huge problem; however, it [7]_____ bad – and we [8]_____ some money as a consequence.

4 What was the project's biggest success?

When we finally [9]_____, the cart looked great and the company is getting a lot of business from it.

5 What would you do differently next time and why?

In future, we need to make sure that the team is coordinated. Everyone was very focused on their own contribution, but this [10]_____ to problems when the elements came together. Overall, we think having shorter meetings more often will improve communication among team members.

4 _____ his design expertise, George's contributions were particularly helpful.
5 The client cancelled the order at the last minute. _____, they lost their deposit.
6 _____, we plan to build extra time into the schedule for possible delays.
7 Our communication wasn't clear at times, and there was some confusion _____ .
8 _____, we think the project was a success, but some aspects could have been improved.

8 21st CENTURY OUTCOMES

Write a similar debriefing of a project you have worked on using the questionnaire in Exercise 6 as a model. You can choose something serious from your job or school or something less serious, such as preparing a family meal.

9 Exchange debriefing documents with your partner. Read the debriefing document. Has each section been explained clearly?

LISTENING

1 🎧 **48** Read the introduction and listen to the extracts from a radio programme about how three companies deal with waste. Then say if each sentence below is true (T) or false (F).

1 Boxcycle doesn't allow people to buy or sell anything using their website.
2 Boxcycle manages a facility that recycles all kinds of paper and cardboard, mostly for boxes that are no longer usable.
3 Hipcycle features art and functional items that are made from junk.
4 Hipcycle takes bicycles that no one wants and repairs them so that they can be ridden again.
5 Marriott Construction builds buildings entirely from waste materials.
6 Marriott's innovation resulted in reduced traffic, noise and pollution on their construction site.

2 Read the definitions. Which word could be used to describe the activities of all three companies? Which company does each of the other two words describe?

1 **Downcycling** is turning waste material into something that is of lower quality than the original material.
2 **Upcycling** is turning waste material into something that is of higher quality or value than the original material.
3 **Recycling** is using a product or material again after it has already been used at least once.

Boxcycle, Hipcycle and Marriott Construction

BOXCYCLE is devoted exclusively to matching up people who need cardboard boxes with people or companies who have spare ones.

HIPCYCLE is a marketplace for art and household items created from materials that were otherwise going to have been thrown away.

MARRIOTT CONSTRUCTION is a builder that immediately reuses waste products on building sites to create materials that in the past had to be bought and delivered.

hipcyc
UPCYCLED PROD

GRAMMAR

3 Complete the text with six of these eight expressions.

arose from	because	contributes to	make
fosters	killed	the result of	results in

Architect Marcio Kogan's decision to build a shop out of discarded shipping containers ¹ _____ his client's request for a low-budget furniture showroom that could be built quickly. ² _____ they didn't want to damage palm trees on the site, the design needed to be narrow – making the 2.5-metre-wide containers the perfect choice. It's part of a new wave of shops and homes made from used containers, which is ³ _____ a growing desire worldwide to recycle and to minimize carbon footprint. The six containers, stacked two high, are each painted a different bright colour, which greatly ⁴ _____ the overall eye-catching look of the place and ⁵ _____ the shipping containers themselves being more noticeable. Glass windows at either

end of the containers ⁶ _____ the inside of the shop light and airy rather than cramped.

4 Complete the text with the correct simple or continuous form of the verbs. In some cases, more than one form is correct.

I ¹ _____ (collect) sculpture made from junk metal for about ten years, and my collection ² _____ (grow) bigger all the time. I ³ _____ (buy) my first piece in Barcelona. I ⁴ _____ (study) the Catalan language there one summer and ⁵ _____ (get) to know some local artists because I ⁶ _____ (hang out) in local art galleries a lot. I ⁷ _____ (not look) for artwork to buy – especially not steel sculpture, because it ⁸ _____ (be) very heavy – but I ended up buying one and paying a lot to ship it home. The pieces I ⁹ _____ (like) the most are animals, because they ¹⁰ _____ (look) so real. Next month, I ¹¹ _____ (go) to a major art show in Croatia.

Right now, I ^{12} _____ (research) the artists whose work will be shown there. I ^{13} _____ (want) to find something special for my collection, but here in Croatia, I ^{14} _____ (look) for smaller items that are cheaper to ship!

VOCABULARY

5 Complete the interview with the correct verbs.

A: As a site manager of a construction team, how do you make sure your team works effectively and safely?

B: One of the most important things a building site manager can do is to help a construction team ^{1} _____ as a group.

A: How do you do that?

B: By example. If you're in charge of a building site, make sure everyone can see that you ^{2} _____ your weight. This will establish your authority, but it will also show that you ^{3} _____ a team player.

A: So you join in on some tasks?

B: Right. When I ask a group of workers to do something, I need to be willing to ^{4} _____ the load sometimes.

A: How important is it that workers ^{5} _____ a sense of belonging in the workplace?

B: It's incredibly important. When people ^{6} _____ a part of things, it creates a culture where people feel proud to ^{7} _____ their fair share of the work and to ^{8} _____ the extra mile to help others when necessary.

6 Complete the expressions with *mind* in the text.

I ^{1} _____ something ^{2} _____ mind that I'd like to share. I read recently that 500 billion plastic bags are used globally each year. That number ^{3} _____ my mind! And picture this in your mind's ^{4} _____ : there's a patch of plastic rubbish in the middle of the Pacific Ocean that's the size of France! We're drowning in plastic! And the fact that we recycle doesn't really ^{5} _____ my mind because it takes most plastic 500 to 1,000 years to degrade. Having said all that, I think it's important for us to ^{6} _____ our minds to reducing the amount of plastic we use. If, every day, you ^{7} _____ in mind the ever-growing plastic problem and stop using plastic, one bag and one bottle at a time, we may be able to solve the problem. Of course with so much plastic packaging, you'll have to keep ^{8} _____ mind about what products you choose or accept the inconvenience of buying loose, unpackaged goods. If you're in a shop and you're ^{9} _____ minds about whether you need a plastic bag, just say no. Once you get used to it, knowing that you're doing something good for the world will give you ^{10} _____ mind.

DISCUSSION

7 Work in pairs. Discuss the questions.

1 Are there examples in your area of recycling, upcycling or downcycling? If not, can you think of any opportunities that exist for these activities?

2 Can you think of a building that is especially suited to its immediate environment – the size or shape of the site, the local climate, or the use of the building? What features make the building special?

3 In many places around the world, paper, cardboard and plastic are collected and recycled. What products are created from these recycled materials? Do you use any?

SPEAKING

8 Tom, Jo and Lena are discussing one of the two locations of the art gallery they run, which sells work by local artists. Put the phrases and sentences (a–h) in the correct order. Then use them to complete the conversation below.

a me / to / likely / seem / doesn't / That / that / all
_____

b I / Could / finish / just / I / what / saying / was
_____

c the / start / like / I'd / to / discussion / sales / talking / by / about
_____

d It / seems / highly / probable / that
_____

e you / say / continue, / Before / just / I / can
_____

f be / in / I'd / interested / views, / your / hearing / Tom
_____

g a / explanation / likely / seems / That
_____

h imagine / I / because / it's / of
_____

Jo: ^{1} _____. Why have they dropped off in our Dean Street location in the past few months?

Tom: ^{2} _____ the increased parking charges. People are really upset about them.

Lena: ^{3} _____. I think there's a more obvious explanation. We really need to consider whether …

Jo: ^{4} _____ that I've met with a group of other shop owners in the area, and everyone agrees that customers are staying away because of the parking charges. So what we need …

Lena: ^{5} _____? I think we really need to consider whether Dean Street is still the best area for us. ^{6} _____ the area has lost its artistic edge. In the past two years, several national chain shops and expensive coffee shops have opened, and it feels like any high street.

Jo: ^{7} _____.

Lena: So as I said, I think we need …

Jo: Sorry for interrupting, Lena. ^{8} _____.

9 Stress and relaxation

Alexandra Kosteniuk, Russian chess Grandmaster, competing at the 2015 Women's World Chess Championship in Sochi, Russia.

TEDTALKS

ANDY PUDDICOMBE wants you to take a break – not just from work, but from your own mind, which is so full of anxieties about the world and anxieties about its own anxieties. To help you do that, Puddicombe, a former Buddhist monk, co-founded Headspace, a project to make meditation more accessible to more people in their everyday lives. Andy Puddicombe's idea worth spreading is that if we meditate for just 10 minutes a day, we can feel more focused and experience the world with more calm and clarity.

BACKGROUND

1 You are going to watch a TED Talk by Andy Puddicombe called *All it takes is 10 mindful minutes.* Read the text about the speaker and the talk. Then work in pairs and answer the questions.

   1 What types of things typically cause people anxiety?
   2 What do people do to try to cope with stress and anxiety?
   3 What comes to mind when you hear the word 'meditation'?

KEY WORDS

2 Read the sentences (1–6). The words in bold are used in the TED Talk. First guess the meaning of the words. Then match the words with their definitions (a–f).

   1 If we learn to be **mindful**, it's easier to deal with life's challenges.
   2 My pace of life is **frantic** and my mind is always busy.
   3 Our lives can become so busy that we rarely do anything **spontaneous** anymore.
   4 You can avoid getting so stressed by taking some simple **preventative** measures.
   5 I wish I felt less **restless** and more relaxed at the weekends.
   6 We sometimes feel **inundated** by work and other people's demands.

   a faced with more than we can easily deal with
   b intended to stop something from happening
   c unable to be still
   d very hurried and using a lot of energy
   e aware of the state and activity of our own thoughts
   f able to act without a plan

AUTHENTIC LISTENING SKILLS
Understanding mid-sentence changes in direction

Sometimes we begin a sentence, but part-way through it, we go off in a different direction. This often happens because, as we're speaking, we think of a better way of making the point and sometimes the change in direction might be used for a particular effect. But it can mean that the second part of the sentence doesn't always match the first part. If you can focus on the ideas contained in the sentence as a whole and not worry about 'the missing part of the sentence' (grammatically), it can help you to understand the speaker's message.

3a 🎧 **49** Look at the Authentic listening skills box. Listen to this sentence. What do you notice about the speaker's way of constructing this sentence?

3b 🎧 **50** Listen to another sentence. What did you expect to hear the speaker say after 'than we'?

3c 🎧 **51** Read two more extracts from the talk. How do you think the sentences might end? Now listen to find out.

   1 But when you sit down and you watch the mind in this way, you might see many different patterns. You might find a mind that's really, sort of, restless and –
        _____ .

   2 You might find a mind that's very, sort of, dull and boring, and it's just, almost mechanical, it just, sort of, seems it's as if you're getting up, going to work,
        _____ .

9.1 All it takes is 10 mindful minutes

TEDTALKS

1 ▶ **1.1** How much do you know about meditation? Decide whether you think each statement is true or false. Then watch the TED Talk and say whether Andy Puddicombe sees them as true (T) or false (F).

1 Meditation involves basically doing nothing.
2 Meditation is a way of caring for the mind.
3 The purpose of meditation is to stop thoughts, get rid of emotion and control the mind.
4 Meditators try to watch their thoughts come and go without getting too involved in them.
5 Meditation needs to be done while sitting on the floor.

2 ▶ **9.1** Watch the first part (0.00–3.38) of the talk again. Answer the questions.

1 Puddicombe lists a series of things that we rely on our mind for. Note down as many as you can.
2 What does Puddicombe say happens when we fail to care for our mind properly?
3 Puddicombe talks about his past view of meditation as an Aspirin (headache tablet) for the mind. What does he mean by this?
4 In his twenties, when Puddicombe's life became very stressful, where did he go and what did he do?

▶ round and round **BR ENG**
▶ around and around **N AM ENG**

▶ mum **BR ENG**
▶ mom **N AM ENG**

3 ▶ 9.1 Watch the second part (3.39–6.49) of the talk again. Choose the best options to complete the sentences.

  1 When he became a monk, Puddicombe learned to be very aware of the workings of his *mind / emotions*.

  2 Research shows that we spend nearly half of our lives thinking about *how to find happiness / something other than what we're actually doing*.

  3 Puddicombe says that meditation is basically a way of getting to know *ourselves / the present moment*.

  4 Puddicombe uses the balls to illustrate the way *physical activity / focus* affects our mind.

  5 According to Puddicombe, the key to successful meditation is *balance / total relaxation*.

4 ▶ 9.1 Watch the third part (6.50 to the end) of the talk again. Which statement (a–c) best gives the main idea of Puddicombe's TED Talk?

  a Meditation doesn't give you a different perspective, but it does give you some control over your thoughts and emotions.

  b Meditation won't change what happens to us in life, but it can help us respond to life in a different way.

  c Meditation is a good way to stop feeling bored by the cycle of waking up, going to work, eating, and sleeping.

5 If you've tried meditation, has it been effective for you? If you haven't, would you like to try it?

VOCABULARY IN CONTEXT

6 ▶ 9.2 Watch the clips from the TED Talk. Choose the correct meaning of the words.

7 Complete the sentences in your own words. Then discuss with a partner.

  1 I like to reminisce about …

  2 When I want to take my foot off the gas, I usually …

  3 I would like to feel more clarity in my life about …

CRITICAL THINKING Understanding the speaker's technique

8 Speakers use different techniques to engage us with their ideas. Match each sentence (1–4) from Andy Puddicombe's TED Talk with the best description of the technique it demonstrates (a–d).

  1 'We spend more time looking after our cars, our clothes and our hair than [our minds].'

  2 'There was a research paper that came out of Harvard, just recently, that said on average our minds are lost in thought almost 47 per cent of the time.'

  3 'It just kind of seems tragic, actually, especially when there's something we can do about it.'

  4 'If you think about the last time, I dunno, you had a wobbly tooth.'

  a referring to scientific studies

  b using everyday images that the audience can relate to

  c appealing to emotions

  d appealing to common sense

9 Which technique do you think is the most effective in Puddicombe's talk?

10 Read these comments* about the TED Talk. Which part of the talk are they referring to? Find it in the transcript on page 179.

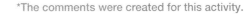

Viewers' comments

  N   **Nell** – Andy's description near the beginning of the talk, about the stressed mind and all the confusion of thoughts going round, really hit home for me. It makes the human condition seem hopeless!

  U   **Uwe** – Yes, but that's if you choose to focus on the negative! Remember, he says it doesn't have to be that way!

  S   **Seb** – I agree with Uwe. What I'm taking away from this is that we have the power to change things.

*The comments were created for this activity.

11 Do you agree with the viewers' comments? Why? / Why not? What techniques did you notice him using in the section they describe?

PRESENTATION SKILLS Thinking about your audience

TIPS

Consider your audience and imagine the talk from their perspective. Ask yourself the following.

- What will they already know, or what assumptions will they have about the topic?
- What will get them excited?
- What jargon or technical language should I avoid because the audience won't know it?

12 ▶ 9.3 Look at the Presentation tips box. Then watch the clips from Andy Puddicombe's TED Talk and answer the questions.

  1 What does Puddicombe assume the audience believes about meditation?

  2 What idea(s) does Puddicombe think the audience may get excited about?

  3 Did you notice any words that might be considered technical language and jargon?

13 Think of a practical way of dealing with stress. Prepare a short presentation about it. Remember to think about the points in the Presentation tips box.

14 Work in pairs. Take turns to give your presentation.

▶ quit my degree **BR ENG**
▶ dropped out of school **N AM ENG**

▶ wobbly tooth **BR ENG**
▶ loose tooth **N AM ENG**

9.2 Even holidays are stressful

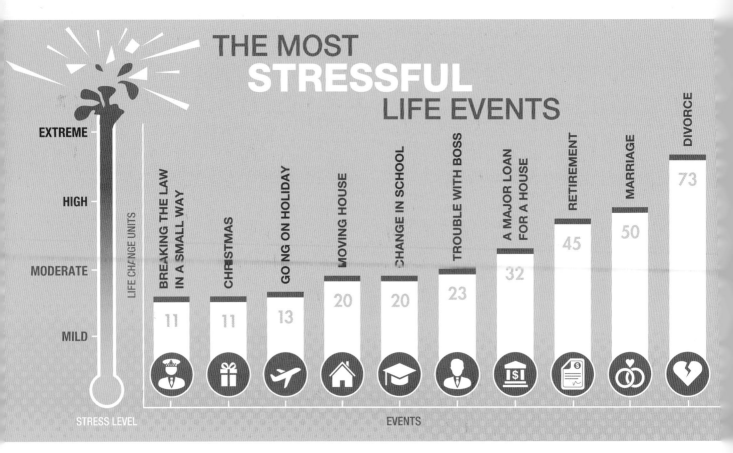

THE MOST **STRESSFUL** LIFE EVENTS

EXTREME

HIGH

MODERATE

MILD

LIFE CHANGE UNITS

STRESS LEVEL

EVENTS

Event	Units
BREAKING THE LAW IN A SMALL WAY	11
CHRISTMAS	11
GOING ON HOLIDAY	13
MOVING HOUSE	20
CHANGE IN SCHOOL	20
TROUBLE WITH BOSS	23
A MAJOR LOAN FOR A HOUSE	32
RETIREMENT	45
MARRIAGE	50
DIVORCE	73

GRAMMAR Intensifying adverbs

1 Work in pairs. In a typical week, what are the three most stressful situations you have to deal with?

2 Look at the table. What do 'life change units' measure?

3 Read the text in the Grammar box. Answer the questions (1–7) about the bold words in the text.

INTENSIFYING ADVERBS

Stress can make you ill. In extreme cases, severe stress can **utterly destroy** a person's health, confidence and well-being. Early research in this area was begun in the late 1960s by psychologists Thomas Holmes and Richard Rahe, who were **quite** certain that there was a link between stress and health and **really wanted** to get to the bottom of it. They asked 5,000 North Americans to rank the degree of stress caused by certain events in life, then assigned 'life change units' to each one. Then they added up the units in each person's life for a total stress score.

The results of their research made the connection **absolutely undeniable**: people who had more life change units for the previous year also had more health problems. One **extremely interesting** finding was that even supposedly relaxing activities like going on holiday were never completely stress-free. This shouldn't be **in the least bit surprising** if we think what is involved in getting away. It can also be **quite difficult** to relax if we've been very busy beforehand. But don't worry. Apparently we start to relax by the end of the third day!

1 Which adverb modifies a gradable* adjective?

2 Which adverb modifies an ungradable** adjective?

3 Which adverb modifies another adverb?

4 Which adverb can modify gradable and ungradable adjectives and verbs?

5 Which adverb is generally used with negative verbs and adjectives?

6 Which negative adverbial construction modifies a verb?

7 Which of the two uses of *quite* is an intensifying adverb? Is the adjective gradable or ungradable?

Check your answers on page 156 and do Exercises 1–6.

* gradable adjectives can be measured on a scale

** ungradable adjectives express extreme or absolute qualities

4 Complete the sentences with the expressions. Some words may fit in more than one sentence.

not at all   quite literally   so   totally   utterly   whatsoever

1 A: We had a scary taxi ride from the airport.
   B: Scary? It was _utterly_ terrifying!
2 A: The weather was a bit rainy.
   B: A bit rainy? It _quite literally_ rained the whole time.
3 A: The first hotel wasn't cheap.
   B: Not cheap? It was _so_ expensive!
4 A: It's a bit silly to get lost if you have a map.
   B: Silly? In a complex city like Tokyo, I think it's _totally / not at all_ understandable!
5 A: The hotel's staff weren't very helpful.
   B: Weren't very helpful? They were _not at all_ interested in their guests.
6 A: The tour guides didn't give us much information about travel arrangements.
   B: Not much? They gave us no information _whatsoever_!

5 Complete the three texts with the correct options.

Text 1

My first holiday abroad was to Singapore. I felt [1]*extremely / utterly* nervous about using the local public transport and getting around, but once I discovered the [2]*so / absolutely* amazing food in the markets, I began to feel [3]*really / entirely* happy with my choice of destination.

Text 2

My holiday in Australia was of no benefit [4]*in the least / whatsoever* for reducing stress. I'd bought cheap plane tickets several months before I went, but I didn't make a hotel reservation before leaving. The first night, I ended up in a business hotel that was [5]*not at all / completely* pleasant – the room smelled of cigarette smoke – and I spent the whole next day trying to find a nicer place to stay. Rather than make last-minute arrangements, it would have been more relaxing to cancel the trip [6]*extremely / entirely*.

Text 3

I had a [7]*totally / so* boring holiday! That was definitely my first and last 'staycation' – you know, going on holiday near home rather than going abroad. I had a reasonably relaxing time, but it wasn't [8]*not at all / the least bit* exotic, so it didn't feel [9]*at all like / entirely* a proper vacation. Next summer, I definitely want to go further from home!

6 Complete the conversation with appropriate intensifying adverbs. There is more than one right answer for most gaps. Don't use the same word twice.

A: How was your long weekend?
B: It was [1]_____ stressful.
A: Oh, no! It was a music festival, right? When you told me about it, your plans sounded [2]_____ brilliant!
B: Right. I mean, we [3]_____ expected it to be a brilliant weekend, but it … got off to a very bad start.
A: So can I ask what went wrong?
B: Well, first, I have to say, I accept the blame [4]_____. But basically, what happened is we went to the wrong place … or I booked the hotel in the wrong place.
A: The wrong place … you mean the wrong part of town?
B: No, I [5]_____ literally booked a hotel in the wrong city – in a city far away.
A: Oh, no! But it was Spain, right? Girona?
B: Well, that's where we flew to. But the hotel I booked was a thousand kilometres away – in Gerena, near Seville.
A: Gerena … Girona …
B: I know … it's [6]_____ embarrassing! There's no excuse [7]_____!

Pronunciation Stress with intensifying adverbs

7a Look at the sentences with intensifying adverbs. Underline the words you think will be stressed.

1 The weather was incredibly stormy.
2 The flights were so expensive.
3 I'm quite certain that was the worst holiday ever.
4 The hotel rooms were absolutely lovely.
5 The guidebook was of no help whatsoever.
6 Our host was really kind.

7b 🎧 52 Listen and check your answers. Then practise saying the sentences with natural stress.

SPEAKING Holiday lessons learned

8 Think of the most relaxing holiday you've ever had. Work in small groups and discuss the questions. Then do the same with the least relaxing holiday you've ever had.

• Where did you go?
• Who were you with?
• What did you do?
• Why was it relaxing/unrelaxing?

9 *21st* CENTURY OUTCOMES

Use the group's responses to the questions in Exercise 8 to create a list of tips and hints for how to have a really relaxing holiday. Think about the following.

• planning
• where to go
• how to get the details right

10 Share your tips and hints and your holiday with another group.

9.3 Alert and alive

READING Can stress be good for you?

1 Look at the photo. Work in pairs. Discuss the questions.

   1 Why do you think people do activities like this?

   2 What do you think the woman is thinking or feeling at this moment?

   3 Have you ever done anything that made you feel that way? Or would you like to?

2 Work in pairs. Look at the title of the article. Do you think stress can be good for you?

3 Read the introduction. Does the writer think stress can be good for us?

4 Read the article and answer the questions.

   1 In what ways does the article say that stress can be good for us?

   2 As very few people in the world are ever actually chased by wild animals, why does Elizabeth Kirby compares a burst of stress to being chased by a bear?

   3 In what ways could moderate stress make people more effective in a job?

5 Match the words (1–7) and (8–10) with their definitions (a–g) and (h–j).

Nouns

   1 adrenaline
   2 awareness
   3 burst
   4 exposure
   5 immune system
   6 thrill
   7 vaccination

Adjectives

   8 alert
   9 chronic
  10 clinical

   a the state of knowing about something
   b the state of having no protection from something
   c the parts and processes of the body that fight illness
   d a chemical produced by the body when we feel excited or frightened
   e a short period of emotion or energy
   f a medicine given to prevent disease
   g a sudden feeling of excitement or pleasure

   h lasting for a long time
   i relating to the treatment of patients
   j very awake and aware

6 Do you think it would be possible to have too little stress in your life? If so, what problems could it cause? If not, what would be the benefits of having a totally stress-free life.

VOCABULARY Idioms related to parts of the body

7 Complete these three expressions with parts of the body in the text. What does each mean?

   1 on your _____ (line 14)
   2 a shot in the _____ (line 41)
   3 in over your _____ (line 48)

8 Look at the expressions in bold and discuss what each one means.

   1 I**'m up to my eyeballs** in work. I really need a break!

   2 **Keep your chin up** – things will look better in the morning.

   3 It really **makes my blood boil** when people drive slowly in the fast lane on the motorway.

   4 It's good to go out with colleagues and **let your hair down** a bit.

   5 Handing in that report will **be a** big **weight off your shoulders**, I imagine.

   6 You look nervous. Are you **getting cold feet** about asking for a pay increase?

   7 Can we talk? I'm having problems and I need to **get some things off my chest**.

   8 All of this unnecessary paperwork I'm supposed to complete **is a pain in the neck**.

9 Use six of the expressions in Exercises 7 and 8 to make six sentences about your own life.

SPEAKING Talking about stress

10 **21st CENTURY OUTCOMES**

Work in small groups. Discuss the questions.

   1 What can people do to avoid getting into a situation where they have constant stress?

   2 If people are in a situation where they are stressed too often, what techniques can they use to cope with it? Diet and nutrition tips? Exercise? Relationships? Using mobile phones and other devices more thoughtfully?

   3 What ways other than stress do you use to stimulate your brain?

CAN STRESS BE **GOOD** FOR YOU?

Google 'stress' and the search results paint a very negative picture: stress is a problem with symptoms, causes and treatments – something that needs to be defeated, like an illness. And indeed, chronic stress is a proven cause of many major health problems such as heart disease and cancer. But did you know that a degree of stress can be good for you? Recent research by Dr Staci Bilbo, an associate professor of psychology and neuroscience at Duke University in the USA, and others, indicates that the effects of stress are more complicated than we think.

KEEPING US ON OUR TOES?

5 Our bodies and minds naturally respond to our environment, to the things going on in the world around us. What's interesting is that whether our experience is negative or positive, the body's reaction is the same. It doesn't distinguish between the feelings we experience when we're under

10 pressure at work – the boss asks us as the last minute to give a complex presentation – or the ones associated with a thrill such as parachuting out of an aeroplane; it just releases a chemical called adrenaline. This is called the 'fight or flight' response; adrenaline gives us a burst of energy either to face

25 a challenge (fight) or run away from it (flight). In moderate amounts, adrenaline makes us feel alert and alive, though a big burst of adrenalin can be unpleasantly overwhelming. Dr. Pamela Peeke, an internationally recognized expert, physician,

30 scientist and author says, 'What stress does is it keeps us on our toes, it keeps us energetic, it keeps us engaged', adding that of course, too much stress can lead to real problems.

STIMULATING THE BRAIN?

Adrenaline and the 'fight or flight' response are only the

35 beginning, though. Clinical research shows that short periods of stress may help the brain work better. When we're stressed, the brain releases cortisol, a chemical that calms the mind. According to brain researcher Elizabeth Kirby, the moderate amount of cortisol produced during a brief burst of stress –

what she compares to being chased by a bear – provides an 40 energizing shot in the arm and motivates a quick response. In these amounts, cortisol improves the brain's ability to learn and remember. The key difference between good stress and bad stress is how long it lasts, according to Kirby. 'If a bear chases you all day, every day', she says, then the system will 45 be activated constantly, giving us a high and steady dose of the body's stress chemicals, which in the long run is harmful rather than helpful. So constantly feeling that you're in over your head at work may make you ill. And that can lead to serious health issues. 50

HELPING US LEARN TO DEAL WITH ANXIETY?

The mind isn't the only part of us that responds when the going gets tough. Our bodies also react in a variety of ways: a stiff neck, a tight stomach, tense shoulders. These symptoms are unpleasant because they cause discomfort, but they can also 55 be helpful, as we can use them to increase our awareness of the sources of anxiety – and therefore become more able to identify and deal with them. If we're mindful of how it affects us, we can practise improving our response and thereby slowly reduce the negative effects stress can have on us. But 60 there's more. Research has also shown that if, as children, we experience moderate stress – for example separation from our parents as part of the weekly routine – we grow into healthier, more relaxed adults. Practice dealing with low-level childhood anxiety can make it much easier to deal with more intense 65 grown-up pressures.

BOOSTING THE IMMUNE SYSTEM?

There's one more clear physical benefit of stress. We know that strong exercise 'stresses' the body and causes the release of adrenaline in much the same way that a sudden shock or 70 thrill does. Researchers have discovered that strong physical activity before certain medical procedures can improve their effectiveness. For example, when cancer patients have a fast workout just before receiving a dose of cancer treatment, it 75 improves the effectiveness of the drugs. Similarly, recipients of a vaccination can increase the body's ability to fight disease by doing a short but intense run just beforehand.

Stress can unarguably cause serious problems, but if we understand how it works, we can learn to use it 80 advantageously. So next time your boss gives you two hours to come up with the best presentation of your life and you're feeling seriously stressed, remember: it may be good for you!

9.4 Have you got a minute?

LISTENING Dealing with awkward situations

1 Work in pairs. Tell you partner what you would do in each of the following situations.

1 In the company car park, you accidentally scratch your boss's car while parking. No one sees it happen.

2 You left your company smartphone on the table in a restaurant. When you went back to look for it, it was gone and no one had turned it in. It holds sensitive information, including details of clients.

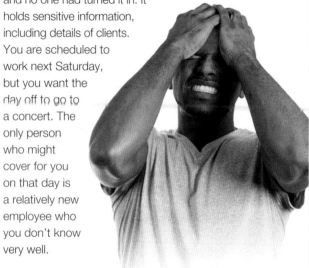

3 You are scheduled to work next Saturday, but you want the day off to go to a concert. The only person who might cover for you on that day is a relatively new employee who you don't know very well.

2 🎧 **53** Listen to five conversations. Answer the questions.

Conversation 1

1 What does the woman want?
2 What does the man say?

Conversation 2

3 What does the woman tell the man?
4 What is the man's reaction?

Conversation 3

5 What did the man do?
6 How does the woman react?

Conversation 4

7 What does the woman want the man to do?
8 How does the man react?

Conversation 5

9 What does the man want?
10 How does the woman respond?

3 🎧 **53** Listen again. Tick the sentences you hear in the Useful expressions box.

HAVING DIFFICULT CONVERSATIONS

Starting a conversation

Could I have a word?
Have you got a minute?
Sorry, but if you have a moment …

Accepting a request to speak

What's on your mind?
What's up?
What can I do for you?

Raising an awkward topic

There's something I wanted to ask you / talk with you about.
I've got a confession to make.
I have to apologize.
I have a favour to ask.

Explaining the situation

The thing is …
There's a slight / a bit of a problem with …

Asking a favour

I don't suppose … ?
You couldn't … could you?
Is there any way … ?

Responses

That's a shame, but I understand.
Actually, that's a bit tricky / awkward.
Don't worry. It doesn't matter / It's not important.
Unfortunately, …
I'm sorry, but …

Pronunciation Polite and assertive intonation

4a 🎧 **54** Listen. Which version of the sentence is polite (write P)? Which is more assertive (write A)?

1 I'm really sorry, but I'm going to have to ask you to pay for the damage.
2 I'm really sorry, but I'm going to have to ask you to pay for the damage.
3 Could you possibly help me out?
4 Could you possibly help me out?
5 That's an awkward situation, isn't it?
6 That's an awkward situation, isn't it?

4b Practise saying the sentences both politely and assertively.

SPEAKING Having difficult conversations

5 Work in pairs. Have conversations imagining you are in these situations. Use the language in the Useful expressions box. Deal with the situation in a way that feels natural to you.

Student A	Student B
You were trying to unjam the only office photocopier, and instead of fixing it, you caused it to spark and start smoking. Tell your boss (Student B).	You are Student A's boss. Have a conversation, then propose a solution.

Student A	Student B
You are Student B's colleague. Have a conversation, then propose a solution.	You want to go out after work. You have two-year-old son, and you need a babysitter. Ask your friend (Student A), who you know has a very busy life, to babysit for you.

Student A	Student B
You were supposed to give some extremely important research results to your colleague (Student B) yesterday, but you noted the date incorrectly in your diary. You will need another day to complete the work. Tell your colleague about the situation.	You are Student A's colleague. Have a conversation, then propose a solution.

Student A	Student B
You are Student B's friend. Have a conversation, then propose a solution.	You borrowed your friend's (Student A's) leather jacket to wear to a party. Unfortunately, someone at the party spilled food on the jacket and there's a big stain on it now. Tell your friend.

WRITING A record of a meeting

6 Read the report. Answer the questions.

1 Why did David Peters believe he wasn't given a pay increase?
2 What is probably the real reason he wasn't given a pay increase?
3 What will happen next?

RECORD OF MEETING: DAVID PETERS

Today at 10:45, I met with David Peters regarding his pay. During the meeting, Mr Peters claimed that his pay had not increased as quickly as he had expected it to. He alleged that he was being treated unfairly and even accused me personally of not liking him and therefore not recommending a pay increase.

In response to that, I acknowledged that his request for a pay increase hadn't yet been approved, but denied that this had any connection with my personal feelings about him. I urged him to consider the fact that he had arrived late for work more than 50 per cent of the time in the previous six months. He admitted that he had indeed been late to work frequently, but insisted that he still performed his job as well as anyone and refused to admit that being on time is a basic part of doing acceptable work.

In order to assist Mr Peters in improving his performance, I proposed that he start arriving at work on time or a few minutes early every day and suggested that we have a follow-up meeting after one month. He agreed with this suggestion.

Signed: _M. Davis_   Date: _06/15/15_

Print name: _Melanie Davis_

Writing skill Reporting verbs

7a Find twelve verbs in the report that paraphrase something that was said.

7b Match each statement (1–6) with the correct reported version (a–f).

1 It was my fault.
2 I'm sorry, I should have been more careful.
3 The data was left without password protection.
4 That's not quite right, actually.
5 You really should consider apologizing.
6 I absolutely didn't do it.

a He confirmed what had happened.
b I urged him to say he was sorry.
c He accepted responsibility for the mistake.
d He apologized for what had happened.
e He refused to admit he'd done it. / He denied doing it.
f He contradicted Ms. Fung's version of the story.

8 **21st CENTURY OUTCOMES**

Choose one of the conversations you had in Exercise 5 or imagine a similar conversation. Write a record of it using reporting verbs to summarize the conversation.

9 Exchange emails with the partner you worked with in Exercise 5. Were your reports similar?

10 Risk

Workers erect scaffolding at a construction site near the financial district in Panama City, Panama.

TEDTALKS

DEL HARVEY works at Twitter to ensure user safety and security, balancing the need for free and open communication on the social network with the need to protect users from online abuse. The security expert spends her days thinking about how to prevent bad things from happening while giving voice to people around the globe. Del Harvey's idea worth spreading is that companies have the responsibility to keep every user safe, by imagining the worst and designing products to avoid it happening.

BACKGROUND

1 You are going to watch a TED Talk by Del Harvey called *Protecting Twitter users (sometimes from themselves).* Read the text about the talk and the speaker, then answer the questions.

1 Harvey believes it's important for Twitter to give a voice to people around the globe. What kinds of stories or news do you think are spread by Twitter and other social media users?

2 What do you think is meant by the term *online abuse*? How do some people use social media to hurt others?

3 What do you think it means to protect Twitter users from themselves?

KEY WORDS

2 Read the sentences (1–6). The words in bold are used in the TED Talk. First guess the meaning of the words. Then match the words with their definitions (a–f).

1 We need to **root out** possible abuse and stop it.

2 If users' personal information were stolen, it would be a real **calamity**.

3 At first the tweet looked threatening, but it turned out to be **innocuous**.

4 The situation wasn't **cut and dried** because the tweet was genuinely intended as a joke.

5 With product safety, the **stakes** are high because people can get seriously hurt.

6 The couple's **prenuptial agreement** helped prevent a legal battle when they split up.

a risks, potential losses
b find and indentify
c clear and already decided
d disaster
e a legal contract made before a wedding stating how the couple will divide their money and possessions in a divorce
f not likely to hurt anyone

AUTHENTIC LISTENING SKILLS Avoiding frustration

When you listen to authentic English speech, it's easy to feel frustrated, because it can be difficult to understand. However, regular exposure to natural speech will help you develop your English. Try these tips.

• Before you listen, try focusing your thoughts on the topic. What do you already know about it? What do you think the speaker might say?

• When you listen, don't try to translate every word and don't worry if you don't understand everything. Relax and do your best to get a general sense of the message from the words you do understand.

• Keep practising. Regular listening related to topics you're interested in will help train your ear.

3a 🎧 55 Look at the Authentic listening skills box. Then listen to the opening sentences from the TED Talk. Focus on the general sense. In what order (1–2) does Del Harvey do these things?

a She explains Twitter's growth.
b She talks about her obligations to Twitter's customers.

3b 🎧 56 Listen to the next few sentences from the TED Talk. Try to get the general sense. Which of these things (1–4) does Del Harvey do?

1 She explains that Twitter is generally very safe.
2 She gives specific examples of risky behaviour.
3 She continues to explain the idea of 'scale'.
4 She mentions how Twitter protects users' private data.

3c Work in pairs. Tell your partner what you understood.

10.1 Protecting Twitter users (sometimes from themselves

TEDTALKS

1 ▶ **10.1** Watch the TED Talk. Take notes on the following topics:

The size of Twitter:
The size of risk:
Examples of users' behaviour:
Examples of risk:

2 ▶ **10.1** Watch the first part (0.00–2.21) of the talk again. What do these numbers refer to?

1 two million	**5** 500
2 500 million	**6** 99.999
3 six	**7** 150,000
4 24,900	

3 ▶ **10.1** Watch the second part (2.21–4.44) of the talk again and answer the questions.

1 What does Del Harvey say makes her job especially challenging?

2 What example does Del Harvey give of each of the following?
  a Possible spam (sending the same message to a lot of people)
  b Possible phishing (trying to steal people's personal information)

▶ 2009 = two thousand nine **N AM ENG**
▶ 2009 = two thousand and nine **BR ENG**

▶ behavior **N AM ENG**
▶ behaviour **BR ENG**

4 ▶ **10.1** Watch the third part (4.45 to the end) of the talk again. Answer the questions.

1 Harvey says she could imagine a situation where tweeting a picture of her cat could lead to her death. How could that possibly happen?

2 'Odds' are numbers used to express how likely something is to happen. For example, the odds of being born in January are 1 in 12 because there are twelve months. Harvey finishes her talk by saying that for Twitter, 'a one-in-a-million chance is pretty good odds'. What does she mean by this?

VOCABULARY IN CONTEXT

5 ▶ **10.2** Watch the clips from the TED Talk. Choose the correct meaning of the words.

6 Complete the sentences in your own words. Then discuss with a partner.

1 My country's most famous landmarks are …
2 A lot of bystanders usually gather when …
3 When I feel gloomy, I try to cheer myself up by …

CRITICAL THINKING Analogies

7 In her TED Talk, Del Harvey says her job is like writing your wedding vows and your prenuptial agreement at the same time. Why does she make this comparison? Choose the best explanation (a–d).

a To put forward the argument that the work she's doing is as important as thinking carefully when getting married.
b To give an explanation of the very different considerations involved in her job.
c To argue that people must think very carefully before sending out tweets.
d To explain that the level of risk in using Twitter is very low.

8 Read the comments* about the TED Talk. Do you think the analogies are effective or not? Which one do you agree with the most?

Viewers' comments

 Kumiko – Harvey's job seems very interesting. She's a kind of psychologist – trying to understand what people are thinking.

Jack – I think it's more like being a police officer. But I don't think any of the 'crimes' she's fighting are so serious. I can't really see why her job is necessary.

 Theodora – To me, Harvey is like a lifeguard in a swimming pool. There isn't usually any problem, but she's got to watch carefully to keep everyone safe. That's why it seems to me like a really important job. She is keeping Twitter users safe.

 Arturo – Harvey's main point is that even a small percentage of 500 million tweets is a lot. Think of it this way: 0.5% of the world's population (7 billion) seems tiny, but it's still an incredible 35 million people!

The comments were created for this activity.

PRESENTATION SKILLS Pace and emphasis

TIPS

Pay attention to the pacing of your words. Pause for emphasis at the most essential points of your talk.

- In general, speaking clearly and not rushing through your points will help you relax and make it easier for the audience to follow your talk.
- You can speed up slightly for asides – short statements that may be interesting but aren't part of the main message.
- Pauses can help emphasize essential points and grab the audience's attention – but don't overuse this.

9 ▶ **10.3** Look at the Presentation tips box. Then watch the clips to see how Del Harvey varies the pace of her TED Talk. Answer the questions.

1 What information does Harvey slow down for and say in a very clear way?
2 When she says 'People do weird things', what effect does the emphasis have?
3 When talking about phishing, what does Harvey slow down for? Why do you think she chooses to emphasize these words?
4 What question that she always asks herself does Harvey emphasize? What answer does she give that describes a big part of her job?

10 You are going to give a short presentation on a risk you took at work or outside work. Make some notes about what happened.

- What was the risk?
- When did it happen?
- Why was it dangerous?
- What were the possible consequences?
- How did you avoid them?

11 Work in pairs. Take turns to give your presentation. Vary your pace. Slow down to emphasize key information.

THE MOST DANGEROUS SPORTS

Every year, there are ten million sports injuries in the USA. So what are the ten most dangerous sports? When we think of dangerous sports, we think of rock climbing and skydiving, but those aren't even on the list. The top ten are ...

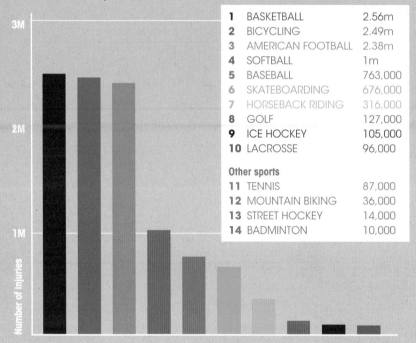

1	BASKETBALL	2.56m
2	BICYCLING	2.49m
3	AMERICAN FOOTBALL	2.38m
4	SOFTBALL	1m
5	BASEBALL	763,000
6	SKATEBOARDING	676,000
7	HORSEBACK RIDING	316,000
8	GOLF	127,000
9	ICE HOCKEY	105,000
10	LACROSSE	96,000
Other sports		
11	TENNIS	87,000
12	MOUNTAIN BIKING	36,000
13	STREET HOCKEY	14,000
14	BADMINTON	10,000

DIFFERENT WAYS TO MEASURE INJURIES

IF YOU TAKE INTO ACCOUNT THE **NUMBER OF PEOPLE** WHO PARTICIPATE IN A SPORT, **AMERICAN FOOTBALL IS THE MOST DANGEROUS**

IF YOU CALCULATE THE NUMBER OF INJURIES PER 1,000 HOURS*:

 RUGBY: 91

 COMPETITIVE SURFING: 13

 INDOOR WALL CLIMBING: 0.02

*ACCORDING TO A GERMAN SURVEY

GRAMMAR Passive reporting verbs

1 Work in pairs. Have you ever tried a sport that is seen as risky? Would you like to? Why? / Why not?

2 Look at the infographic. Answer the questions.

   1 Which sport is the most dangerous?
   2 Which sport is the safest?
   3 Which sport would you never want to try?

3 Read the text in the Grammar box. Answer the questions (1–3).

4 Rewrite the sentences using the passive form of the reporting verbs.

   1 People say that skateboarding causes 676,000 injuries a year.
     Skateboarding _is said to cause_

   2 Studies have shown that cycling is more dangerous than football.
     Cycling _has shown to be_

   3 The newspaper reported that horseriding is the seventh most dangerous sport.
     Horseriding _is reported to be_

PASSIVE REPORTING VERBS 1

As safe as ice hockey?
Ice hockey **has** long **been considered** to be one of the most dangerous North American sports, because the puck – the hard rubber piece that the players hit and score with – can travel at 170 kilometres per hour, causing painful injuries when it hits a player. However, according to recent research, basketball **has been shown** to be America's most dangerous sport. Why? One reason may be that ice hockey players wear equipment to protect them from injury, while basketball players have none. Basketball **is estimated** to cause about 2.5 million injuries each year, compared with ice hockey, which **is reported** to cause only about 100,000.

1 What grammatical form follows the bold passive reporting verbs?

2 Do we know who the agent of each passive reporting verb is?

3 Why is a passive verb used, rather than an active verb?

Check your answers on page 158 and do Exercises 1 and 2.

4 Records show that golf is more dangerous than ice hockey.
Golf _is shown to be_.

5 Hospitals expect to see a million baseball injuries this year.
A million baseball injuries _are expected to be seen_.

6 Doctors understand that softball can cause serious injuries.
Softball _is understood to cause_.

5 Read the text in the Grammar box. Answer the questions (1 and 2).

PASSIVE REPORTING VERBS 2

Climbing: Not as risky as you thought

When the first indoor climbing gym was opened in Seattle in 1987, **it was thought** that it would provide a relatively safe indoor training alternative for serious climbers. Now **it's been shown** that indoor climbing is less risky than both surfing and rugby. A study in Germany discovered that indoor wall climbers have an average of 0.02 injuries per 1,000 hours spent climbing, while **it's estimated** that competitive surfers have on average 13 per 1,000 hours, and rugby players 91. **It's expected** that the publication of this data will boost Germany's already popular indoor-climbing business.

1 What grammatical form follows the passive reporting verbs in bold?
2 Which of the sentences refers to something that will occur in the future?

Check your answers on page 158 and do Exercises 3 and 4.

6 Complete the text with passive reporting structures with *it*, using the words in brackets.

These days ¹_it is expected_ (expect) in any given year that hundreds of climbers will reach the top of Mount Everest. But after climbers George Mallory and Sandy Irvine failed to return alive from the peak in 1924, ²_it was widely bel_ (widely believe) that the great mountain would never be climbed. This was especially true after the failure of ten more expeditions in the next 30 years. Then in 1952, ³_it was reported_ (report) that an attempt would be made the following year by a British team. The group, consisting of about 400 people, arrived on the slopes of the mountain early in 1953. ⁴_it was estimated_ (estimate) that their baggage, containing food, camping gear and scientific equipment, weighed more than 4,500 kg. As spring came, they waited for a safe weather conditions for climbing. Finally, on May 26, ⁵_it was revealed_ (reveal) that Edmund Hillary and Sherpa Tenzing Norgay would attempt the summit. However, because of terrible weather conditions at the top, ⁶_it was announced_ (announce) that there would be a delay. Finally, on May 28, 1953, ⁷_it was proved_ (prove) that Everest could be climbed when Hillary and Norgay reached the summit

and returned to tell the story. Though Everest is the highest mountain in the world, ⁸_it is thought_ (think) today that several other mountains are more dangerous, including Annapurna, the world's tenth highest mountain.

7 Rewrite the following statements as they might appear in a news article, using passive reporting verbs.

1 We know that BASE jumping is very risky. (It)
It's known that BASE jumping is very risky.

2 We think there are a few thousand cave divers in the world.
There are _thought to be a few thousand_

3 A medical study reported that head injuries were the most common white-water rafting injuries.
It was _reported that head injuries_

4 We expect injuries in big-wave surfing to increase as more people try the sport.
Big-wave surfing injuries _are expected to increase_

5 We hope that BMX teams will set a good example by always wearing head protection.
It _will be hope that BMX set..._ ↳ _is hoped_

SPEAKING A TV news story

8 **21st CENTURY OUTCOMES**

Work in pairs. You're going to create a short TV news story about the following situation using passive reporting verbs.

> An unknown person climbed to the top of a university building and hung a banner from the roof.

The news story should answer the following questions:
- Who was the person?
- What did they do?
- Where did it happen?
- When did it happen?
- Why did they to it?
- How did they do it?

The person was believed to be …

The message banner which read 'Just say no' is thought to refer to …

9 Present your news story to another pair. Were your stories similar?

10.3 Follow your gut instinct

READING Understanding risk

1 Look at the risks. Number them in order of what you think is most likely (1) to least likely (5) to happen.

- **a** ___ Being killed by a bee sting
- **b** ___ Being injured by a toilet this year
- **c** ___ Being killed by an asteroid impact
- **d** ___ Being attacked by a shark
- **e** ___ Being struck by lightning in your lifetime

2 Check the answers to Exercise 1 on page 183. Then answer the questions.

1 Which possible event seems the scariest to you? Why?
2 Has anything ever happened to you that seemed extremely unlikely or an amazing coincidence?
3 What is your attitude to risk? Do you avoid it as much as possible, or can some risk make life exciting?

3 Read the article. Put the four headings (1–4) in the correct place (A–D).

1 Look critically at statistics.
2 Be sceptical of expert advice.
3 Follow your gut instinct.
4 You probably know more than you realize.

4 Read the article again. Answer the questions.

1 Why might choosing to drive make things worse?
2 What sort of evidence do you think supports the claim about transport safety?
3 What is the usual result of visiting the doctor frequently, and why does Gigerenzer think they are problems?
4 How did Gigerenzer choose good investments?
5 What are two signs that a person is likely to make good choices based on feelings?
6 In 2011, what did the news media incorrectly report as having increased?
7 What factors work together in our minds to calculate risk – even if we aren't aware that we're doing it?

5 Find these words and expressions in the text and explain their meanings in your own words.

1 (line 4) make matters worse
2 (line 8) get behind the wheel of a car
3 (line 9) statistically
4 (line 29) medication
5 (line 45) intuition
6 (line 45) gut instinct
7 (line 59) following your heart
8 (line 64) antidepressant

6 Which statements are supported by the article?

1 I'm safe driving a car because I'm in control, and I'm a good driver.
2 I visit the doctor when I know I'm ill, but not before.
3 I don't have a good enough understanding of business to be a good investor.

4 I've been in this business a long time and I just had a bad feeling about the company, which turned out to be right!
5 If the newspaper says that something is based on statistics, it's very likely to be true.
6 We aren't always completely aware of our thinking process when we solve problems and make decisions.

7 Would you use Gigerenzer's method for choosing companies to invest in? Why? / Why not?

VOCABULARY Risk and probability

8 Complete the sentences with these verbs.

are	increases	is	poses	reduces	run

1 Increasing sugar consumption ___poses___ a threat to public health.
2 Regular exercise ___reduces___ the odds of developing heart disease.
3 There ___is___ a one-in-11.5 million chance of being attacked by a shark in the USA.
4 Regularly eating fresh produce ___increase___ the likelihood of a long and healthy life.
5 The chances of recovering from many types of cancer ___are___ high.
6 People who collect honey ___run___ the risk of bee stings.

9 Complete the sentences with the correct form of the expressions from Exercise 8.

1 What do you think are the best ways to _____ of becoming ill later in life?
2 What's something unexpected that has happened to you that felt like it was _____?
3 What do you think _____ to global public health?
4 What medical developments have made the _____ from many diseases high?
5 Do you ever break the rules and _____ of getting caught or do you prefer be careful and stay safe?
6 What's the best way to _____ of success in your work or studies?

10 Work in pairs. Discuss the questions in Exercise 9.

SPEAKING Facing risks

11 **21st CENTURY OUTCOMES**

Work in pairs. Each think of a country and the possible risks of travelling there. Write advice to a visitor, using the Internet if it is available. Think about food, accommodation, health, climate, transport, customs, etc. Take turns to tell your advice to your partner but don't mention the country. Your partner should guess which country you are talking about.

understanding RISK

Risk expert, Gerd Gigerenzer, believes that we talk a lot about risk, but that we don't really understand it very well. In particular, Gigerenzer believes that in trying to avoid risk, sometimes we make matters worse rather than better.

For example, when we hear a news story about a frightening incident involving an aeroplane, many of us will choose to avoid air travel and instead get behind the wheel of a car. But statistically, there is clear evidence that even though scary things happen in aeroplanes, driving clearly poses a greater threat to personal safety than flying does. According to the World Health Organization, 1.24 million deaths occurred on the world's roads in 2010 while the per-year average for deaths while travelling in an airliner is 720 people globally.

Here are three lessons we can draw from Gigerenzer's research.

A

According to Gigerenzer, we're all aware of the risk of various common diseases – cancer, heart disease and so on – and many people choose to go for regular medical checkups to try to avoid these. They believe expert advice will help them reduce the odds of developing a serious illness. But Gigerenzer isn't convinced. 'I follow the evidence', he says, pointing out that there are not fewer cases of disease among those who visit the doctor regularly. 'They just get more treatment, take more medication, and worry more often', he says, adding that this is another example of creating problems by trying too hard to avoid them.

Gigerenzer once did an experiment. He stopped people in the street at random, gave them a list of companies, and asked them a single question: Which ones have you heard of? He then invested in those companies, and also in companies recommended by financial experts. Which investments performed better? Perhaps surprisingly, the ones named by people in the street. And it turns out that this isn't just random luck. There's actually a correlation between how well companies perform and how well known they are – though Gigerenzer admits that of course there are many exceptions.

B

In politics and business, feelings and intuition – gut instincts – are not openly considered a good guide for assessing risk and making important decisions. People often feel that if they rely on their heart rather than their head, they run the risk of making serious mistakes. However, Gigerenzer points out that people with a lot of experience who have shown good judgement in the past are very likely to be able to assess situations unconsciously, and will often have a better understanding of a situation than can be expressed by complex data or statistical predictions. One reason that gut instinct is important is that many systems – the global financial system, for example – behave in ways that are ultimately unpredictable. So when the evidence is unclear or extremely complex, following your heart can be a good solution.

C

In 2011, England's National Health Service reported that the number of individual prescriptions for antidepressants in the country had increased. The news media immediately interpreted this to mean that more people were depressed, and ran headlines about the 'depression crisis'. But statistics expert Dr Ben Goldacre points out that while you might think the only reason for more antidepressants would be more depression, it could easily be the case that doctors are writing more frequent prescriptions for smaller amounts to reduce the risk of patients taking too many pills. Goldacre cautions strongly against assuming relationships between the statistical information available and possible underlying causes.

D

In all areas of life, people regularly need to make quick decisions in situations where there is uncertainty or a lack of complete information. The mind can be seen as a set of tools: your ability to learn, your memory and your ability to reason. Whether you're aware of it or not, they work together whenever you have to make a choice or decision or calculate a risk. That doesn't mean you'll always get it right, but it does mean your mind may have a natural capacity to calculate risk – one that maybe you didn't even know about.

10.4 All things considered ...

LISTENING Assessing risk

1 Look at the photo. Work in pairs. Discuss the questions.

1 What kind of seat do you use for your work or studies?
2 Do you know about any non-traditional office chairs such as the one in the photo?
3 What are the risks of sitting for long periods of time in an unsuitable chair?
4 Does your country have strict rules about workplace safety, including safe seating?

2 🎧 **57** Listen to three people who are deciding which chairs to buy for their new office. Number the chair options (A–E) in the order they are discussed.

3 🎧 **57** Listen again. Complete the sentences.

1 The most obvious one is _____ .
2 In light of the research, ball chairs probably aren't _____ .
3 On the plus side, the high stool isn't _____ .
4 One downside of standing desks is _____ .
5 A final option that might do the job is _____ .

4 Work in pairs. Discuss the questions.

1 What are the pros and cons of each chair?
2 What type of chair do you think they choose?
3 Is it the same chair you would choose?

Pronunciation Saying lists

5a 🎧 **58** Listen to two people saying lists of options for sports activities they'd like to take part in during the work day. Which list sounds complete? Which list does the speaker leave open for more suggestions?

5b Name your top three favourite foods as a 'closed' list. Then make another list, describing ways you try to stay fit, leaving the list 'open'.

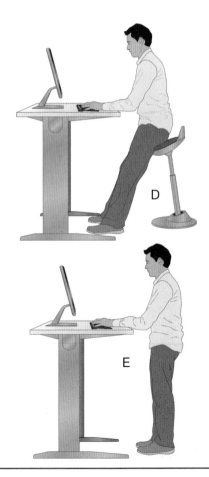

SPEAKING Health and safety issues

6 Work in groups of three. Read the new health and safety measures. Discuss options and decide the best way to implement them.

MEMO

RE: Health and Safety Measure Enforcement

From next week, all offices must enforce the following health and safety measures:

- All workers must have access to outdoor space in which to play sport.
- Equipment for at least three different ball sports must be supplied.
- At least three healthy options must be included in all food or drinks machines.
- All employees must have access to at least one organized indoor physical fitness session per day: a basic exercise class, yoga, martial arts, etc.

DISCUSSING ALTERNATIVES

Presenting options

There are some pretty interesting options to choose from.
Possibly the most obvious one is … as long as …
A third alternative that might do the job is …
… is another option to consider.

Discussing pros and cons

One downside/drawback of this option is …
What's not so great about this choice is …
On the plus side, …
On the minus side …
… makes this a very attractive possibility.

Considering options

Considering the price, I'm not sure this is the best option.
In light of the research, ball chairs probably aren't the best option.
All things considered, it makes sense to go with …
Ultimately, the best choice seems to be …

WRITING A consumer review

7 Read the online reviews of a ball chair. Match each star-rating/summary (1–3) with the correct review (A–C).

1 ★ ★ ★ ★ ★ I love it
2 ★ ★ ★ Pretty good
3 ★ ★ Not worth it

A I purchased this chair in an effort to address my lower-back problems – I work all day at a fairly demanding desk job. I can sit on this chair reasonably comfortably for periods of about twenty minutes, but after that I need to get up for a stretch. But maybe that's the point? My back pain hasn't gone away, but after two weeks with the chair, it is slightly better, so I'll continue using it.

B Considering it's sold as an office chair, I was a bit surprised to find that it's lower than a conventional office chair and therefore too low for my desk. I feel like a ten-year-old kid sitting at a grown-up's desk! If I use the chair at my desk, I'm sure it will mess up my back. So overall, the ball chair has been rather disappointing. On the plus side, I quite like using it when I'm not at my desk, but what I really need is a desk chair I can use.

C When I ordered this, I was a little concerned that it would be of poor quality, considering the fairly low price. As turns out, this chair is actually rather a good deal! I find that a standard desk chair gets uncomfortable for me pretty quickly – a matter of twenty minutes or half an hour. But with this one, I'm able to sit for long periods of time, and my back problems, which have always been a bit of an annoyance, are now non-existent.

Writing skill Using qualifiers

8a Look at these words from the reviews. Answer the questions.

fairly	reasonably	slightly	a bit
rather	quite	a little	pretty
rather a	a bit of		

1 What kind of word is being qualified in each case?
2 What effect does the qualifier have on this word?

See page 154 for more information about qualifiers, and do Exercises 5–7.

8b Add the qualifiers to the sentences.

1 You've been working hard recently so you deserve a holiday. (quite)
2 I'm afraid we were late arriving at the meal last night. (a little).
3 They had a quiet day at the office because most of the staff were on a course. (rather)
4 I'm having a problem with my computer crashing all the time. (a bit of)
5 They finished the work quickly. (reasonably)

9 **21st CENTURY OUTCOMES**

Think of something you have bought recently that you would give a three-out-of-five (3/5) star rating. Write an online review of it. Use qualifiers.

10 Exchange your review with your partner.

LISTENING TRIODOS BANK

1 🎧 **59** Read the introduction and listen to the podcast about Triodos Bank. Then answer the questions.

1 What were some of the results of the global financial crisis of 2007 mentioned in the podcast?
2 What types of business does Triodos support with investment?
3 What sector of business is each of the three named examples engaged in?

Triodos Bank, with its headquarters in Zeist, in the Netherlands, offers sustainable banking services to nearly 100,000 savers and provides finance for hundreds of organizations such as social enterprises, fair trade businesses, organic farms and renewable energy generators.

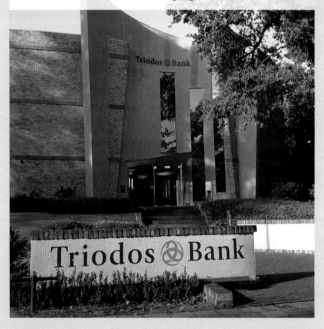

2 🎧 **59** Listen again. Choose the correct word or phrase (a, b or c) to complete these sentences.

1 Many customers moved to sustainable banking because they _____.
a didn't like increased regulation
b no longer trusted mainstream banking
c wanted to earn more from their savings

2 Triodos would not invest its customers' money in a company that was involved in _____.
a making weapons
b food production
c social work

3 Triodos's philosophy is that a bank _____.
a shouldn't make a profit
b can't be both ethical and competitive
c can be ethical and offer good returns

4 In addition to growing food, Belle Vue Farm _____.
a hosts music festivals
b offers accommodation
c manufactures camping gear

5 Key Driving Competences _____.
a makes in-car electronics
b trains people to drive electric cars
c has developed an alternative fuel source

6 Escuela del Actor has students _____.
a from the national government
b who work in factories
c of all ages

3 Would you like to do business with an ethical bank such as Triodos? Why or why not?

GRAMMAR

4 Complete the text with the correct form of the reporting verbs.

¹_____ (It / believe) that the concept of money, as we know it today, didn't appear in one place all at once, rather it emerged gradually in many different cultures around the world. The first 'cash' ²_____ (say / be) commodities: grain and cattle, used like money to buy and sell other things, as long ago as 11,000 years. And seashells ³_____ (know / use) as currency on every continent as a type of coin. The first true cash – metal coins as we know them today – ⁴_____ (think / make) independently in Greece, India, Turkey and China around 2,700 years ago. Until just a few years ago, ⁵_____ (it / not thought) that the world would ever be without notes and coins. However, despite its long history, cash ⁶_____ (report / be) under threat as more forms of electronic payment, including contactless cards and mobile phone payments, become more common.

5 Choose the correct options to complete these sentences.

A: I heard something ¹*really / the least bit* surprising today.
B: What was that?
A: City buses are going to stop taking cash ²*incredibly / entirely*. You have to pay either by contactless credit or debit card, or with a transport card.
B: You mean they'll take no cash ³*whatsoever / totally*?
A: Right. It will be ⁴*absolutely / very* impossible to travel without a card of some kind. It's going to be ⁵*completely / extremely* cashless.
B: That won't be ⁶*utterly / at all* convenient for out-of-town visitors who don't have a card, will it?

VOCABULARY

6 Complete the texts with words related to the body.

It makes my [1] _____ boil when I read about cyber criminals stealing people's bank details – and their money – over the Internet, so I don't use the Internet for banking. Sometimes it is a pain in the [2] _____ going out to the bank, but I'm sure it's safer.

When I borrowed a lot of money for university, I worried that I was getting in over my [3] _____ financially, but I'm glad I got my education. When I finally finished paying off the loans, it was a big weight off my [4] _____ . I was very lucky to get a job quickly. Sometimes I complain when I'm up to my [5] _____ in work and feel too busy, but a little stress keeps you on your [6] _____ , doesn't it? It's certainly better than being unemployed.

Last year, I almost borrowed a large sum of money for a new car, but at the last minute, I got cold [7] _____ and didn't take the loan. I decided instead to carry on cycling and using public transport. When the opportunity came up for me to leave my 9–5 office job in England and work for a year on an organic farm in Australia, I was able to do it, because I had some savings. Arriving in a hot country was a real shot in the [8] _____ . I loved working outdoors and was finally able to let my [9] _____ down.

7 Match the two parts of the sentence.

1 Some say that too much regulation in banking is
2 Regular saving reduces
3 There is much less than
4 Careful financial planning increases
5 The chances are
6 If you aren't careful with your credit card details, you run

a a one-in-a-million chance of a big win in the lottery.
b high that there will be another global economic crisis.
c a threat to economic growth.
d the risk of being a fraud victim.
e the odds of ending up with no money in retirement.
f the likelihood of reaching your financial goals.

DISCUSSION

8 Work in pairs. Discuss the questions.

1 In addition to banking, what other ethical or sustainable businesses are you aware of? What features make them ethical or sustainable?
2 What features do you look for in a bank? Good interest rates? Good customer service? Something else?
3 What are the pros and cons of a cashless society?

SPEAKING

9 Two friends are discussing which tablet to buy. Put the phrases (a–l) in the correct order. Then use them to complete the conversation below.

a are / choose / from / interesting / options / pretty / some / There / to
   _____

b a / got / Have / minute / you
   _____

c On / side / the / plus
   _____

d can / do / for / I / What / you
   _____

e an / attractive / it / makes / possibility
   _____

f minus / on / side / the
   _____

g a / ask / favour / have / I / to
   _____

h any / could / I / Is / there / way
   _____

i All / considered / things
   _____

j doesn't / Don't / it / matter / worry,
   _____

k a / Actually, / awkward / bit / that's
   _____

l is / The / thing
   _____

A: [1] _____ ?
B: Sure. [2] _____ ?
A: I want to buy a new tablet, and I know you just bought one. Which one do you think is the best?
B: [3] _____ . The first thing to think about is size. Do you want a 175 millimetre one, or a 250?
A: Which size did you buy?
B: I went for a 175. [4] _____ , it's very small and light to carry, but [5] _____ , the screen is pretty small and can be hard to read, sometimes. Of course the lower price [6] _____ .
A: You're right about that! [7] _____ , I'll probably go for the smaller size. But … [8] _____ .
B: Yes?
A: [9] _____ , I've just started my new job, but I have to wait a couple of weeks for my first pay cheque. [10] _____ borrow some money from you?
B: [11] _____ .
A: [12] _____ .

11 Vision

Cliff-hanging walkway on Tianmen Mountain in Hunan Province, China.

TEDTALKS

DIÉBÉDO FRANCIS KÉRÉ grew up in Gando, a small village in the African nation of Burkina Faso. After completing his education and starting work as an architect, he decided to give back to the community that raised him. He does that through the power of architecture. In this talk, Kéré shows off some of the beautiful structures he's helped to build in his small village. Diebedo Francis Kéré's idea worth spreading is that we all benefit from and can give back to our communities, and that those contributions can have profound effects.

BACKGROUND

1 You are going to watch a TED Talk by Diébédo Francis Kéré called *How to build with clay … and community*. Read the text about the speaker and the talk. Then work in pairs and answer the questions.

> **1** What do you know about Burkina Faso? What do you think life is like there?
>
> **2** In Burkina Faso, Kéré builds with clay. What do you think might be the advantages of building with clay? What about the disadvantages?
>
> **3** What building materials are the most common in the place where you live?

KEY WORDS

2 Read the sentences (1–6). The words in bold are used in the TED Talk. First guess the meaning of the words. Then match the words with their definitions (a–f).

C **1** When glass was first put in windows, it was considered a major architectural **innovation**.

F **2** We tested the **prototype** and discovered several ways we could improve it.

D **3** We need to improve the **ventilation** because the building gets far too hot in the summer.

A **4** Very thin clay walls are beautiful but can be **fragile**.

E **5** The builders **cast** concrete to make the walls of the building.

B **6** The dirt on the road was **compressed** by the traffic and became very hard.

> **a** easily broken
> **b** flattened, pressed down
> **c** a new method or idea
> **d** a system of providing fresh air to a room or building
> **e** pour liquid into a pre-made shape, so it hardens and makes something solid
> **f** the first version of something

AUTHENTIC LISTENING SKILLS Dealing with accents: different stress patterns

> Sometimes, non-native English speakers such as Diébédo Francis Kéré stress different syllables in a word or words in a sentence from those that a native English speaker would stress.
>
> For example, he says *rainy **seas**on* rather than the standard English ***rain**y season* .
>
> Being aware of this and listening to a variety of accents will help you be able to pick out familiar words and phrases even when they are not pronounced as a native English speaker would say them.

3a 🎧 **60** Look at the Authentic listening skills box. Listen to this sentence pronounced first by Kéré in his TED Talk and then by a native British English speaker. Compare the pronunciation of the underlined word.

> I would like to show you how <u>architecture</u> has helped to change the life of my community.

3b 🎧 **61** Listen to this sentence pronounced by Kéré and then by a native British English speaker. Underline the word that is stressed by the speaker in each version of the sentence.

> **1** What does it look like to grow up in a place like that?
> **2** What does it look like to grow up in a place like that?

3c 🎧 **62** Listen to another extract. Complete the text.

> I am an ¹ _____ of that. I was born in a little ² _____ called Gando. In Gando, there was no electricity, no access to clean ³ _____, and no school. But my father wanted me to learn how to read and write. For this reason, I had to leave my ⁴ _____ when I was seven and to stay in a city far away from my village with no contact with my family. In this place I sat in a class like that with more than 150 other ⁵ _____, and for six years.

11.1 How to build with clay and community

TEDTALKS

1 ▶ **11.1** Watch the TED Talk. Note down details about Diébédo Francis Kéré's life.

Hometown and early life:
School days:
University:
Return to Gando:
Challenges of the first project in Gando:
Other projects in Gando:
Other challenges in Gando:
A final story from his childhood:

2 ▶ **11.1** Watch the first part (0.00–6.07) of the talk again. Are the statements true (T) or false (F)?

1 Today, Gando is much more modern than when Kéré was a child.
2 When he was an architecture student, Kéré raised US $50,000 to build a school.
3 At first the people of Gando didn't like Kéré's plans for building the school.
4 Clay is never used as a construction material in Burkina Faso.
5 The main design considerations for the building were to make it large enough and cheap to build.

3 ▶ **11.1** Complete the notes on the second part of the talk. Then watch the second part (6.08–9.18) of the talk again and check your answers.

cast mud	clay pots	clay walls	extension
high school	library	prototype	rain

- The school [1]_____ : built a(n) [2]_____ to test whether the construction was strong enough
- The [3]_____ : used [4]_____ in the roof structure to allow heat out and light in
- The [5]_____ : used [6]_____ – very similar to concrete
- The fragile [7]_____ : had to be protected from the [8]_____ during construction

4 ▶ **11.1** Watch the third part (9:19 to the end) of the talk again. Answer the questions.

1 In addition to the buildings, what benefit has Kéré's work brought to his community?
2 What is Kéré's main motivation for doing his work?
3 Why, according to Kéré's mother, did the women of his community give him money?

VOCABULARY IN CONTEXT

5 ▶ **11.2** Watch the clips from the TED Talk. Choose the correct meaning of the words.

6 Complete the sentences in your own words. Then discuss with a partner.

1 For me, it would be a privilege to …
2 I would be happy to participate in fundraising for …
3 When … , I was over the moon.

CRITICAL THINKING Relevance

7 Kéré says he hopes he was able to prove the power of community and show that architecture can inspire communities to shape their own future. Why was each of the following relevant to the talk?

1 He tells us about the poverty in Gando.

   This is relevant because it helps us understand the community he comes from.

2 He talks about fundraising while an architecture student in Germany.
3 He explains the traditional process of making a hard clay floor.
4 He talks about Burkina Faso's climate.
5 He explains that usually, young men from Gando have to leave the village and work far away.

8 For both speakers and commenters, it's important to focus on ideas that are relevant. Read the comments* about the TED Talk. Which two are relevant to Kéré's talk? Which one is not?

Viewers' comments

J JJ312 – I love this talk. We so often think of buildings as places in a community, but Kéré shows that the process of building is just as important as the result and that working together can make a community stronger. That's a very valuable lesson that we all should learn.

C Cowboy – As Kéré points out, the rains are definitely a big feature of life in Burkina Faso. They're necessary for farmers or for anyone who is trying to grow food for the community or raise animals. When the rains don't come, it can create serious problems for the community.

C ClarkKent – It's wonderful to see that Kéré's designs work with nature. He doesn't try to find a way to generate electricity in Gando to run air conditioning – he instead designs a building that will be naturally cool and light. Great work!

The comments were created for this activity.

PRESENTATION SKILLS Varying your tone of voice

TIPS

Your tone of voice is the overall quality of your voice, including pitch and volume. When you're nervous, you may sound more hesitant or speak in a monotone, without raising or lowering your voice. Try to vary your tone of voice. Doing so can:

- help keep your audience interested
- emphasize key ideas
- convey your enthusiasm for what you're saying

For example, when you briefly lower your voice and speak quietly, for emphasis, it can grab the audience's attention more than raising it. However, it's important not to change your voice so much that it's artificial.

9 ▶ **11.3** Look at the Presentation tips box. Then watch the clip from the TED Talk and notice how Kéré varies his tone. Answer the questions.

1 At the start, is Kéré's voice more excited and passionate or calm and quiet?
2 What's his tone of voice when he describes the finished floor, saying 'And then you have this result, very fine'? What do you feel this tone communicates?
3 What's his general tone as he says 'It can be 45 degrees in Burkina Faso', and then describes his design?
4 What tone does he end on?

10 Think of a time when something exciting happened to you, for example, you won something, accomplished a difficult task, or had a nice surprise. Prepare how you will describe it to a partner. Think of the tone of voice you will use at each stage.

11 Work in pairs. Take turns to give a presentation in which you tell your story.

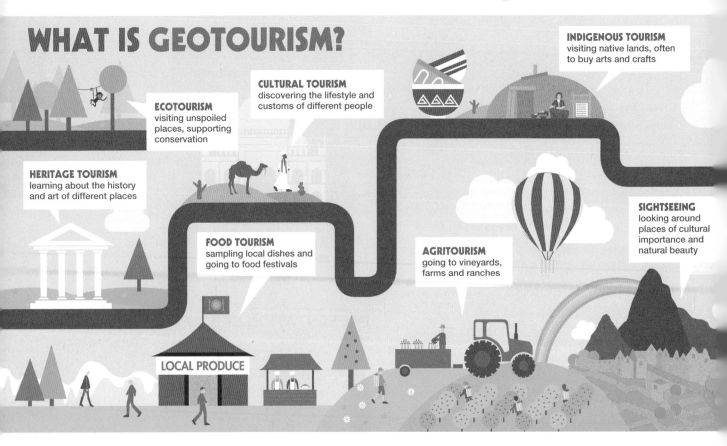

WHAT IS GEOTOURISM?

ECOTOURISM
visiting unspoiled places, supporting conservation

CULTURAL TOURISM
discovering the lifestyle and customs of different people

INDIGENOUS TOURISM
visiting native lands, often to buy arts and crafts

HERITAGE TOURISM
learning about the history and art of different places

FOOD TOURISM
sampling local dishes and going to food festivals

AGRITOURISM
going to vineyards, farms and ranches

SIGHTSEEING
looking around places of cultural importance and natural beauty

LOCAL PRODUCE

GRAMMAR Subordinate clauses

1 Work in pairs. Discuss the questions.

1 Is your country popular with tourists? Why? / Why not?
2 Where have you travelled / would you like to travel?
3 What benefits / problems can tourism bring to a country?

2 Look at the infographic. Answer the questions.

1 What kinds of places are ecotourists most interested in seeing?
2 Which type of tourism is concerned with native people? history? farming?

3 Read the text in the Grammar box. Answer the questions (1–5).

SUBORDINATE CLAUSES

Considering that global tourism is often blamed for ruining popular holiday destinations, the notion that tourism could save the world might seem surprising. But that's what geotourism's supporters claim, **in spite of the fact that** this is an apparent contradiction. **In case** you are unfamiliar with the idea of geotourism, the most popular definition of this very 21st century concept is leisure travel that enhances the environment, culture, and the well-being of tourist destinations.

Compared to mainstream tourism, which often comes at the expense of unwanted change to local communities, geotourism:

- unites communities and encourages local people and businesses to work together to provide visitors with a real experience.
- informs both visitors and hosts. Residents discover their own history **when** they learn what is interesting to visitors.
- brings economic benefits to the hosts **provided that** businesses use local workers, services and supplies.

While geotourism's vision can't solve all of the world's problems, perhaps it can nonetheless make the world a better place.

Which expression in bold means that:

1 something will happen at the same time as something else? (time)
2 you are referring to a factor that is already known? (cause)

Check your answers on page 160 and do Exercises 1–6.

3 something will happen only if something else happens? (condition)
4 something will happen even though something else seems in conflict with this idea? (contrast)
5 something might or might not be a factor? (precaution)

4 Complete the text with these conjunctions.

> although by the time given that in spite of in view of

¹_____ many people think of tourism as a jet-age pastime, some would argue that it's actually been around since ancient times. ²_____ the fact that travel was difficult and dangerous, we have several accounts including Pausanias's *Description of Greece* written in the second century, and the journals of fourteenth-century Arab traveller Ibn Batutta to prove that tourism has been popular for many hundreds of years. ³_____ Batutta returned home for the last time, he had been all over Africa, Asia, Eastern Europe and the Middle East – keeping a journal throughout. He's still considered one of the greatest travellers of all time. However, ⁴_____ the fact that all of this travel was such hard work, is it really right to call it tourism? Some people have described Petrarch's climbing of Mont Ventoux – also in the fourteenth century – as the first instance of 'modern' tourism, ⁵_____ his purpose in climbing the mountain was simply to enjoy the view.

5 Join the two sentences using the conjunction in brackets. There may be more than one position in the sentence you can place the conjunction. Use appropriate punctuation.

1 The country has beautiful beaches. Tourists hardly ever visit them. (although)
2 Upper-middle-class people are generally comfortable financially. They frequently travel abroad. (since)
3 Students often spend a few months abroad before starting university. They can save enough money for their travels. (providing that)
4 The weather is terrible. Visitors stay in the hotel rather than going out on a tour. (in the event that)
5 Visitors first arrive in the jungle camp. They're amazed at how beautiful it is. (every time)
6 One study found that single working people prefer to take holidays abroad. Families with young children often like to holiday closer to home. (whereas)

6 Look at the statements about travel. Expand them with your own ideas to write eight sentences with subordinate clauses. Try to use each of the six types of conjunction (cause/reason, condition, contrast, time, precaution, other).

1 Tourism can be great for a local economy.
   Given that tourists usually pay for hotels, food and entertainment, **tourism can be great for a local economy.** (cause/reason)
2 Extensive tourism may mean that most of the well-paid jobs in popular destinations are tourism-related.
3 Geotourism makes people feel good about international travel.
4 International travel contributes to the world's environmental problems.
5 The widespread use of English makes communication easy.
6 Some environmentalists feel that some parts of the world should be completely closed to tourism because any visitors to remote areas can cause problems for wildlife.
7 Local people such as the Masai in Kenya become a tourist attraction themselves.
8 Many Masai give up farming or other traditional activities because being photographed earns more money.

Pronunciation Intonation in subordinate clauses

7a Read the sentences. In each one, would you expect the intonation to rise or fall at the end of the subordinate clause?

1 Although geotourism brings benefits to both the visitors and the hosts, some environmentalists feel that there are parts of the world that should be completely closed to tourism.
2 Considering that the local Masai people in Kenya have become a tourist attraction themselves, it may be worth re-thinking ecotourism.
3 By the time thousands of divers have visited a popular diving spot, damage has been done that can never be repaired.

7b 🎧 **63** Listen and check your answers. Then practise saying them.

SPEAKING Looking after what matters

8 **21st** CENTURY OUTCOMES

Work in small groups. Discuss the questions.

- Geotourism is seen by many as being environmentally friendly. Can you think of other activities or products that are described as 'green', when in reality, the greenest thing might be to avoid them altogether?
- It's predicted that in the foreseeable future, 639 known languages will no longer be spoken by anyone. 457 languages (9.2 per cent of the world's total) already have fewer than ten speakers. Is this inevitable, or should something be done to stop it? If so, what?

11.3 A personal calling

READING Visionaries

1 Read the short definition of visionary. Then discuss the questions.

> **visionary (n)** a person with original ideas about what the future will or could be like; a person who sees ways to solve problems that no one has thought of, or takes action that no one else is taking.

1 Can you think of anyone who is or was a visionary in …
 a business? b science? c politics?

2 What qualities do visionaries often have?

3 Can you think of examples of how some visionaries have been treated by society?

2 Read the article about four visionaries. What is each person's vision for?

1 Peace Pilgrim: a vision for *world peace*

2 Jiro Ono: a vision for …

3 Georges Bwelle: a vision for …

4 Albina Ruiz: a vision for …

3 Read the article again. Are these sentences true (T) or false (F)?

1 Peace Pilgrim's main activity was to raise money for people in countries at war.

2 Peace pilgrim relied on people to offer her life's basic necessities.

3 Despite the success of his restaurant, Jiro Ono doesn't feel that he has completely mastered the art of making sushi.

4 Ono has tried several different occupations but always returned to making sushi.

5 Georges Bwelle became a doctor so that he could better care for his own father, who was ill.

6 Bwelle now spends all of his time in a rural hospital giving free medical treatment.

7 Albina Ruiz found a way to turn an activity that people were already doing into a business.

8 Ruiz's vision wasn't to end poverty, but to slightly improve the lives of people living in difficult circumstances.

4 Work in groups of four. Make notes on the following. Then share your answers with the group.

Student A: The qualities the four people in the text have in common

Student B: The qualities that some, but not all, of them have

Student C: Anything we know about the specific motivation of the speakers – the thing that started them on their path

Student D: How each person's vision has affected other people's lives

5 In your groups, decide where each visionary is on this scale.

a personal, ----|-----|-----|-----|-----|--- a practical vision
inward vision   for a better world

6 Work in pairs. Discuss the questions.

1 Which visionary would you most like to join for one day? Why?

2 If you had unlimited time and money, what vision – personal, or for the world – would you like to pursue?

VOCABULARY Expressions with *look* and *see*

7 Choose the correct options to complete the sentences.

1 Jiro *overlooks / oversees* a team of people who make sushi.

2 People don't always *look / see* eye to eye about what constitutes an ethical life.

3 As far as I can *look / see*, the only thing to do is to keep trying.

4 Let's make some changes, then wait and *look / see* what happens.

5 Can you *look and see / see and look* what time tomorrow's meeting is?

6 I *looked / saw* him in the eye and told him that I really admire his work.

7 I'm on the *lookout / see out* for an opportunity to try something new.

8 We need to *look / see* into why the delivery was late.

9 I'm going to *look / see* about volunteering for a charity.

10 I *look / see* up to my mother because she followed her artistic vision.

8 Make sentences that are true for you using five expressions from Exercise 7.

I'm on the lookout for a good second-hand car.

SPEAKING Talking about visionaries

9 21st CENTURY OUTCOMES

Work in pairs. Discuss the questions.

1 Think of a well-known visionary. What vision did/do they pursue?

2 How do they communicate their vision to others?

3 How are they generally portrayed in the media? Does the media support them? Question them? Some of both?

VISIONARIES

How four people have made the world a better place

We all look at ourselves and our world and imagine how things – and we – could be better. Visionaries, however, devote themselves to following their vision and to bringing reality closer to the ideal that sometimes only they can see.

Peace Pilgrim

On January 1, 1953, 44-year-old Mildred Lisette Norman left her home in California with just the clothes on her back. She didn't stop walking until her death in 1981. The reason? To promote peace. She adopted the name Peace Pilgrim, and by 1964, she had walked 40,000 kilometres. Peace Pilgrim found freedom in living simply. She had no possessions other than her clothes, carried no money, and never asked for food or shelter. She vowed to 'remain a wanderer until mankind has learned the way of peace, walking until given shelter and fasting until given food'. Her message? 'One little person, giving all of her time to peace, makes news. Many people, giving some of their time, can make history.'

Jiro Ono

Jiro Ono's story shows that an intensely personal vision can be as powerful as the desire to save the world – and can touch people's lives. Ono was born in 1925 and has been making sushi since he left home at the age of nine. At 85, he said 'All I want to do is make better sushi.' 'Once you decide on your occupation', says Ono, 'you must immerse yourself in your work. You have to fall in love with your work. Never complain about your job. You must dedicate your life to mastering your skill. That's the secret of success.' Although he's been working at it for most of his life, Jiro remains constantly on the lookout for ways to improve. Years ago, he learned to massage an octopus for 30 minutes before preparing it. Then he realized that a 45-minute massage improved the texture of octopus, so he added fifteen minutes to the process. The deep admiration that Jiro's food inspires, and the respect his customers have for his art make his restaurant in Tokyo one of the hardest in the world to get a reservation for.

Georges Bwelle
50

'To make people laugh, to reduce the pain, that's why I'm doing this', says Dr Georges Bwelle. You might not think Bwelle has much to laugh 55 about, having experienced, from both sides, the sadly underresourced medical care in his home country of Cameroon, Central Africa. 60 For 21 years, Bwelle cared for his father through a long illness. What started as a broken arm turned into an infection that eventually spread to the brain. Whenever the situation became worse, he'd take his father to hospital only to find that the necessary medical equipment 65 and experience simply didn't exist in his country. Eventually, his father lost the battle and died. As a direct result of these experiences, Bwelle decided to pursue a career as a doctor. In 2008, he started a nonprofit organization offering free medical assistance to people in need of a doctor. Now, every Friday, 70 he and 30 other volunteers, including medical students, drive long distances over difficult roads to visit rural villages that need medical help. They've treated tens of thousands of patients. 'I am so happy when I am doing this work', Bwelle said. 'And I think about my father. I hope he sees what I am doing.' 75

Albina Ruiz

When Albina Ruiz left her rural village in Peru in the 1990s to study in Lima, she was shocked to find 'waste 80 pickers' crawling over piles of garbage, trying to make a living out of what they found there. Most of them had bare feet and hands and 85 were frequently ill. As far as she could see, there was no reason for this situation to continue. Upon completing her university studies, Albina devoted herself to helping the waste pickers, setting up a business providing uniforms, masks and 90 gloves so that the refuse collectors could work safely. She also supplied them with carts so they could deliver waste to recycling stations in return for payment. In addition, she gave the workers a management system that included training, affordable equipment and clothing, and a reliable source of pay. 95 Perhaps most importantly, she gave them a voice. Her group – Ciudad Saludable (Healthy City) – has, in addition, trained waste-management business professionals from other countries in how to create effective waste-handling systems and created employment for workers in countries as far away as India. 100

11.4 A dream come true

LISTENING Life coaching

1 Work in pairs. Discuss the questions.

1 When you were a child, what did you want to be when you grew up?
2 Do you know of anyone who from a very young age had a vision for themselves that they followed into adulthood?

2 Read the definition. Would you like to work with a life coach? Why? / Why not?

---

life coach (n) a person who helps others develop a vision for the future and to make and meet personal and professional goals. A life coach's main aim is to help others become happier and more satisfied in all areas of life.

---

3 🎧 **64** Listen to a life coach talking to her client. Choose the correct options to complete the sentences.

1 Carly asks Mike to talk about things he *hopes to do / he dreams of doing*.
2 Mike talks about *making / designing* furniture.
3 Mike talks about things that seem *very difficult to him / exciting to him*.

4 Mike *has already spent some time / likes the idea of* living and studying abroad.
5 Carly suggests one way that Mike could *use Spanish / learn Chinese*.

4 🎧 **64** Listen again. What does Mike say? Complete the sentences.

1 I've always fancied …
2 I could see myself …
3 If money were no object, I'd …
4 I'd love to …
5 Wouldn't it be great …

Pronunciation Sure and unsure tones

5a 🎧 **65** Listen. Mark each sentence S (sure) or U (unsure).

1 I could see myself writing a novel.
2 I've always fancied learning an African language.
3 I can envisage really enjoying a year's travel.
4 I'd like to spend some time studying business.
5 Wouldn't it be great to get a job on a cruise ship?
6 I can't see myself spending all day just relaxing.
7 I can see myself working in a restaurant.
8 If money were no object, I'd stop working.

5b Practise saying the sentences with both sure and unsure tones.

SPEAKING Talking about a vision of the future

6 Roleplay being a life coach and a client. Take turns being Student A and Student B.

Student A – The life coach
Tell Student B you'd just like to hear a bit about some things that really excite Student B, or things Student B could envisage doing in the future. Be encouraging and ask questions for more information where appropriate.

Student B – The client
Respond to Student A. Use the expressions in the Useful expressions box and your own ideas. Use appropriate intonation to show whether you're sure or unsure.

SHARING DREAMS AND VISIONS OF THE FUTURE

I've always fancied learning a new language.
I could/can see myself studying medicine.
If money were no object, I'd buy my own plane.
I can envisage opening my own restaurant.
I'd love to see Antarctica.
Wouldn't it be great to work as a volunteer?

WRITING An endorsement

7 Read the online endorsements (1–3). What do you think the relationship of each endorsement writer was to the person being described? How can you tell?

Writing skill Persuasive language

8a Look at the positive, persuasive words and expressions in bold in the first recommendation. Then underline the positive, persuasive words and expressions used in the other two recommendations.

8b Choose the best options to complete the sentences.

1 Working with Beatta was a real *privilege / asset*.
2 I was very *honoured / pleased* with Heitor's computer programming skills.
3 Shelagh is extremely *real / good* at managing multiple tasks.
4 Joe was *an inspiration / confident* to the whole team, especially when times were tough.
5 Melinda is *impressed / proactive* and doesn't need to be told what to do.
6 Bernard has *a strong sense / an ambition* of personal responsibility.

1

I had the **privilege** of working alongside Tomas Burak for six months. He **worked hard** to fulfil his ambition of improving our team's sales performance, and was **a great example** for the rest of us. He's **proactive, focused** and **hard-working**. He's **extremely good** at setting goals and reaching them. I **feel confident** that Tomas would be a **real asset** to any team he joins.

2

Melody Wong joined my team as an intern three years ago. From her first day working with us, we were all impressed by her ability to understand our project's vision and to work toward helping us achieve it. I was extremely pleased when she agreed to stay on working part-time when her internship ended and even more pleased when she joined us full time after completing her degree. Melody is a great team player with a strong sense of personal responsibility.

3

Jorge Benevades is an inspiration for his whole staff. When I started working on his team, I didn't have much of a sense of professional direction. However, Jorge had vision and recommended training and project work that helped me develop skills I didn't even know I had. Rather than telling his team what to do, he leads the way and shows us what's possible. I felt very honoured to work under him. Any company he joins will be lucky to have such an inspiring leader.

9 Write an endorsement for the person you worked with in Exercise 6. You may write as their colleague, or imagine that you are their boss or their employee. Remember to focus on the positives.

10 Share your endorsement with the person you wrote about. Do they think it was a fair an honest assessment of their strengths and abilities? Was it persuasive?

12 The future

BACKGROUND

1 You are going to watch a TED Talk by Matt Mills and Tamara Roukaerts called *Image recognition that triggers augmented reality.* Read the text about the speakers and the talk. Then work in pairs and answer the questions.

    1 What types of Internet content are you the most likely to share with friends, and how do you share it?

2 What do you think augmented reality is, and what do you think it could be used for?

3 Have you heard of or used an app like Aurasma? If so, describe it. If not, would you like to try one? Why? / Why not?

TED TALKS

MATT MILLS and **TAMARA ROUKAERTS** demonstrate Aurasma, an app that places animated images on top of a user's view of the world using a smartphone. Point your phone at a building, and on your phone's screen you'll see an interactive map. Point it at a film poster, and you'll see a clip of the film. Mills's and Rouakerts's idea worth spreading is that cutting-edge augmented reality tools will allow our devices to see and understand the world more like the human brain does – and enable us to blend virtual and physical realities in amazing ways.

The past meets the future in Medellin, Columbia

KEY WORDS

2 Read the sentences (1–6). The words in bold are used in the TED Talk. First guess the meaning of the words. Then match the words with their definitions (a–f).

F **1** Image **recognition** software allows computers to 'remember' and identify items and people in pictures.

C **2** When you point your phone at a certain image, it will **trigger** a video in the phone's memory.

A **3** **Augmented reality** will change how we see the world.

E **4** When I point my camera at the Eiffel Tower, an **aura** appears on my phone giving lots of information.

D **5** The software can **overlay** the background image with maps and other information.

B **6** We can **tag up** textbooks so that a video clip plays when the smartphone camera is pointed at it.

a digital content that is placed on top of reality on a smartphone screen

b mark or label something

c cause something to happen

d put one thing on top of another

e technology that allows digital information to be viewed 'on top of' something real

f the action of knowing and identifying something or someone

AUTHENTIC LISTENING SKILLS Listening for grammatical chunks

It isn't necessary to hear and process everything a native speaker says in order to understand their message. A lot of natural spoken English is delivered in 'chunks' – small groups of words that function as grammatical units, for example *in order to*, and *A lot of* in the sentences above. Grammatical chunks are often spoken quickly and are unstressed because they don't carry the key meaning. Listeners can learn to ignore the unstressed chunks and focus on the main, stressed content words – usually nouns, adjectives and main verbs.

3a 🎧 66 Look at the Authentic listening skills box. Then listen to the start of the TED Talk and write the main words you hear. Work in pairs. Try to reconstruct the extract.

3b 🎧 67 Now listen to the same extract slowed down. What words did you hear this time that you didn't hear last time?

3c 🎧 66 Listen to the extract at normal speed again. Did you notice more content words within the grammatical chunks?

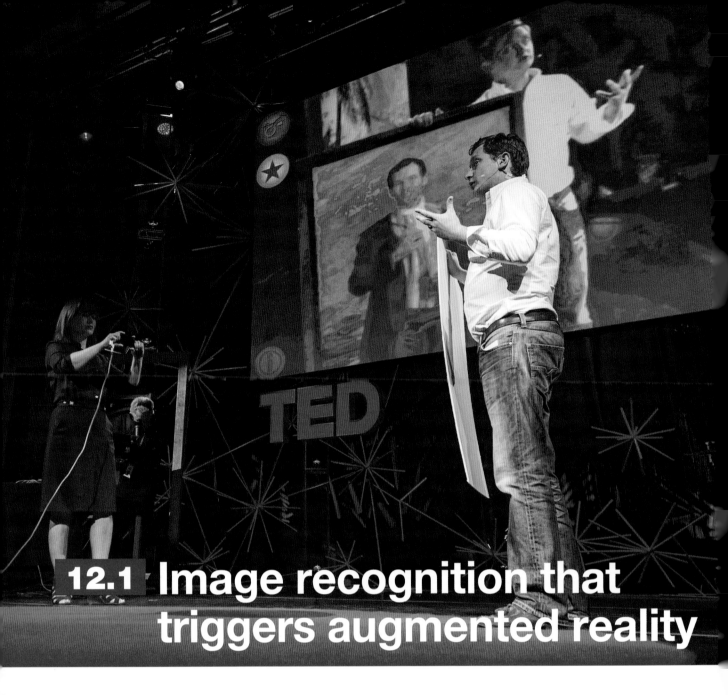

12.1 Image recognition that triggers augmented reality

TEDTALKS

1 ▶ **12.1** Watch the TED Talk. Choose the correct words to complete the sentences.

1 Mills and Roukaerts are demonstrating their app using a *normal* / *specially adapted* mobile phone.
2 The picture that Mills holds up is a *modifed 'digitally readable'* / *traditionally painted* image.
3 Mills's phone *records* / *recognizes* the newspaper and the router (an electronic device for connecting computers together).
4 The dinosaur is an example of *a tag* / *an aura*.
5 After Mills and Roukaerts take a video of the audience doing a 'stadium wave', Mills describes *how people have used Aurasma* / *how simple Aurasma is to use*.
6 Pointing the camera at Mills's conference badge *triggers* / *records* the content that is overlaid on the badge.

2 Throughout the presentation, what real-life objects do Mills and Roukaerts either use or describe using as triggers for auras?

3 ▶ **12.1** Watch the first part (0.00–3.19) of the talk again. What exactly do the words in bold refer to in the following statements by Matt Mills?

1 'There's nothing done to **this image**.'
2 'All the processing to do that was actually done on **the device** itself.'
3 'And that linking of **the digital content** to **something that's physical** is what we call an aura ...'

4 ▶ **12.1** Watch the second part (3.20–6.20) of the talk again. Answer the questions.

1 Who is not very animated (doesn't show much emotion)?
2 What has increased a lot in the past year?
3 What does Mills say that teachers have tagged up?
4 How do their students react?

▶ cell phone **N AM ENG**
▶ mobile phone **BR ENG**

▶ router /ˈraʊtər/ **N AM ENG**
▶ router /ˈruːtə(r)/ **BR ENG**

5 ▶ **12.1** Watch the third part (6.21 to the end) of the talk again. Discuss the questions in small groups.

1 Mills says that with Aurasma, 'we can literally take the content that we share, we discover, and that we enjoy and make it a part of the world around us.' Having seen his demonstration, can you explain how the app works?
2 Do you like the idea of auras? Would you use them?
3 What do you think they would be useful for?
4 What kind of information would you share using Aurasma?

VOCABULARY IN CONTEXT

6 ▶ **12.2** Watch the clips from the TED Talk. Choose the correct meaning of the words.

7 Work in pairs. Discuss the questions.

1 What sort of trickery do people use to deceive other people on the Internet?
2 What technical advancements have taken place during your lifetime that you now feel you can't do without? Which ones do you wish had never happened?
3 A paradigm shift occurred when people realized that the world wasn't flat. Can you think of another example?

CRITICAL THINKING Thinking about the speaker's motivation

8 Look at some of the phrases Matt Mills uses in his TED Talk. What do they all have in common?

Wouldn't it be amazing …
The thing that's incredible about this …
What's great about this …
It's completely free to download …
This process is very, very quick …

9 What does Mills's use of language suggest about his motivation for speaking about Aurasma? That he's trying to teach us how to use the technology? 'Sell' a product to us? Share his enthusiasm for a new idea?

10 Read these comments* about the TED Talk. Which do you think most accurately describes Mills's main motivation for speaking? Why?

Viewers' comments
R **Rick** – Truly amazing! I really want to try Aurasma. Mills obviously wants to help the public understand the benefits of augmented reality.
D **DLM** – What an incredible educational tool! Mills clearly shows how augmented reality will soon become part of every child's education.
J **Jolly89** – Mills does a wonderful job of showing off Aurasma. He promotes the product brilliantly – I'm definitely going to download it!

*The comments were created for this activity.

PRESENTATION SKILLS Being concise

TIPS

Being concise is saying what you want to say using a limited but effective number of words. It compels you to concentrate on your main message and edit out any 'filler'. Try to:

- prepare a talk that isn't lightweight, but also isn't overly repetitive or too dense
- be very clear in your own mind about what you want the audience to take away
- keep sentences relatively short and straightforward
- avoid unnecessary words. Words such as *kind of*, *sort of* and *actually* can be useful, but they can also be overused
- practise and revise your talk a lot. When you practise, you'll usually find that you're able to communicate your message with fewer words.

11 ▶ **12.3** Look at the Presentation tips box. Then watch the clips from Matt Mills's TED Talk. Answer the questions.

1 How would you rate the content of the TED Talk?

|----------------|----------------|----------------|----------------|

too lightweight   just right   too dense

2 How would you rate the presentation of the talk?

|----------------|----------------|----------------|----------------|

not enough   just right   overly
explanation   repetitive

12 Think of a product or service that you use. You are going to explain how it works and why it's useful, and give several reasons why you think others should use it, too.

13 Work in pairs. Take turns to give your presentation. Follow the suggestions below and remember the advice from the Presentation tips box.

- Introduce the product or service.
- Explain how it works.
- Explain why it's useful, and therefore why you think people should use it.
- Summarize.

14 Rate your partner's explanation using the two questions in Exercise 11.

▶ world /wɜrld/ **N AM ENG**
▶ world /wɜː(r)ld/ **BR ENG**

▶ processing /ˈprɑsesɪŋ/ **N AM ENG**
▶ processing /ˈprəʊsesɪŋ/ **BR ENG**

12.2 They saw it coming

Predictions made in 1900 ...
when 2000 was the

DISTANT
FUTURE

GRAMMAR Future in the past

1 Work in pairs. Discuss the questions.

1 How do you think the world will be different ten years from now?

2 How about 100 years from now?

3 Can you think of any technological developments of the last ten years that your grandparents' generation probably never even dreamed of?

2 Look at the infographic. What predictions does it make? Which ones have come true?

FUTURE IN THE PAST

When centuries turn, people invariably look to the future, and the year 1900 was no exception. Following the great inventions of the 1800s, the twentieth century **was bound to** be a time of further technological achievement. In 1900 the Wright Brothers **were about to** make the first powered aeroplane flight, and the horse **was unlikely to** rule the roads for much longer because Henry Ford **was going to** turn the automobile into a mass-market product. 1900 was the year that engineer John Elfreth Watkins **was to** write an article entitled 'What May Happen in the Next Hundred Years'. The article predicted that in the year 2000, people **would** send colour photographs and moving images using electrical signals (digital photography and television) and that trains **were likely to** travel 240 kilometres per hour. It also said that, given the increasing use of electrical power, farmers in the year 2000 were going to grow fruit and vegetables under electric lights. Amazingly, all of those came true. His predictions weren't perfect, though. Watkins also said that the letters C, X and Q were bound to be dropped from the alphabet because they were unnecessary, and that in cities, bridges and underground tunnels would separate all vehicle traffic from pedestrians.. Neither of these turned out to be correct.

Check your answers on page 162 and do Exercises 1–6.

3 Read the text in the Grammar box on page 132. Which expression in bold means:

> **1** *were at the point of*?
> **2** *was planning to*?
> **3** *was almost certain to*?
> **4** *was/were going* to to describe something in the past as if seen as a future prediction? *(×2)*
> **5** *probably would*?
> **6** *probably wouldn't*?

4 Choose the correct options to complete the text.

From 1965 to 2003, the television show *Tomorrow's World* tried to predict how the world ¹*would* / *was bound to* change in the near future. Here are some things they got mostly right:

In 1967, the show featured a 'home computer terminal' capable of organizing a diary, updating the user with banking information, and sending and receiving messages. According to the show, the home computer ²*was going to be* / *was* so convenient and easy to operate that it ³*was bound to be* / *was about to be* standard in every home by 1987 – and as cheap to rent as a telephone.

A 1968 episode asserted that gardeners everywhere were ⁴*about to* / *unlikely to* replace their plants with artificial ones because they were much easier to care for. While this didn't happen, by the 1980s top football clubs began installing fake grass on their grounds.

In 1994, unknown inventor Trevor Bayliss said that his battery-less radio ⁵*was going to* / *was about to* revolutionize communications in poorer countries if he could find funding to produce it. As a result of his going on the show, the Freeplay radio ⁶*would* / *was going to* become a huge success.

And one they didn't get right:

In 1981, *Tomorrow's World* featured a robot that played the game snooker*. The programme suggested that robotic snooker players ⁷*wouldn't* / *were going to* become commonplace – which we now know was never ⁸*going to* / *about to* happen.

_____

*snooker** (n) a British table game played with sticks and balls

pool

5 Complete the sentences. Use these words. Some have more than one possible answer. Have you or has anyone you know had similar experiences to those described?

> bound   going   just about   never going   unlikely

1 For years, I thought I was ___going___ to get a job in computing, but I ended up in something completely different.
2 I really loved being near my friends and family, so I was ___unlikely___ to move abroad.
3 I reckoned that if I kept studying and doing my school work, I was ___bound___ to find a subject I really loved eventually.
4 I was ___never going___ ever to have a career as a singer, so I decided I'd better get an education and find a steady job.
5 I was ___just about___ to catch up on some work when my friend phoned and asked me to go out.

Pronunciation Sentence stress in explaining outcomes

6a 🎧 **68** Listen. Underline the word that's stressed in the two versions of the sentence. Which one emphasizes that an intention was changed? Which one emphasizes that an intention was followed through?

1 I wanted to study biology.
2 I wanted to study biology.

6b 🎧 **69** Practise saying these sentences with natural stress. Then listen and check your answers.

1 I always thought I was going to be a teacher (and I was right).
2 I always thought I was going to be a teacher (but I became a mechanic).

SPEAKING Past views of the present

7 **21st CENTURY OUTCOMES**

Work in small groups. Discuss the questions. Try to include future in the past expressions.

1 When you were a child, what did you think you would do when you grew up? Think about work, where you'd live, family, children, travel, and so on. Did any of your ideas come true?
2 And what did you think the world would be like when you grew up? Consider technology, the environment, transport, homes, space travel, cities, communication and so on.
3 Which of the things you discussed in question 2 have come true?
4 Which have not come true? Do you think any of them will come true in the future?

12.3 Half full or half empty?

READING Is pessimism really so bad?

1 Work in pairs. Discuss the questions.

  1 Do you feel generally positive about the future, generally negative, or neither?

  2 Do you ever feel annoyed by people who are very positive or very negative? Why? / Why not?

2 Complete the sentences with *optimist, pessimist* or *realist*.

  1 'The _____ sees difficulty in every opportunity. The _____ sees the opportunity in every difficulty.' – Sir Winston Churchill

  2 'The point of living, and of being a/an _____, is to be foolish enough to believe that the best is yet to come.' – Sir Peter Ustinov

  3 'Optimism means better than reality; pessimism means worse than reality. I'm a/an _____.' – Margaret Atwood

  4 'It's a good idea to borrow money from a/an _____ because they don't expect to get it back.' – Anonymous

  5 A man interviewing for a job said, 'I'm a/an _____.' The interviewers said, 'Can you give me an example?' The man said, 'When do I start?'

3 Read the article. Then choose the best options to complete the sentences.

  1 _____ people in the world are realists.
    a The vast majority of   b Relatively few

  2 Some psychologists now believe that our _____ may change and adapt, depending on circumstances.
    a attitude   b personality

  3 Pessimism leads to a positive outcome _____ .
    a in no situations   b in some situations

  4 Realism _____ pessimism and optimism.
    a offers more benefits than   b doesn't offer the same benefits as

  5 The greatest emotional benefit is likely to come from _____ mindset.
    a an appropriate   b a realistic

4 Read the article again. Which of the following statements are supported by the article?

  1 There's a time to give up and to say you've been beaten.

  2 If you expect great things, great things will come to you.

  3 If you believe enough, you will get what you want.

  4 Optimists rarely get a pleasant surprise.

  5 With the power of positive thinking, there's no limit to what you can achieve.

  6 You're more likely to get what you want if you don't think too much about what's standing in your way.

  7 Taking a pessimistic view of a situation may make a positive outcome feel even more positive.

5 Work in pairs. Discuss the questions.

  1 The article talks about the benefits of optimism and pessimism. Can you think of a time when thinking realistically about a situation is the best approach?

  2 Can you think of a time when you had a pessimistic outlook and were pleasantly surprised?

  3 What kinds of things do you think we can feel optimistic about when we look at the future of the world?

VOCABULARY Optimism and pessimism

6 Expressions relating to optimism often use light or brightness as a metaphor and expressions of pessimism often use darkness as a metaphor. Complete these expressions from the article.

  1 The optimist sees the world through _____ .

  2 The pessimist always sees _____ on the horizon.

7 Match the two parts of the expressions.

The optimist says:	The pessimist says:
F **1** The glass is	D **5** The glass is
E **2** There's light	B **6** There's no hope
A **3** Every cloud has	C **7** If something
G **4** Look on the	

  a a silver lining
  b in sight.
  c bad can happen, it will.
  d half empty.
  e at the end of the tunnel.
  f half full.
  g bright side.

8 Which expressions from Exercises 6 and 7 could describe the following situations? Sometimes there's more than one possibility.

  1 I've lost my job, but it was time for me to make a change anyway.

  2 We had a flat tyre on the way to the airport – of course.

  3 This project has been incredibly difficult, but I'm really looking forward to handing it over next week.

  4 My job is going great, but you just never know when things are going to change for the worse.

  5 I don't like my job, and the promotion I've been offered only means that it will get a lot harder.

  6 There's absolutely nothing bad about my life.

SPEAKING Talking about financial decisions

9 *21st* **CENTURY OUTCOMES**

Work in pairs. Student A turn to page 172, Student B turn to page 183.

Is **pessimism** really so **bad**?

There's a simple test to determine whether you're generally an optimist, or a generally a pessimist. When you see this glass of water, if you describe it as half full, you're an optimist, but if you describe it as half empty, you're a pessimist.

And there's a third option: the realist, who sees the water as taking up 50 per cent of the volume of the glass. The truth about realism, though, is that people are rarely completely neutral.

Optimists are often seen as the happy, healthy people who cheerfully overcome hardship and always see light at the end of the tunnel. The glass-half-empty crowd, by contrast, are usually thought of as bringing everyone down and maybe even making themselves ill in the process. When you're trying to get a job, no expert would advise that you think negatively. And no one would ever suggest that you'd be better off always looking out for the next dark cloud on the horizon. In fact it's quite the opposite in many cultures, where there can be huge pressure to be optimistic, and to avoid pessimism at all costs.

But have we got it wrong? Are there times when a little less optimism and little more pessimism could be helpful?

For decades, psychologists have told us that optimism and pessimism were largely matters of disposition – that most people tended one way or the other, while the self-help industry has been built on helping people work to overcome negativity and train themselves to be more optimistic. However, recent research by Edward Chang, a professor of psychology at the University of Michigan, seems to indicate that the situation is actually far more complex than that. His view is that rather than being a pure optimist or pure pessimist, there are many contexts in which people choose to adopt one or the other mindset depending on the individual situation they're facing, and further, that people often choose the attitude that will lead to the best outcome. It's important to note that the research found that people rarely approach situations as realists, they usually choose to see things either as slightly better than they actually are, or slightly worse. A key conclusion is that pessimism isn't 'bad' and optimism 'good', but rather that they're both functional. Current psychology supports the following example of strategic use of optimism and pessimism.

A woman starting a new business knows it won't be easy, though she doesn't know exactly what the challenges will be. If she chooses to be pessimistic and imagine that the business venture will be more difficult than she can handle, she might decide it's too much trouble and quit without even trying. However, if she decides to be optimistic, she will accept that she will face obstacles, but will also feel confident that she'll find ways to overcome them. Optimism, in this case, would motivate her to start and very likely carry her through the difficulties to success.

After a few successful years, as a result of an economic downturn, the woman is facing the almost certain collapse of her business and needs to decide what to do. If she adopts an optimistic mindset – looking through her rose-coloured glasses – she may imagine that somehow the business will survive, even though all evidence indicates otherwise. She might waste months or even years hoping for the best, only to eventually fail. However, if she takes a pessimistic view and sees the business as already doomed, she will then do what she needs to do to close the business quickly and move on to the next thing. This is as close to success as she could hope to come.

It's important to point out that we aren't simply talking about realism, which has no emotional power. In both starting and finishing the business, the realist would look at the future and say that it's largely unknown, but would have no strong emotional motivation in either direction. However, both optimism and pessimism enhance the view of reality with feelings that can lead us to action in a way that simple realism cannot.

Another way that optimism and pessimism can both serve us well, depending on the circumstances, is in the management of emotions. It easy to see that optimism can help us see the silver lining to the dark cloud and help us overcome worry and anxiety in difficult situations. What's less often appreciated is the way pessimism can protect us from disappointment by keeping our expectations low. For example, if you were pessimistic about applying for a job you know you might not get, then the blow of not getting the job would be less painful. At the same time, if you got the job, your joy would be even more powerful because of your pessimistic outlook. So in this case, pessimism leads to a more positive outcome, whether you get the job or not.

So next time someone tells you to cheer up, you can make an informed choice about whether optimism or pessimism really is the best way forward.

12.4 Is Friday good for you?

LISTENING Arranging to meet

1 Work in pairs. Discuss the questions.

  1 How do you usually make arrangements? Email?
Face-to-face conversation? By telephone? By text
message?

  2 What are the pros and cons of making arrangements
with each type of communication?

2 🎧 **70** Listen to the three conversations. Note
down the arrangements as you listen. Then answer the
questions.

  1 What are Phil, Linda and Mr Dean meeting about?

  2 Where and when have they decided to meet?

  3 What two things does Phil need to do next?

  4 How is Phil's speech different when he speaks with
Mr Dean?

3 🎧 **70** Listen to the conversations again. Complete
the sentences.

Conversation 1

  1 I _____ make a meeting next week?

  2 I _____ have a work trip then, but it was
cancelled.

Conversation 2

  3 I'm afraid Wednesday _____ me.

  4 Friday's _____ for me.

Conversation 3

  5 I _____ pick up some things in town.

  6 Nine _____ place.

Pronunciation Sentence stress in making
arrangements.

4a 🎧 **71** Listen. Which words are the most strongly
stressed?

  A: Is Monday any good for a meeting?

  B: I'm afraid not. I'm away till Wednesday. How about
Thursday?

  A: I was supposed to have a work trip then, but it's been
cancelled. Thursday at ten?

  B: Ten would be perfect.

4b Practise the conversation using natural stress.

SPEAKING Making arrangements

5 Work in groups of three or four. Imagine that you need to
meet outside of class time to plan a class party. Use your
own diary. Find a time and place that you can meet.

MAKING ARRANGEMENTS

Asking about availability

I was wondering if you could make a meeting next week?
Does/Will/Would next Wednesday at eight work for you?
Is Thursday any good for you?
How about Monday?

Saying yes

Sure, yeah, I'm around.
That should be OK.
That would be good.
Yeah, I can make that.
That's not ideal, to be honest, but if we make it nine instead of eight, I can manage that.

Talking about changing plans already in place

I was going to have a team meeting at that time, but maybe I can reschedule it.
I'm supposed/meant to be meeting John but I may be able to postpone that.
I was supposed/meant to have a work trip then, but it's been cancelled.

Saying no

Wednesday? I'm afraid not. I'm away overnight that night.
Tuesday's out for me, but Thursday would work.

Agreeing

Nine next Thursday, my place. OK, I think that'll work.
Let's pencil it in.
Sounds great.

FROM: PhilJames@xyzemail.com

TO: Oak Park Residents   CC:

SUBJECT: Summer street party update

Hi All,

The planning committee met recently to discuss plans for the upcoming summer street party. Various suggestions were made about entertainment. One proposal was to host an 'open mic' session so that local residents could demonstrate their talent, but not everyone agreed that this was a good idea. Another suggestion was to hire a band with a local reputation. The objection to this was that it would be difficult to choose a musical style that everyone would enjoy. We were unable to reach a final agreement.

We also discussed food. Several ideas were put forward, including asking a local restaurant to cater the event, but with several good choices, we found it difficult to choose one. The suggestion was also made that we could invite residents of Oak Park to work together to cook for the entire group, but that wasn't seen by everyone as a good option.

In the end, it was agreed that the best thing to do would be to create on online survey for residents to complete and share their views about plans for the party. When the survey is complete, I'll send a link. We'll make arrangements for the party based on the results.

Best regards,

Phil

WRITING A group email

6 Read the email. Answer the questions.

1 What suggestions were made about entertainment?
2 What suggestions were made about food?
3 What action did they agree to take to help come to an agreement?

Writing skill Impersonal language

7a Underline the phrases that the writer uses to avoid naming people directly when reporting what was said. Why was this technique used?

7b Rewrite the sentences from the email. Use the words given to make them impersonal.

1 Lucian proposed hiring a karaoke system.
(proposal) One _____ .

2 Justine didn't think it was a good idea.
(everyone/agree) Not _____ .

3 Harry said it would be difficult to limit the number of participants.
(objection) The _____ .

4 Leila suggested that we change the date.
(suggestion) The _____ .

5 Bill, Sara and Raul all said that more research was needed.
(agreed) It _____ .

8 21st **CENTURY OUTCOMES**

Work in groups of three. Have a five-minute meeting to plan a class party. Brainstorm the following topics and then make a decision about each one.

- Food
- Music
- Venue

9 Write a group email about it.

10 Exchange emails with another group. Is the message clear? Does it use impersonal language correctly?

READING

1 Read the article about Mellowcabs. Then say if each sentence below is true (T) or false (F).

1 Mellowcabs hopes to take market share from motorised taxis.
2 Mellowcabs offer the first two kilometres free, and after that, charge a small fare.
3 Every Mellowcabs is fitted with a tablet computer.
4 Local landmarks will be tagged as triggers for auras.
5 Pedicabs have been popular in South Africa since the 1920s.
6 Du Preez and Breytenbach raised finance for their venture by selling shares.
7 Mellowcabs will not directly own all of the vehicles in its fleet.

2 Are there taxis similar to Mellowcabs in your area? Who uses them? Or do you think they would be popular if they were introduced? Why? / Why not?

Mellowcabs

One of the strongest positions a company can find itself in is to have no direct competitors, which is currently the case with South Africa's Mellowcab. With an estimated 60 per cent of South African commuters travelling by taxi, it may be hard at first to understand how the company can claim to have no competition. But consider these facts:

- 65 per cent of urban journeys are shorter than four kilometres, and Mellowcabs is the only company that has made short distances its sector.
- The company is currently the only one that earns its money not from fares, but from advertising – so every ride is free.
- Unlike typical mainstream taxi companies, Mellowcabs alone uses fully electric vehicles with zero direct emissions, so they're environmentally friendly.

In addition to more traditional advertising on the cabs, each taxi also has an on-board tablet with location-sensing software, so as the taxi approaches shops or restaurants that are Mellowcab's advertising clients, the tablet displays promotional offers for those businesses. The company plans to add augmented reality to its tablets, too. Passengers will be able to point the on-board tablet at a local landmark – a historical building, for example – and the tablet will display information about it. There will even be the option to choose different languages, so the tablet can be used as a kind of guidebook.

When co-founders, Neil du Preez and Kobus Breytenbach, started Mellowcabs in 2012, their aim was to develop the pedicab industry in South Africa. Pedicabs are bicycle taxis that have been operating in the cities of Europe and North America for at least twenty years, and in Asia for much longer, but not, until now, in South Africa. Du Preez and Breytenbach started Mellowcabs using their own money, most of it to manufacture the first eight vehicles, and also to pay their drivers and maintenance staff. The company wants to provide employment opportunities and is aiming for 60 per cent of their drivers and technicians to be young people and for at least fifteen per cent to be women. The company also has an owner-driver scheme that means some of the vehicles belong to the people who drive them.

Cities everywhere need clean, efficient transport for short journeys, so with any luck, the Mellowcab idea will catch on and spread around the world.

EVERY MELLOWCAB:

- is made in South Africa
- has 110 km daily range
- has a solar panel on the roof, supplying up to 35% of the vehicle's charge
- conforms to international vehicle safety standards
- has a shell made from recycled plastic
- uses regenerative braking, which means the energy from the braking process is used to charge the battery
- features illuminated body panels to increase safety and display the adverts
- has pedals, not to directly power the vehicle, but to extend battery life

GRAMMAR

3 Complete the text with these words.

although	bound	by
considering	going	in spite of
provided	was	in view of the fact that
when	would later	was about

[1] _____ Tokyo merchant and cart manufacturer Akiha Daisuke put the first *jinrikisha* (literally 'human-powered vehicle') on sale in 1869, he probably had no idea he [2] _____ to start a personal mobility revolution. [3] _____ the idea was incredibly simple, it had the effect of shrinking cities. The business [4] _____ to become a runaway success first in Japan, then in the rest of Asia and eventually beyond.

The rickshaw, as it [5] _____ come to be known, reached Shanghai and Hong Kong in 1874, and by 1875, there were 100,000 of them on the streets of Tokyo alone. Its speed ([6] _____ you had a strong man pulling it), convenience, style and relatively low cost meant that it was [7] _____ to become a hit in the rapidly modernizing cities of Asia. In spite of its huge popularity around the turn of the twentieth Century, the cycle-powered version was soon [8] _____ to revolutionize things further.

[9] _____ that it was such an important innovation to a hugely popular mode of transport, it's amazing that no one knows who first got the idea of marrying the bicycle and the rickshaw to create the trishaw – also called a pedicab. The new hybrid vehicle almost certainly emerged in Singapore. [10] _____ the end of the Second World War, in 1945, the pedicab had almost completely replaced traditional rickshaws. And [11] _____ the fact that cars and motorcycles rule today's roads, the pedicab still has a place. It's estimated that as many as five million pedicabs still play a vital role in daily transport in India alone, and [12] _____ traffic problems and environmental concerns are a part of daily life, the future of the pedicab seems secure.

VOCABULARY

4 Choose the best options to complete the texts.

A pedicab business partnership proves that differences between people don't prevent a strong partnership.

Helena Roberts My business partner and I almost never [1] *see / look* eye to eye. If I say there's light at the end of the [2] *tunnel / cloud*, he says he can't see any hope in [3] *sight / view*. If I say the [4] *glass / bright side* is half full, he'll [5] *look / see* me in the eye and say no, it's half [6] *gone / empty*. However, as far as I can [7] *see / look*, we're going to stick together, because our differences are part of our success.

Jerry Bronski I [8] *oversee / look and see* the maintenance for our fleet of pedicabs. I need to keep them on the road, earning money, so it's part of my job to assume that if something [9] *can have a silver lining / bad can happen*, it will. I'm constantly [10] *on the lookout for / looking into* potential problems: worn tyres, loose nuts and bolts, and quite literally, [11] *rose-tinted / dark* clouds on the horizon – because the cloth coverings over the cabs need to keep passengers dry in all weathers. When it comes to vehicle maintenance, you can't [12] *wait and see / see about* what problems develop, you have to stop them before they arise.

DISCUSSION

5 Would Mellowcabs be a profitable business in your area? Consider the following questions.

- Are pedicabs already in use?
- Do many people need to make short journeys? If so, who?
- Are there tourists to your area who would use them? Why or why not?
- Would the climate make pedicabs an attractive option?

6 Would you invest in a local Mellowcabs business? Why or why not?

SPEAKING

7 Complete the conversation with these expressions. Then practise it with a partner.

I think	I was supposed	I was wondering
I'm around	let's	see you
we make it	work for you	

A: [1] _____ if you could make a meeting next week?

B: Sure, yeah, [2] _____ .

A: Would next Tuesday at ten [3] _____ ?

B: That's not ideal, to be honest, but if [4] _____ midday, I can do that.

A: [5] _____ to be meeting Henry for lunch at 12.30, but that's been cancelled.

B: [6] _____ pencil it in.

A: OK, next Tuesday at twelve. [7] _____ that'll work.

B: Great! [8] _____ then!

THE PERFECT ASPECT

English verbs carry two kinds of meaning: tense, which tells us when the action occurred in time (past, present or future) and aspect, which tells us how we view this time – whether it's completed, ongoing, temporary, etc. There are two aspects in English: perfect and continuous. We use the perfect aspect to look back from one point in time to an earlier time.

Present perfect

Simple

Have + past participle
To look back from now to situations or actions in the past that have a connection to the present. It can be used:

- for complete actions that have an importance in the present
  *I'vo **bought** a now tolovision.* (= I have the television now.)
  ***Have** you **had** lunch?* (= You're not hungry, are you?)

- to refer to a time period that has continued into the present and with time expressions that mean 'up to now', for example *this month*, *today*
  *I'**ve** always **lived** in small flats, so I don't have much stuff.*
  ***Have** you **used** the car today?*

- with time expressions *just, already, yet, recently, for* and *since*
  *I haven't been here long. In fact I've **just** arrived.*
  *It's only four. Have you **already** finished work for the day?*
  *I'm waiting for her call, but she hasn't phoned **yet**.*
  *We've had this television **for** ten years / **since** our wedding.*

- with stative verbs (*have, be, know,* etc.) for unfinished actions and situations that continue into the present
  ***Have** you **known** Leo for a long time?*

Continuous

Have been + *ing*
To talk about situations or actions that started in the past and are still continuing. It can be used:

- for temporary situations
  *How long **have** you **been waiting**?*

- for repeated actions
  *I'**ve been using** the clothes dryer far too much.*

- with the time expressions *for, since, recently, all day/week/month/year*
  *We'**ve been managing** without heating **for** two weeks now.*

▶ Exercises 1 and 2

Past perfect

Simple

had + past participle
To look back from a point in the past to an earlier situation or action. It can be used:

- for single completed events or repeated actions that happened before other events

*He'**d enjoyed** a good lifestyle before the recession hit.*
*She'**d used** her MP3 player only four or five times before it stopped working.*

- after verbs of thinking and feeling
  *As soon as I shut the door, I realised I'**d left** my keys inside.*

- with stative verbs (*have, be, know,* etc.) to talk about unfinished actions and situations that continued into the point in the past from which the speaker is looking back
  *The wifi **had been** down for three days.*

With two events that happen one after the other using expressions such as *after, as soon as* or *when* we can usually use the past simple, as the sentence doesn't involve looking back to an earlier time.
*After we **(had) settled in**, we went to call on the neighbours.*

Continuous

had been + *ing*
To look back to a situation or action that was in progress before a given time in the past.
*How long **had** you **been living** in London before you could afford to buy your own house?*

We don't usually use stative verbs (*have, be, know,* etc.) in the past continuous.
*I'**d had** a car for years (Not I'd been having a car for years.)*

▶ Exercise 3

Future perfect

Simple

will have + past participle
To look back from a point in the future to a completed action. It is used:

- with a time expression such as *by, in, at* or *before* to indicate when the action is going to be completed
  *I'**ll have finished** using your laptop in about an hour.*

- to make predictions about the present
  *You should call him. **He won't have realised** you've moved.*

- with stative verbs (*have, be, know,* etc.) to talk about unfinished actions and situations that will continue into the point in the future from which the speaker is looking back
  *By Thursday, we **will have been disconnected** for a week!*

Continuous

will have been + *-ing*
To talk about an action that is going to be in progress at some time before and/or until a given time in the future. It is usually used with a time expression such as *by, in, at* or *before*.
*In a week, I'**ll have been living** in this flat for two years.*

▶ Exercise 4

EXERCISES

1 Choose the best options to complete the sentences.

1 I haven't *had* / *been having* this book for very long. In fact I've *already* / *just* bought it.

2 We've *owned* / *been owning* this car *for* / *since* three years.

3 I used to see Peter every morning on the train, but I haven't *seen* / *been seeing* him *recently* / *yet*.

4 Have you *lived* / *been living* in this house *for* / *just* a long time?

5 *Are you still working* / *Have you worked* on your project or have you *already* / *since* finished it?

6 She's *arrived* / *been arriving* at the office late *yet* / *all week*. ~~She has~~

7 I've *tried* / *been trying* to find my keys *for* / *since* an hour.

8 I haven't *used* / *been using* my computer *since* / *all* last Tuesday.

2 Rewrite these sentences in the present perfect continuous. Use the verb and time expressions in brackets.

1 My sister repairs bicycles. She started when she was a kid. (repair, since)
My sister *has been repairing bicycles since she was a kid.*

2 James is using the washing machine again. He's used the washing machine every day this week. (use, all)
James *has been using the washing machine all week.*

3 How much longer until we get to New York? We left London five hours ago. (fly, already, for)
How much longer until we get to New York? We *have been flying already for five hours.*

4 Aren't they hungry? They started work at nine o'clock! (work, since)
Aren't they hungry? They *have been working since nine o'clock.*

5 I live in this apartment. I moved here twelve months ago. (live, all)
I've *been living in this apartment all year.*

3 Choose the correct form of the verb.

1 I'd never *been using* / *used* Skype before you suggested it.

2 He'd *been starting* / *started* saving for his daughter's university education before she finished primary school.

3 They hadn't *been turning on* / *turned on* their air conditioning once in five years, so they got rid of it.

4 *You'd been working* / *You've been working* there for ten years by the time you left, hadn't you?

5 Until I bumped into Alexi last week, I *didn't see* / *hadn't seen* her since we left university.

6 It's going well but we *haven't finished* / *didn't finish* painting the bedroom yet.

4 Complete the sentences using the future perfect simple or continuous form of the verb.

1 How long *we will have been driving* (we / drive) by the time we reach Los Angeles?

2 She *won't have completed* (not complete) her degree before she starts her job.

3 By the time I retire next month I *won't have had* (not have) a single day off in ten years.

4 I don't think we need to rush. Jason and Jessie *won't have arrived yet* (not arrive) yet.

5 By the end of this afternoon, you *will have been talking* (talk) for about three hours, so your voice will need a rest.

6 *Will you have studied* (you / study) English for six years by the time you move to New York?

7 I need to speak to Claire. Do you think they *will have finished* (finish) the meeting by now?

8 Ross *won't have seen* (not see) the new Bond film already, will he?

5 Complete the text using the correct perfect form of the verb. Use the continuous where possible.

My partner and I [1] _____ (just / decide) to have an adventure and go sailing around the world. In a year we [2] _____ (sell) our house where we [3] _____ (live) for 18 years now, and if all goes well, we [4] _____ (sail) for a month by this time next year. I'm excited because until we started planning this trip I [5] _____ (never do) anything adventurous, even though before our first child was born [6] _____ (talk) about doing something like this. We [7] _____ (have) sailing lessons for 18 months now but we [8] _____ (not complete) our training for another 6 months.

6 Correct the mistake in each sentence.

1 I know Simon for six years.
_____

2 They're working in this office since 2012.
_____

3 Have you been talking for long before your phone died?
_____

4 I already posted the letter before I realized the address was wrong.
_____

5 By this time tomorrow, I finish my final exam.
_____

6 By the end of September, I have been walking to work every day for ten years.
_____

AMOUNTS AND COMPARISONS

Quantifiers

How much/how many

We use quantifiers with nouns to talk about how much or how many of something there is. Basic quantifiers include *some*, *any*, *much*, *many*, *a lot of* and *no*.

> Did **many** people come to the product launch event?
> Sorry, I don't have **a lot of** time right now.

Fractions and percentages

We use quantifiers such as *a little over*, *about*, and *nearly* with fractions and percentages to express approximate quantities. These are often used when we're talking about data.

With countable or uncountable nouns	A little over a quarter of	the students	have a credit card.
	About half of Nearly three quarters of Fifty per cent of	the class	has a credit card.

Note: Phrases with these expressions can function as singular or plural, depending on the nouns they modify. The verb agrees with the noun, not with the quantifier.

Describing large quantities

We use the following quantifiers to express large quantities.

With uncountable nouns	A large amount of A great deal of	illegal activity takes place online.
With countable nouns	The (vast) majority of A considerable number of	international criminals speak two languages.
With both	A sizeable portion of	fraud that's committed is never reported. the victims never get their money back.

Note: Phrases with *a large amount of*, *a great deal of*, and *a sizeable portion of* are always followed by singular verbs. Phrases with *the vast majority of* and *a considerable number of* function as plural nouns and are always followed by plural verbs.

Describing small quantities

We use the following quantifiers to express small quantities.

With uncountable nouns	A small amount of A small portion of	his income is from illegal sources.
With countable nouns	A (small) minority of A handful of A tiny number of	of the cases of identity theft involve stolen passports.
With both	Virtually none of	

Phrases with *a small amount of* and *a small portion of* are always followed by singular verbs. The other expressions above function as plural nouns and are always followed by plural verbs.

Comparing amounts

We use the following quantifiers to compare two amounts.

With uncountable nouns				
We had	half as much twice as much	identity theft this year	as	we had last year.
With countable nouns				
We had	half as many twice the number of / twice as many	cases of identity theft this month	as that	we had last month.
With both				
Today's earnings were	about the same as / similar to	yesterday's.		

• few → to little
No enough

A few → Some

• Little → No enough

A little → Some

• Handful → Some
many

EXERCISES

1 Choose the correct option to complete the sentences.

1 Nearly three quarters of our budget *is* / *are* spent on research and development.
2 Over 50 per cent of our materials *come* / *comes* from local suppliers.
3 A great deal of money *seem* / *seems* to be missing.
4 The majority of phones reported stolen *is* / *are* never recovered.
5 A sizeable portion of my work *involve* / *involves* using the computer.
6 A small amount of wasted time *isn't* / *aren't* a problem.
7 Virtually none of the products I need *is* / *are* available.
8 Only a handful of shareholders *attend* / *attends* the AGM each year.

2 Match the two parts of the sentences.

1 A large amount   **a** my salary goes into a retirement plan.
2 There were twice   **b** number of our students will go to top universities.
3 A small portion of   **c** as many teachers as students at the party.
4 A handful   **d** patients today as he had yesterday.
5 A considerable   **e** of money was stolen last night.
6 The doctor had half as many   **f** of my friends speak English.

3 Choose the correct option to complete the sentences.

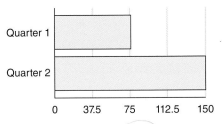

1 We sold twice as *many* / *much* units in the second quarter.

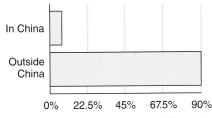

2 *A small portion* / *The vast majority* of our customers are outside China.

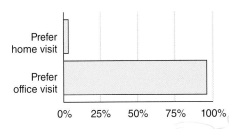

3 A *considerable number* / *handful* of our clients prefer a home visit.

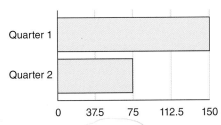

4 We had *half as many* / *a sizeable portion of* faulty products returned in the second quarter.

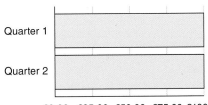

5 Net income in the second quarter was *the same* / *similar* as net income in the first quarter.

4 Complete the sentences with these expressions.

majority	none	per cent
portion	quarter	similar

1 Nearly 50 _____ of Mr Smith's personal wealth was stolen.
2 The vast _____ of Internet users share some financial details online.
3 A small _____ of local police time is spent investigating online crime.
4 Virtually _____ of the information that was stolen was password-protected.
5 This year's income was _____ to last year's.
6 A little over a _____ of my work time is spent writing emails.

5 Correct the mistake in each sentence.

1 Nearly three quarter of the applications included false information.
_____

2 A great deal fraud is conducted across international borders.
_____

3 There were twice number of reported cases this year.
_____

4 This month's crime figures are similar of last month's.
_____

5 A handful of passports was stolen in February.
_____

6 We had half as many case of credit card fraud reported as usual for this time of year.
_____

CLEFT SENTENCES → Complex sentences

Cleft means 'divided'. A cleft sentence is one which is divided into two parts. The introductory part of a cleft sentence often uses *wh-* words, *it* or *the thing* + the verb *be*.

My business partner really understands accounting. ➔
What my business partner really understands is accounting. or
Accounting is **what** my business partner really understands. or
It's accounting that my business partner really understands. or
The thing my business partner really understands is accounting.

Cleft sentences create focus or emphasis on part of a sentence.

Cleft sentences with *wh-* words + noun

We use *wh-* ... *be* / ... *be wh-* to emphasize a noun or noun phrase:

Their day-to-day management makes established companies successful. ➔
What makes established companies successful is their day-to-day conflict management.
or
Their day-to-day conflict management is **what makes established companies successful.**
I love their office layout. ➔
What I love is their office layout.
or
Their office layout **is what I love.**

Cleft structures with *What* are often used with verbs of emotion such as *like, enjoy, hate, love, prefer, want*, etc.

We really enjoyed the cultural life when we were in Berlin.
➔ **What we really enjoyed when we were in Berlin** was the cultural life.
or
The cultural life in Berlin **is what we really enjoyed when we were in Berlin.**

Cleft sentences with *wh-* words + verb

Notice that when the verb in the *wh-* clause is in the past, the verb *be* is also in the past.

We hired a new consultant. ➔
What we did was hire a new consultant.
We met Gina at a conference and offered her a job. ➔
What happened was (that) we met Gina at a conference and offered her a job.

Cleft sentences with *it.*

We use preparatory *it* + *is/was* + the language we want to emphasize + relative clause:

The smallest disagreements can grow into the biggest problems. ➔
It's the smallest disagreements that can grow into the biggest problems.
You need to talk to Bill Adams. ➔
It's Bill Adams (who) you need to talk to.

Cleft sentences with *the thing / thing to do*

We make cleft sentences with *the thing* to emphasize:

- the noun
  I don't have time for email ➔
  The thing I don't have time for is email.
  or
  Email is **the thing** I don't have time for.
- the verb
  Find an expert. ➔
  The thing to do is find an expert.

Cleft sentences with *the place*, *person*, *reason*, etc

To introduce and emphasize information about a place, person, or reason that something is/was done, we use *The place (where)*, *The person (who)*, *The reason (why)*. They are formed the same way as cleft sentences with *the thing*.

Two is the perfect number because fewer co-founders means fewer arguments. ➔
The reason why two is the perfect number **is** that fewer co-founders means fewer arguments.

Cleft sentences with *the way*

To introduce and emphasize information about how something is/was done we can use *the way* + verb. In these examples, *the way* replaces *by*.

You can get to know people by going to conferences. ➔
The way to get to know people is by going to conferences.
or
Going to conferences is **the way to get to know people**.

EXERCISES

1 Choose the correct options to complete the sentences.

1 *What* / *How* we did was offer the app as a free download.
2 *Where* / *The thing* you can save money is in your office expenses.
3 *What's* / *It's* the details you really need to pay attention to.
4 *Who's* / *The thing* to do is hire the best designer you can find.
5 *The reason* / *place* why it didn't work is that we didn't plan carefully.
6 *It's* / *The way* to learn a new job is to do it.

2 Match the two parts of the sentences.

1 It's the regular planning meetings *d*
2 The thing *c*
3 What I like *e*
4 What we need is *a*
5 What they did was *b*

a   more time for relaxed communication.
b   go out for a long lunch every Friday.
c   I benefit from is the on-site gym.
d   I like.
e   is the simplicity of having only one business partner.

3 Choose the correct options to complete the sentences.

1 *The reason* / *The way* you can make your work easier is by attaching your computer to two monitors.
2 *The thing* / *Where* they went wrong was not estimating the size of the crowd very well.
3 *It's* / *The person is* my boss you want to speak to, not me.
4 *The way* / *The thing* that can really help is having regular team meetings.
5 *The reason* / *It's* why the instructions are downloadable is so that we can update them easily.
6 *The place* / *What* you need to be is next door, in room 57.

4 Complete the short conversations using cleft sentences.

1 A: I need some help with my laptop. Is Rob around?
   B: Not today. (The person / need to talk to / Ella)
   The person who you need to talk to is Ella

2 A: I'm not familiar with the London Underground. I'm worried about getting lost.
   B: Don't worry. (One good thing about the Underground / the maps and signs / easy to follow)
   One good thing about the Underground is that the maps and signs are easy to follow

3 A: My printer's not working. I need the instruction manual.
   B: Joe just tried to fix it. (It / new printer / need / not the instruction manual)
   It's a new printer that you need, not an instruction manual.

4 A: Were they late for their flight?
   B: No, they weren't. (What happened / flight cancelled)
   What happened was that their flight was cancelled

5 A: Should I pay for the course now?
   B: No, that's not necessary. (What / do / pay online)
   What you do is pay online.

6 A: I hear you missed the last bus last night. Did you have to get a taxi?
   B: No. (What / did / stay at my friend's house.)
   What I did was stay at my friend's house

5 Complete the cleft sentences.

1 I want more information.
   What I want is more information

2 Write your name on this list.
   What you need to do is write your name on this list

3 I really like the view from the office window.
   The thing I really like is the view from the office window

4 I'm emailing you because I don't have your phone number.
   The reason I am emailing you is because I don't have your phone number

5 I like the variety of salads they have in that restaurant.
   The thing I like is the variety of salads that they have in the restaurant

6 My uncle introduced me to running.
   The person who introduced me to running was my uncle

6 Correct the mistake in each sentence.

1 What I would like more time in the office.
   is

2 Where you need go is upstairs to the third floor.
   Where you need to go is upstairs to the third floor

3 Is our chief programmer you need to talk to.
   It's our chief programmer you need to talk to.

4 The thing to do is going online and try to find some information there.
   is go online

5 The why I'm calling is I have several questions.
   The reason why I am calling

6 What happens was I lost his phone number and couldn't phone him.
   What happened

145

APPROXIMATION

With numbers

We use approximations when we talk about amounts to emphasize the scale of numbers rather than the exact amount.

These expressions mean *at* or slightly *above* or *below* the given number.

I spend	approximately around about more or less roughly some	four hours a day on electronic communication.

[handwritten: around - about (combine with number)]

Note: *Some* is often used in more formal contexts or where we want to emphasize that the number is high.
> He's written **some** 30 novels.

We use **nearly** to mean a bit lower than the given number.
> There were **nearly** 50 people in the meeting – 48, to be exact.

We use **just over** to mean a bit higher than the given number.
> I wrote **just over** twenty emails before lunch. I think I wrote twenty-two.

We use **as much as / as many as** to emphasize that we think the given number is a large amount.
> I sometimes send **as many as** 35 text messages.
> Some days, **as much as** 50 per cent of my time is spent on the phone.

We use **as little as / as few as** to emphasize that we think the given number is a small amount.
> You can buy a good guitar for **as little as** $300, although they usually cost more.
> Teams can consist of **as few as** three players, but if you have five, you've a better chance of winning.

We use **at least** to emphasize we mean this number or above.
> You should arrive at the airport **at least** three hours before your flight departure time.

We can also use the following expressions to approximate numbers.
> There were sixty **or so** people at the party.
> I saw a hundred-**odd** bicycles chained to the fence.
> We had **hundreds of** applications for the job.
> My MP3 player has a thousand songs, **or thereabouts.**

Vague language

Sort of and *kind of*

We use *kind of* or *sort of* when we can't think of a better way to describe something or to show we're not being very precise in our description. They are used with:

- adjectives
  > It's **kind of** hard to keep up with all the communication we receive every day.
  > The message he sent was **sort of** confusing.

- verbs
  > I **kind of** expected that he would disappoint us.
  > They **sort of** said they weren't interested.

- nouns
  > I think working alone in the garden shed is **kind of** a man thing.

Note: *Sort of* often comes between the article and the noun.
> They were driving a **sort of** motorcycle, but with three wheels.

-ish

We can add the suffix *-ish* to approximate a number, or when we can't think of a better way to describe something or we want to approximate a quality. We use a hyphen except with very frequent collocations such as *tall*, *short*, etc. Note that the spelling rules are the same as for comparatives (eg *late* → *latish*, *fat* → *fattish*)
> He's **tallish** – you know, taller than I am but not super tall.
> Let's meet at **two-ish** for a late lunch.

Some

We use *some* plus a singular noun to refer to an unknown or unnamed person or thing.
> I'm always getting junk mail from **some** company in California.
> I read about using an email filter in **some** computer magazine I read.

We can use *some* with a time reference, to talk about vague or undecided plans.
> You should come and visit **some** weekend.
> I'll visit Peru **some** day.

We sometimes add *or other*, which can give the feeling that we aren't being completely serious or respectful.
> Don't worry, we'll get **some expert or other** to review our product. It will be fine.
> He showed up **with some colleague or other** who wanted to join us for a meal.

Stuff and *things*

When we don't know the name of an object, substance or material, or when the name isn't important, we use *stuff*, which is uncountable, and *things*, which is countable.
> He put some green **stuff** on his mosquito bites.
> Whose **things** are these on the chair?

EXERCISES

1 Choose the best answer (a–h) for each question (1–8).

1 How many people came to the presentation? C
2 Was the factory tour interesting? f
3 What does Ken Arnold look like? e
4 Who was that on the phone? d
5 What's in the bag? a
6 How many tickets do we need to buy to get a group discount? b
7 Is your new computer working out? h
8 When do you want to meet? g

a My stuff.
b Roughly twenty.
c As few as ten, according to their website.
d Some sales representative from an office supplies company.
e He's tallish, about 40.
f It was actually kind of frustrating because I couldn't hear the guide.
g Three-ish?
h Actually, it's sort of annoying. It isn't as good as I expected it to be.

2 Choose the best options to complete the sentences.

1 I thought it was *kind of* / *roughly* strange that the restaurant didn't have our reservation.
2 Can you drop by my office at *just over four* / *four-ish* for a quick meeting?
3 She spends *sort of* / *around* 13 hours a day online.
4 David gets as *many* / *little* as ten text messages a day from a gym he's not even interested in joining.
5 Yusuf says that 78 per cent of his email is junk mail. That's *as much as* / *more than* three quarters!
6 She spent just *over* / *under* a month on the project. Three weeks and four days to be precise.
7 He was reading *some* / *a sort of* book or other about management, but it didn't help.
8 How much *stuff* / *things* do you usually take with you for an overnight business trip?

3 Choose the best approximation (a or b) for each expression in bold.

1 I have **22** notifications on Facebook.
   a nearly twenty
   b just over twenty
2 I spend **an average of two hours and 26 minutes** a day dealing with text messages.
   a about two-and-a-half hours
   b approximately two hours
3 We arrived at **6:05**.
   a six or so
   b nearly 6:00.

4 My friend Jeremy gets **no more than** five or ten emails a day.
   a nearly
   b as few as
5 It took me **two hours and five minutes** to go through my email this morning.
   a roughly two hours
   b roughly two hours and five minutes
6 **A man I don't know** keeps sending me contact requests on LinkedIn.
   a Some colleague
   b Some guy
7 We expect **205 people** at the conference.
   a 200 people or thereabouts
   b thereabouts 205 people
8 We need **98** chairs for the presentation.
   a 98-odd
   b a hundred-odd

4 Rewrite the expressions in bold using these expressions.

| a little under | as few as | hundreds of | –ish |
| kind of | –odd | some | stuff |

1 He had **$5,023.28** in his bank account.
   He had $5,023.28-odd in his bank account.

2 We drove **475** kilometres without seeing another car.
   We drove hundreds of kilometres without seeing another car.

3 I felt **a little** ill on the flight.
   I felt kind of ill on the flight.

4 Thomas arrived at the party **quite late** – at about 11:30.
   Thomas arrived at the party latish – at about 11:30 pm.

5 The trip took **five hours and 55 minutes**.
   The trip took a little under six hours.

6 Oh, no! I left my **notebooks, pens and laptop** on the bus!
   Oh, no! I left my stuff on the bus!

7 We met at **a pizza restaurant**, but I've forgotten **its name**.
   We met at some pizza restaurant but I have forgotten its name.

8 Some days, **only two or three people** visit the shop.
   Some days a few or two or three people visit the shop.

5 Correct the mistake in each sentence.

1 They bought a car that's a sort a yellow colour.

2 You can rent a room here for as few as £500 per month.
   You can rent a room here as little as 600 per month.

3 We have 600 employees, and thereabouts.

4 Pietro is tall or so and will be wearing a blue suit.
   tallish

5 They got some or other politician to open the event.
   some politician or other

6 Have you got a lot of stuffs to move?

UNREAL PAST

Some expressions in English can be followed by past-tense forms even when the meaning is present or future. These are used when we talk about unreal or hypothetical situations.

I wish and **if only** are used with the past simple to express wishes for things that are unlikely to happen. *If only* is more emphatic that *I wish*.

> **If only / I wish** my job **was** closer to home.

I wish and *if only* are used with the past perfect for regrets.

> **If only / I wish** I **hadn't turned down** the job offer in Madrid.

Wish + would is used with the infinitive to express dissatisfaction or annoyance and a desire for change.

> **I wish** you**'d remember** to recharge my iPad after you've borrowed it.

Wish + would and *If only* are used to express a desire for someone else's annoying action to change:

> **If only** he **wouldn't talk** on the phone so loudly.

Would isn't used if both clauses have the same subject.

> **I wish** I **had** a bigger house. (Not ~~I wish I would have a bigger house.~~)

Suppose, **supposing** and **what if** are used to form questions about the consequences of hypothetical or possible situations or to make suggestions. *Suppose* and *supposing* are more formal than *what if*.

> **Suppose** the business **didn't make** any money – what would we do?
> **Supposing** I **were to** help you / I help you find a new job – would you be interested?

We use the present tense when we think something is more likely to happen.

> **What if** we **run** out of cash part way through the trip?

We use **would rather** or **would sooner** + subject + past tense to express a preference.

> **I'd rather / I'd sooner** you **didn't text** during the meeting.

I'd rather and *I'd sooner* + infinitive without *to* can be used when there is no change of subject.

> **I'd rather not talk** to you right now.

It's also possible, though less common, to use the present instead of the past with *would rather / would sooner*.

> **I would sooner** you **get** a job and start earning some money.

○ **It's (high) time** + subject + past tense is used to say that action needs to be taken soon. *High* or *about* can be added for emphasis.

> **It's (high/about) time** I **found** a job where I can use my degree.

For all of the above structures, *were* can be used instead of *was*, especially when the style is more formal.

▶ Exercises 1 and 2

INVERSION IN CONDITIONALS

In more formal and written contexts, we can form conditional sentences by putting an auxiliary verb before the subject, instead of using *if*. This is most commonly done with *had, were* and *should.*

> **Had** I known that so many people were coming to the presentation, I'd have reserved a bigger room.

Were + subject + statement
The **second conditional** is used to talk about a possible but currently untrue statement. Note we use *were* not *was* even for first person.

> **Were I in a position to do so**, I'd offer you a job today.

were + subject + *to* is used to talk about possibilities in the future, but not impossible situations.

> **Were the company to relocate to Hong Kong**, we'd pay for our employees' moving expenses.

Were it not for (*the fact that*) is used to show how a particular event or person has changed a situation.

> **Were it not for the fact that** I have student loans to repay, I would work less.

Had + past is used to
The **third (and mixed conditional)** is used to describe any situation where a specific action or event in the past led to a specific outcome. It is often used for regrets.

> **Had I arranged for some interview coaching**, I might have got the job.

Had it not been for (*the fact that*) is very similar to *Were it not for* discussed above. It is used to show how a particular event or the action of a particular person in the past has changed a situation. Note that the negative auxiliaries are not contracted.

> **Had it not been for the fact that** I bumped into Lee, I wouldn't have heard about the job opening.
> **Had it not been for** my wonderful science teacher, I would never have gone to university.

You can use *should* instead of *if* in more formal contexts.

> **Should** you need any careers advice, don't hesitate to talk with one of our counsellors.
> **Should** you ever want to visit my office, you're welcome any time.

▶ Exercises 3–6

EXERCISES

1 Choose the correct option to complete the sentences.

1 *I rather / I'd rather* you waited until tomorrow to tell your mother about your new job.
2 I'd sooner you *scheduled / would schedule* the job interview for next week.
3 It takes forever for web pages to load. If only our Internet connection *wasn't / isn't* so slow!
4 I wish you *arrive / would arrive* on time to team meetings!
5 *I suppose / Supposing* we can't find a suitable candidate for the job – what then?
6 It's about time *you'll decide / you decided* what you want to do for a career.

2 Rewrite the sentences using the words in brackets.

1 I'd prefer for us to hire a part-time assistant. (sooner)
_____

2 It would be really good if I had a newer car. (only)
_____

3 They'd prefer us to meet at their office. (rather)
_____

4 Should we rent a bigger office? (supposing)
_____

5 I might reduce my workings hours. (what)
_____

6 We need to update our website. (high)
_____

3 Complete the sentences with the missing word or words.

1 Were you to be offered a place on the course, _____ you take it?
2 Had it not been for _____ that the plane was delayed, we would have missed it.
3 Were it _____ my headmistress, I don't know where I'd be today.
4 Should Tuesday's interview be cancelled for any reason, we _____ let you know.
5 _____ I not working full time, I'd be happy to volunteer.
6 _____ you have any questions, don't hesitate to ask.
7 _____ I known Holly was your boss, I wouldn't have said anything.

4 Read the situations. Complete the inverted sentences.

1 Pete didn't wear a coat. He didn't expect it to be cold.
Had Pete _____.
2 You may need help filling out the application. Give me a call if you do.
Should _____.
3 You didn't tell me it was a casual dinner. I'm wearing my dinner jacket.
Had you told me it was a casual dinner, I
_____.
4 There was a train strike. We were late.
_____ the fact that there was a train strike, _____ on time.
5 Darius didn't phone. Kate was angry.
_____ phoned, Kate _____ so angry.
6 Bill felt tired because he stayed up so late last night.
_____ stayed up so late last night, he _____ so tired.

5 Match the two parts of the sentence.

1 I wish I hadn't
2 If only I had
3 Supposing you
4 I'd rather you
5 It's high time we
6 Were I in your position, I
7 Were it not for the fact that I studied art at university, I
8 Had I known you needed help, I

a worked harder at university, I could have got a better job.
b didn't leave in the middle of the project, because you will be difficult to replace.
c accepted such a low salary.
d quit your job. What will you do then?
e wouldn't have been offered the job.
f would have come sooner.
g stopped talking and started actually doing something.
h would try to focus on the good parts of the job.

6 Correct the mistake in each sentence.

1 Was I wealthy, I'd buy a bigger house.
_____

2 I'd rather you don't use this phone for personal calls.
_____

3 If only I would have a job!
_____

4 Supposed you didn't receive a pay increase – what would you do then?
_____

5 Its a high time you bought a new car.
_____

6 Were I'm offered £1,000,000, I wouldn't know what to say.
_____

7 Should you've needed any tax advice, don't hesitate to ask Jenna.
_____

8 If it hadn't been so cheap, we didn't book the holiday.
_____

PURPOSE

We use the following structures to express the purpose of doing something.

(In order) to

(in order) to + infinitive. *To* alone is less formal than *in order to*.

> We stopped the car **to** change a flat tyre.
> They put a guard at the entrance **in order to** prevent anyone from entering.
> **In order to** prevent anyone from entering, they put a guard at the entrance.

The negative is *in order not to*.

> We hurried **in order not to** be late.

so (that) / in order (that)

so (that) / in order (that) + a statement. *So that* is less formal than *in order that*, and is more commonly used. They are often used with auxiliary verbs such as *can* or (more formally) *may*.

> Please keep your phone switched on **so that** we can contact you if necessary.
> The company paid for the party **in order that** everyone could attend.

In informal English, we can omit *that* after *so*.

> I always keep my phone switched on **so** I can be contacted easily.
> Let me know when you're in town **so** we can meet up.

Present tense verbs can be used after *so (that)* and *in order (that)* to refer to the future:

> Can you give this to Sheila now **so that** she **has** it at next week's meeting?
> When you land in New York tomorrow, call Edward **so** he **doesn't worry** about you.

When *so (that)* and *in order (that)* are used to talk about the past, *would* and *could* are usually used before the verb.

> We warned everyone about the virus **so that** their computers **wouldn't** be damaged.
> He arrived in Moscow on a Friday in order that he **could** have the weekend to see the sights.
> We gave him a microphone so that he**'d** be more audible in the big hall.

Note that *so that* and *in order that* are often used with a new subject.

In very formal English, we can use *might*.

> They provided each worker with an electronic ID card **so that** they **might** track their movements at work.

so as to

so as to + infinitive without *to*.

> I turn my email off for several hours a day **so as to** be able to concentrate.

The negative is *so as not to*.

> I always keep my phone switched on **so as not to** miss a call.

So as (not) to is always followed by an infinitive without *to*, no matter what time is being referred to.

> They moved to Manhattan **so as to be** closer to Melanie's office.
> I carry my laptop with me **so as to make** good use of the time on the train.
> During the conference, we'll have a day off in the middle **so as to allow** everyone to see a bit of Venice.

to avoid/prevent

Avoid and *prevent* are both used to indicate the purpose of an action taken to make something *not* happen.

We use *to avoid* to talk about an action we take so that something else doesn't happen.

> We took Flower Road **to avoid** the traffic on George Street.

We use *to prevent … (from) + ing* to talk about an action we take to stop a problem before it happens.

> The windows are closed **to prevent** rain **from damaging** the floors.

for

We use *for + noun* to describe the purpose of an action or thing.

> Eric keeps these water bottles **for emergencies**.

For also can be used to describe a purpose that includes someone else's action.

> We bought a phone **for Liz to use** when she visits.

EXERCISES

1 Complete the sentences with these expressions.

for	in order not	in order to	is for
so as	so that	to avoid	to prevent

1 I check email only twice a day _____ myself from wasting too much time dealing with it.

2 Jaime saves time by starting work at 7.30 a.m. _____ the morning rush hour.

3 I'm trying to get more organized _____ work more efficiently.

4 I'd like to meet you next week _____ we can discuss our deadlines.

5 We decided to extend the deadline _____ to take the pressure off the team.

6 This notebook _____ recording the names of the people who attend the workshop.

7 The time management software I use _____ work has helped me a lot.

8 _____ to waste time on social networking, I never use social media when I'm at work.

2 Match the two parts of the sentences.

1 Please let me know your schedule so that
2 This meeting room is for
3 Please be on time so as not to
4 To keep the meeting brief,
5 Please turn off your phone in order to
6 Order your lunch before the session to avoid

a marketing department meetings only.
b please stay on topic.
c we can plan the meeting.
d wasting time during the break.
e minimize interruptions.
f delay the start of the meeting.

3 Choose the best position (a or b) for the words in bold.

1 I / in order to
(a) _____ work more efficiently
(b) _____ answer email only twice a day.

2 Mike / so that he
(a) _____ works late on Friday nights
(b) _____ can take the weekend off.

3 We / so as not to disturb
(a) _____ other customers,
(b) _____ would kindly request that you switch off your mobile.

4 I / in order not to
(a) _____ forget appointments
(b) _____ set an alarm on my phone.

5 Dean and Lola are / to avoid
(a) _____ practising their presentation
(b) _____ making any big mistakes when they give it tomorrow.

6 we have / to prevent
(a) _____ fires
(b) _____ a strict no-smoking policy.

7 this / is for
(a) _____ door
(b) _____ emergency use only.

8 I / To
(a) _____ start work at seven o'clock.
(b) _____ avoid rush hour traffic.

4 Choose the correct options to complete the sentences.

1 The road was closed for about six hours *so that / so as to* they could repair it.

2 I usually take the stairs to *avoid / prevent* the crowded lift.

3 Could you leave your phone number so that Mr Jones *can / will* call you back?

4 I'm trying to be very quiet *so as not / in order* to disturb Kevin's meeting in the next office.

5 I'd like to meet Elsa *to / for* find out what her plans are.

6 *In order that / In order to* we can seat everyone, we've rented two extra tables and some chairs.

7 I left the garage unlocked *for / so* Ollie to put the car away.

8 Ring the bell when you arrive so Davina *would know / knows* you're there.

5 Join the two sentences using the expression of purpose in brackets.

1 They didn't want to miss the flight. They set off for the airport early. (so as not to)

2 More scholarships have been offered. More people will study engineering. (in order that)

3 I gave him my mobile number. He can text me. (so that)

4 Smokers block the entrance. We put up 'no smoking' signs. (prevent)

5 I'm distracted by the noise of people around me. I wear headphones at work. (avoid)

6 I don't usually drink coffee but I keep some in the house. Visitors drink it. (for)

6 Correct the mistake in each sentence.

1 I went to the library in order find some peace and quiet.

_____

2 I set my alarm for six so as I would be on time for work.

_____

3 Let's take a different route so avoid the road works.

_____

4 You should lock your bike to prevent thieves from steal it.

_____

5 I wear these clothes for run.

_____

6 In order to not to lose them, I always put my keys in the same place at home.

_____

CONTINUOUS ASPECT

Continuous verbs are made with *be + -ing*.

Name	Example
Present continuous	I**'m working** on a problem now.
Past continuous	I **was daydreaming** when the phone rang.
Present perfect continuous	They**'ve been talking** for hours.
Past perfect continuous	He **had been studying** for six hours when he took a break.
Future continuous	She**'ll be working** until she finishes the project.

The continuous aspect is used to describe actions that are in progress at a specific time and often connects an action in progress with a later point in time. It is usually used to refer to actions that are temporary and ongoing rather than permanent or completed. The continuous aspect can refer to a past, present or future action.

> Scientists **are scanning** people's brains as part of their research into daydreaming.
> We**'ll be writing** up our results tomorrow.
> We were exhausted. We**'d been working** since five in the morning.

Note that past continuous forms are often used in a sentence with the past simple to indicate that an ongoing action is interrupted by another shorter action.

> When he phoned yesterday I **was daydreaming**.

The continuous aspect is often used:

- to describe a new situation
  I've quit my old job and I**'m working** in a bakery, now.

- to describe a change, development or trend
  It**'s getting** harder to find good workers.
  The average temperature **had been increasing** for years.

- for a temporary, but repeated action
  My laptop **is making** a clicking noise.

Sometimes the choice of verb reflects the speaker's attitude.

Compare:

> I **went** to the gym every day when I was a student (and got really fit)
> I **was going** to the gym a lot last month (but then I got lazy and stopped going).

Note that we can't usually use the continuous when we describe how often something is repeated.

> I fell asleep three times on the bus yesterday. NOT ~~I was falling asleep three times on the bus yesterday.~~

With stative verbs

We rarely use the continuous form with verbs such as *believe, know, realize, suppose, understand, agree, remember, wish* etc. However, we sometimes use continuous forms if a dynamic use is intended. Compare:

> I **realize** you will be disappointed if you don't get accepted for the post.
> I**'m realizing** he's actually quite disappointed about this.

Note some verbs have a stative and a non stative use. Compare:

> I **think** Prague is a very interesting city.
> I**'m thinking** of visiting Prague next year.

We can also use the continuous to make statements, requests and questions with *hope, wonder* and *wish*, etc. less direct.

> I**'m hoping** you'll be able to help me.
> I **was wondering** if you might have ten minutes.
> **Are** you **wishing** we hadn't left the party so early?

This also works with non-stative verbs.

> I need a lift home. **Will** you **be leaving** soon, by any chance?

Special uses of the continuous

- to make complaints and criticisms, using *always* (and other words with a similar meaning)
  He's **always** coming to class late.
  She was **forever** forgetting to lock the door, and it really annoyed me.

Future

- to speculate about what people may be doing now
  His flight was delayed, so he**'ll** just **be arriving** now.

- to talk about planned events in the future
  We**'ll be heading** south on Wednesday. We can't leave before then.

Past

- to soften statements or questions. It is often used in informal speech to report what someone says.
  What were you saying? sounds more polite than What did you say?
  'Did you know Ella was buying a new flat?' 'Yes, she **was telling** us.'

- to make an action seem less significant. Compare:
  I **talked** to the headmaster yesterday.
  I **was talking** to the headmaster yesterday.

EXERCISES

1 Choose the best verb form to complete the sentences.

1 Sam had *been trying* / *tried* to phone you about six times before he finally got through.

2 I dropped my keys somewhere while I *was walking* / *walked* to work.

3 *I'm writing* / *I write* my final history essay right now, to hand in tomorrow.

4 Do you think you *'ll be living* / *live* in Barcelona a year from now?

5 *You're missing* / *You've missed* the bus twice this week, so leave a few minutes early today.

6 *He's always playing* / *He always plays* on his computer when he should be studying.

7 Fred *is always listening* / *always listens* to audio books while he drives to work.

8 I finally *was finishing* / *finished* reading War and Peace.

9 We haven't *tried* / *been trying* to go to the new cinema yet. Shall we go tonight?

10 I *wasn't thinking* / *didn't think* George's joke was funny.

2 Match the two parts of the sentences.

1 Can I call you back in fifteen minutes? I'm having a meeting
2 I was just shutting down my computer
3 She's been working on her proposal
4 We had been working for about twelve hours
5 They'll be staying here in Singapore

a for about six weeks, and it's nearly finished.
b when my boss asked me to do some more work.
c until the project is complete.
d at the moment.
e by the time Joe finally arrived.

3 Choose the best answer to each question.

1 Are you still thinking about hiring an assistant?
   a Yes, I definitely am.
   b Yes, I do.
   c Yes, I'm thinking.

2 What will they be doing right now?
   a They will have flown back.
   b They were flying back home.
   c I guess they'll be on the plane.

3 Had he been working all night when he finally left the office?
   a Yes, he had. He was looking pretty exhausted.
   b Yes, he was. But he said he'd finished.
   c Yes, he did. And it wasn't the first time.

4 George was telling us about your new house.
   a He said that? What happened then?
   b Oh, really? Yes, we were lucky to find it.
   c I know he is. I think he really likes it!

5 I heard you're teaching in Spain now.
   a Yes, you're right. I'm going there next month.
   b Yes, that's right. I started the job last month.
   c Yes, that's correct. I've been there for nearly twenty years.

6 And that's only the beginning!
   a Sorry, are you saying? The band is too loud!
   b Sorry, what will you be saying. It's the music!
   c Sorry, what were you saying? I didn't quite hear.

4 Complete the sentences using the correct continuous form of the verbs.

1 She ___*wasn't listening*___ (not listen) to the teacher because she was extremely tired.

2 This time next year, I _____ (work) in Australia.

3 They _____ (live) in New York for six years before they finally met their neighbours.

4 I _____ (spend) a lot of time this week preparing for my next trip.

5 We _____ (have) dinner when Beata's phone call came through.

6 If it's six o'clock, Luke _____ (arrive) in Singapore.

7 Larry _____ (drive) a lorry for the past fifteen years.

8 I _____ (travel) for three weeks when I realized my passport was out of date.

5 Complete the questions to which the sentences in Exercise 4 might be answers. Use the continuous form.

1 Why ___*wasn't she listening*___ to the teacher?
2 This time next year, _____ ?
3 How long _____ met their neighbours?
4 How _____ your time this week?
5 What _____ phoned?
6 What _____ right now?
7 How long _____ a lorry?
8 How long _____ out of date?

6 Correct the mistake in each sentence.

1 He's living in London since 2012.

_____

2 Right now, I try to repair my computer.

_____

3 This time last year, I'm working for Exxon.

_____

4 When she's graduating from university in two years, she'll be looking for her first job.

_____

5 I've been trying to find the office for 45 minutes when I finally got there.

_____

6 I had a nap when the phone woke me up.

_____

CAUSE AND RESULT

We can use a number of different verbs in English to show how one thing causes or is caused by another.

In sentences with *kills, gives rise to, causes, brings about, leads to, contributes to, makes, produces, fosters* the result follows the expression.

Fog **results in** poor visibility.

In sentences with *is a consequence of, results from, is the result of* and *arises from*, the result comes before the expression and the cause comes after.

Poor visibility **is the result of** fog.

Some verbs tend to be used when the speaker or writer feels that the result is negative, and others when the result is positive. Some can be used in either context.

Usually negative	Can be both / neutral	Usually positive
kills	gives rise to arises from is a consequence of causes brings about leads to contributes to makes produces results from results in is the result of stems from	fosters *promote* * -medical (bad)

Long working hours **kill** employee motivation.
Long working hours **lead to** / **contribute to** reduced concentration.
A sense of dissatisfaction can **arise from** / **result from** having no security.
Many accidents on the job **are a consequence of** / **are the result of** workers being very tired.
Colder weather **gives rise to** minor health complaints.
Noise **causes** the most problems in open-plan offices.
The slight decrease in traffic **resulted from** schools being closed for the day.
The closure of the school **resulted in** a slight decrease in traffic.
This policy has **brought about** significant changes in employment practices.
Training often **produces** improved sales results.
Many studies have shown that being in work **contributes to** feelings of well being.
A relaxed work environment **fosters** good communication.

We can also express cause and result using the conjunctions *since*, *as* and *because*. *Since* and *as* often go at the beginning of the sentence. *Since* is more formal than *as*.

As his daughter was ill, he took the day off.
Since his child was ill, he was obliged to take a day's leave.
He stayed at home **because** his daughter was ill.

The prepositions *due to*, *owing to*, *because of* and *on account of* can also be used explain cause. Strictly speaking, *due to* is adjectival (so used only with a noun or pronoun), whereas *owing to* is adverbial (so used after a verb and where it could be replaced by *caused by*).

Compare:
Due to the flu epidemic, staff numbers were very low.
The high absenteeism was **owing to** the flu epidemic.

In practice, many native speakers use *owing to, due to, on account of* and *because of* interchangeably.

I missed the first day of the conference **owing to / due to / because of / on account of** severe flight delays.

Thanks to is used to explain why something positive has happened.

Thanks to increased funding, we have been able to help 30 per cent more people this year.

We can also express result using adverbs and adverbials: *for this reason, as a result, therefore* (formal), *consequently* (formal) *that's why,* and *thus* (very formal or literary) can all replace *so* to talk about the result of something you've just mentioned.

It's been a very cold winter. **As a result / Therefore**, staff have not always been able to get into the office.
It was snowing heavily. **Thus**, it was decided to abandon the expedition.

We can also use *thus* with a gerund to mean 'in this way'.

It has been a very cold winter, **thus** leading to more work days missed.

EXERCISES

1 Choose the best options to complete the sentences.

1 Too many meetings *kill / result from* motivation at work.
2 Success *leads to / is the result of* luck and hard work.
3 Bad weather usually *arises from people driving / makes more people drive* to work.
4 The failure of the business *fostered / was a consequence of* bad management.
5 Bonuses often *bring about / arise from* improved sales results.
6 The band's appearance in a cola advert *contributed to / was the result of* sales.

2 Complete the sentences with these expressions.

arise	bring	consequence
foster	kill	lead

1 Poor performance is a _____ of low investment.
2 Conflicts often _____ from poor communication.
3 Changes in management can _____ to improved results.
4 Flexitime can _____ a positive attitude among workers.
5 A big success will usually _____ about strong feelings of satisfaction.
6 Strong negative criticism can _____ creativity.

3 Match each sentence (1–6) with a possible ending (a–c).

1 Traffic in the town centre gives rise to
2 Severe traffic problems make
3 Traffic delays often result from
4 Unexpectedly high traffic volumes often produce
5 Traffic jams are often the result of
6 Road works often cause

a road works.
b commuter delays.
c people late for work.

4 Put the words in the correct order to make sentences.

1 hard / is / of / result / success / the / work
_____.
2 contributes / feelings / happiness / of / sunny / to / weather
_____.
3 you / trust / people / makes / honest / being
_____.
4 communication / foster / good / in / offices / open / spaces
_____.
5 consequence / management / low / of / is / a / productivity / poor
_____.
6 high / increased / lead / sales / sales / targets / to
_____.

5 Join the two phrases using the word in brackets.

1 bad diet, poor health (rise)
_____
2 increased productivity, regular breaks (results)
_____
3 back pain, bad posture (contributes)
_____
4 lack of sleep, poor work performance (cause)
_____
5 people angry, inappropriate phone use (make)
_____
6 networking, increased opportunities (lead)
_____

6 Rewrite the sentences using the word in bold.

1 He resigned as he was stressed. **account**
   He resigned on account of stress.
2 Due to increased workload this year, I will no longer be able to play in the football team. **result**
_____
3 She decided to quit her job because she wanted to spend some time travelling. **That's why**
_____
4 Since he had taken early retirement, he wasn't able to draw his full pension. **Consequently**
_____
5 I got a pay rise, so I've been able to start looking for my own flat at last. **thanks**
_____
6 Only one of the team could be promoted, which resulted in tensions in the office. **thus**
_____

7 Correct the mistake in each sentence.

1 Unreasonable demands from managers result unhappy employees.
_____
2 Employee dissatisfaction consequences of low pay and poor working conditions.
_____
3 Poor computer security rises to possible loss of data.
_____
4 Company restructuring leads to employees feel insecure.
_____
5 Constant negativity from management results to frustrated employees.
_____
6 Training contributes a safer work environment.
_____

Grammar summary | UNIT 9

INTENSIFYING ADVERBS

Adverbs modify adjectives, verbs or other adverbs to express time, place, degree or manner. Intensifying adverbs such as *extremely*, *totally* and *so* are a type of adverb of degree, which make the words they modify stronger.

> *My holiday turned into a disaster **incredibly** quickly.*
> *I'm **quite** sure I'll never go there again.*
> *She disagreed with me **entirely**.*

Note that some adverbs collocate more commonly with certain words than others. For example, it's more common to say *absolutely perfect* than to say *really perfect*. A good dictionary will provide the most common collocations.

We use different adverbs to intensify gradable and ungradable adjectives. The intensifier always goes directly before the adjective it modifies.

Gradable and ungradable adjectives

Gradable adjectives can be measured on a scale, e.g. *big*: a house can be more or less big. Ungradable adjectives, on the other hand, are not measured on a scale. They express only extreme or absolute qualities, e.g. *fantastic*, *empty*.

> Gradable: *I thought my flat was **pretty small**, but compared to John's, it's **quite big**.*
> Ungradable: *No one came to the concert. The theatre was **completely empty**.*

When used with an ungradable adjective, verb or adverb, *quite* means 'extremely'. With a gradable adjective, *quite* is not intensifying. See page 158.

> *They were **quite** certain that there was a link between stress and health.*
> *Stress can **quite literally** make you ill.*

Intensifying adverb + gradable adjective

extremely, highly, incredibly, really, so, very

> *One **extremely interesting** finding was that even supposedly relaxing activities like going on holiday were never completely stress-free.*
> *We were incredibly **lucky**.*

Intensifying adverb + ungradable adjective

absolutely, completely, entirely, quite, really, so, totally, utterly

> *The results of their research made the connection **totally clear**.*

Utterly is more commonly used with negative adjectives.

> *Our fridge broke while we were on holiday, and when we got back, it was **utterly** disgusting.*

Also note that *really* can be used with both gradables and ungradables.

> Gradable: *It's **really warm** in here.*
> Ungradable: *It's **really boiling** in here.*

Gradable and ungradable verbs

Verbs, like adjectives, can be gradable or ungradable. For example, *like* is gradable and *adore* is ungradable. You can like something a little or a lot, but *adore* is absolute.

> Gradable: *I **really like** James.*
> Ungradable: *We **absolutely adore** your cousin.*

The verbs most commonly modified by:

- **completely:** *be, have, change, agree, understand, ignore, go, remove, eliminate, lose, do, destroy, cover, satisfy, forget, disappear, get*

- **totally:** *be, agree, have, got, do, understand, change, feel, ignore, forget, lose, make, destroy, relax*

- **entirely:** *be, depend, make, base, focus, do, consist, rely, separate, go, build, disappear*

In sentences with a direct object, the intensifying adverb can go before or after the verb it intensifies, or at the end of the sentence.

> *She **entirely** disagreed with him.*
> *She disagreed **entirely** with him.*
> *She disagreed with him **entirely**.*

When used with negatives, they go before the verb:

> *We **absolutely don't** want to cause any complications.*

Utterly is more commonly used with negative verbs.

> *In extreme cases, severe stress can **utterly destroy** a person's health, confidence and well-being.*

Verbs commonly modified by *utterly*: *destroy, exhaust, disgust, baffle, confuse*

Negative intensifiers

We use these expressions to add negative emphasis.

> *I had **no** experience **whatsoever**.*
> *They were **not (in) the least (bit)** interested in the local culture / not interested in the local culture **in the least**.*
> *The weather was **not at all** what I had expected.*

EXERCISES

1 Choose the correct options to complete the sentences.

1 The holiday was stressful, but the views from the hotel were *quite / very* incredible!
2 I *utterly / really* don't want to talk about the problems we had.
3 Evan was *absolutely / extremely* right to ask for a refund.
4 The airline tickets must have been *totally / incredibly* expensive.
5 I agree *highly / entirely* with Kevin.
6 The tourist buses are always *really / completely* crowded.
7 I'm not *the least bit / whatsoever* interested in taking a city bus tour.
8 The food wasn't *very / in the least* what I expected.

2 Complete the conversation with these words. There is sometimes more than one possibility.

incredibly	the least bit	really
so	totally	very

A: You have to be ^{1}_____ lucky to get a cheap airline ticket these days.
B: I know. They've ^{2}_____ gone up in price, haven't they? But I found a deal on the Internet that was so cheap I was ^{3}_____ sure must be a mistake! I found two London to Hong Kong returns for 99 Euros.
A: I'm ^{4}_____ jealous. When are you going?
B: Next month. But it isn't ^{5}_____ perfect.
A: Oh, no? Why not?
B: It's a(n) ^{6}_____ long journey. We have to change planes three times, and it takes 40 hours.
A: Really?! I'm not ^{7}_____ interested in that kind of bargain. I'd rather pay more and fly direct!

3 Complete the sentences with the intensifiers.

1 We were _____ hungry when we left the hotel, and we were _____ starving by the time we got to the restaurant. **absolutely** / **very**
2 We felt _____ exhausted after three days of walking around New York, and I felt _____ tired the following week at work. **extremely** / **completely**
3 I was _____ confident in our tour guide, because some of the historical information he gave us was _____ incorrect. **n't so** / **utterly**
4 The food on the tour was _____ delicious, but I think some people found it _____ spicy. **totally** / **very**
5 The weather in Mexico was _____ hot, but we _____ roasted on the beach in Egypt. **absolutely** / **very**

4 Choose the best position in the sentence for the word in brackets.

1 The instructions were of no _____ value _____. (whatsoever)
2 I'm afraid his advice was _____ in the least bit _____ helpful. (not)
3 I _____ loved _____ that movie. (absolutely)
4 He said _____ they're hoping to change the system _____. (entirely)
5 His email was _____ surprising _____. (completely)
6 I've had _____ an _____ exhausting morning. (utterly)
7 The house fell apart _____ literally _____. (quite)
8 I don't _____ like _____ my new haircut. (really)

5 Match the two parts of the sentences.

1 They were very
2 We weren't at all
3 She absolutely
4 We've quite
5 I think we need to throw the plan away and start over

a happy with the accommodation.
b literally been running all day.
c tired after the long walk and slept for eighteen hours.
d entirely.
e doesn't need a new car.

6 Correct the mistake in each sentence.

1 The temperature at the beach was extremely boiling.
   _____
2 We were utterly late for the plane, so we missed it.
   _____
3 I had not fun whatsoever sitting around the hotel pool.
   _____
4 The bungalow we stayed in was very perfect.
   _____
5 I'm afraid I disagree with you quite about the hotel being comfortable.
   _____
6 We had so a good time in Bali.
   _____

PASSIVE REPORTING VERBS 1

We can form passive reporting structures like this:

- Subject + *be* + past participle of reporting verb + *to* infinitive.

This structure can be used with present, past or future reference.

> **They are said to be** the best surfers in the world.
> The ship's captain **was presumed to have died** in battle.
> (= It was presumed then) or
> The ship's captain **is presumed to have died** in battle.
> (= it is presumed now of a past event)
> The new energy source **is expected to be** cleaner.

These verbs are often used with this construction: *allege, assume, believe, consider, estimate, expect, find, know, prove, report, say, show, think, understand.*

We can use the passive voice to report actions and events. We use reporting verbs in the passive when:

- we don't know or cannot verify the source or agent of the information
  No injuries have been reported.

- we assume the reader or listener is not interested in who the agent or source is
  They are believed to have started exploring the cave at four in the morning.

- the agent or source is obvious from the context
  100 people **are known to have been arrested.**

- when you want someone to remain anonymous
  You've been reported to be driving without a license.

▶ Exercises 1 and 2

PASSIVE REPORTING VERBS 2

We can also form passive reporting structures like this:

- *It* + *be* + past participle of reporting verb + (*that*) clause
  It is known (that) ancient people climbed mountains.

These verbs are often used with this construction: *agree, allege, announce, assume, believe, claim, consider, decide, estimate, expect, fear, hope, know, presume, report, say, suggest, think, understand.*

This construction can be also used with present, past or future reference.

> **It is said that** they **are** the best surfers in the world.
> **It was presumed that** the ship's captain **died** in battle.
> **It is expected that** the new energy source **will be** cleaner.

Notice the use of *There*.

> It is known that there are many more dangerous sports. →
> **There are known to be** many more dangerous sports.

▶ Exercises 3 and 4

QUALIFIERS

A qualifier is a word or phrase that intensifies or softens the word that comes after it.

Fairly modifies adjectives and adverbs. It means 'to a limited degree'.

> The chair was **fairly** easy to assemble.

Quite often suggests a higher degree than *fairly*. It can also qualify nouns and verbs.

> The instructions were **quite** confusing. I didn't really understand them.
> I **quite** enjoy working standing up.
> It was **quite** a comfortable chair.

With an adjective + noun, *quite* comes before *a/an*.

> The exercise ball came with **quite a** useful set of instructions.

Pretty also modifies adjectives and adverbs, and expresses a higher degree than *fairly* and *quite*. It can also suggest 'more than usual' and 'more than expected'. *Pretty* is slightly less formal than *quite* or *fairly*.

> I assembled the chair **pretty** quickly.

Rather is stronger than *quite*. It can modify adjectives, adverbs, nouns or verbs. It can express disappointment, criticism or surprise.

> It's **rather** uncomfortable.
> It was **rather** a mistake.

When qualifying an adjective + noun, *rather* can come before or after *a/an*.

> It was **rather a / a rather** low chair.

A bit, *slightly*, and *a little* soften adjectives, adverbs and verbs. They can make a criticism sound less direct. *A bit* is less formal than *slightly* and *a little*.

> The price seems **a bit / a little / slightly** high.
> The poor construction of the chair surprised me **a bit / a little / slightly**.
> The poor construction of the chair **slightly** surprised me.

A bit, *a little* and *slightly* can be used before comparative adjectives whereas *quite*, *fairly* and *pretty* cannot.

> The new chair is **slightly** better than the old one. (NOT ~~The new chair is quite better than the old one.~~)

When we use *a bit* or *a little* before a non-comparative adjective, the meaning is usually negative.

> He's **a bit** difficult to get along with. (Not ~~He's a bit nice.~~)

We can use *a bit of a/an* before a noun.

> It's **a bit of a** problem.

▶ Exercises 5–7

EXERCISES

1 Choose the correct options to complete the sentences.

1 The new CEO *is expected / will be* to make big changes.
2 Flying was *been shown / shown* to be safer than driving many years ago.
3 He *thinks / is thought* to have arrived already.
4 *There are / We are* believed to be ten people in the group.
5 The two men were alleged to *have / be* stolen more than a million dollars.
6 The city council is known *to planned / to be* planning major alterations to the town centre.

2 Match the two parts of the sentences.

1 Climbing hasn't always been understood to be
2 The surfing instructor is expected to arrive
3 There were reported to have been
4 BASE jumping is often assumed
5 The shuttlecock in badminton is known
6 BMX racers are often thought to have

a   four bull riders injured in the event.
b   to travel faster than the ball in any sport.
c   a healthy pastime.
d   after four o'clock this afternoon.
e   a kind of addiction to fear.
f   to be more dangerous that it really is.

3 Put the words in order to make make sentences with passive reporting verbs.

1 known / it / is / that / climb / for / the feeling / of / danger / some people
2 has / reported / it / bad weather / that / cancelled / caused / the climb / been / to be
3 revealed / several days / was / the / two climbers / had / that / been / it /missing / for
4 believed / at first / it / that / climbing / would / become / wasn't / so popular
5 places / generally / in the past / it / were / mountains / felt / had / been / that / dangerous
6 feelings / commonly / that / it's / and / similar / excitement / are / known / fear

4 Complete the sentences with the correct form of the verbs.

1 It _____ that there are 3000 protestors in the street at this time. (estimate)
2 It is known that the company _____ creating 200 new jobs. (consider)
3 It _____ in 1954 that the club would open to women as well as men. (decide)
4 It wasn't widely known in the 1980s that the Internet _____ developed. (already / be)
5 It _____ that the new shopping centre will attract business from all over the region. (expect)
6 It isn't thought that many people _____ the band's first few performances. (attend)

5 Choose the best options to complete the sentences.

1 My new chair is *quite / a bit* comfortable.
2 We were pleased because they performed the work *reasonably / a little* skilfully.
3 Jamie has practised a lot and is now *slightly / rather* good at playing the piano.
4 Let's go by train. It's only *a bit / fairly* more expensive.
5 She lives in *quite / pretty* a big house.
6 It's *slightly / fairly* common these days to meet people who speak English.

6 Rewrite the sentences with a similar meaning using the qualifiers in bold.

1 It was a fairly hot day. **quite**

_____

2 Rather a long time had passed since his previous job. **fairly**

_____

3 The announcement slightly surprised me. **a little**

_____

4 The holiday cost rather a lot of money. **pretty**

_____

5 We had a little problem with the car. **a bit**

_____

6 It isn't very comfortable. **rather**

_____

7 Correct the mistake in each sentence.

1 Japanese is estimated to speak by more than 120 million native speakers.

_____

2 Vikings knew to have visited North America hundreds of years before Columbus.

_____

3 The new building is expected to be cost $20 million.

_____

4 Two students are believed to have climbing on to the roof of the building last night.

_____

5 The treasure is assumed by experts in the 1950s to have been lost at sea.

_____

6 20,000 are expected attend tomorrow night's concert.

_____

7 Getting my computer repaired turned out to be a bit nightmare.

_____

8 It was a quite useful meeting in Macau.

_____

SUBORDINATE CLAUSES

A clause is a group of words that contains at least a subject and a verb. A clause can be a full sentence, but is often just part of a sentence:

She sings. (a clause that is a full sentence)
You bring (a clause that isn't a full sentence)

When we want to combine two or more ideas in one sentence, we can use multiple clauses.

The tour bus arrived.
The locals held a welcome party.
*The tour bus arrived **and** the locals held a welcome party.*

When a clause could be a sentence on its own, it's called a main clause. Two main clauses can be joined into one sentence with a conjunction such as *and, but* or *or*.

We use subordinate clauses to give more information about a main clause. The subordinate clause doesn't make sense as a sentence on its own without the main clause, but the main clause makes sense without the subordinate clause. A subordinate clause can be joined to a main clause using a conjunction such as *when, because* or *although*. The clauses usually can go in either order:

***When** you get there, be sure to ask for a local guide.*
*Be sure to ask for a local guide **when** you get there.*

In writing, you may choose to order the clauses so that the most important information is at the end of the sentence. This can help to give it more impact.

Hal shouted for joy after being rescued. ➝
After being rescued, Hal shouted for joy.

Note that we use a comma after a subordinate clause when it begins the sentence.

The main clause and the subordinate clause can have different subjects.

***I** haven't been to Laos, **although David** might have been.*
***We** had to borrow Leanne's map **because I** didn't have mine.*

Time
after, as, as soon as, before, by the time, every time (that), once, since, the first/last/next time (that), until, when, whenever, while
Contrast
although, even though, in spite of the fact that, regardless of the fact that, though, whereas, while
Precaution or provision
in case, in the event that
Condition
as long as, assuming (that), if, providing/provided (that), unless
Cause/reason
as, because, considering (that), given (that), in view of the fact that, since, in light of the fact that
Referring to other ideas, situations or information
as far as … (is concerned), as regards

Note the following:

In case is used to introduce something that might or might not be a factor.

***In case** you are unfamiliar with the idea of geotourism, the most popular definition of this very 21st-century concept is leisure travel that enhances the environment, culture, and the well-being of tourist destinations.*

We use *in case* to describe an action *before* a possible thing happens and *if* to describe an action *after* another possible thing happens.

Compare

*Take these pills with you **in case** you feel seasick on the journey.*
*You should take one pill **if** you feel seasick on the journey.*

In the event that can replace *in case* in a more formal context.

***In the event that** a tourist becomes ill, they should contact the tour guide.*

Given (that), considering (that), in view of the fact that (more formal), *as* and *since* refer to a factor that it already known in order to introduce another fact. *Considering* is usually used in a context that indicates some mismatch between the facts whereas *as* and *since* suggest one factor is usually the logical conclusion to another.

***Considering** global tourism is often blamed for ruining popular holiday destinations, the notion that tourism could save the world might seem surprising.*
*We expected to get good service, **as/since** we'd paid so much.*

Given that can be used in both examples above.

Provided/providing that means that one thing happens only if another happens. *Unless* is used to talk about something that only happens if something else *doesn't* happen.

Compare:

*Geotourism brings economic benefits to the hosts **provided that** businesses use local workers, services and supplies.*
*Geotourism brings economic benefits to the hosts **unless** businesses fail to use local workers, services and supplies.*

In spite of the fact that, although and *even though* are used to suggest that something is true as well as another factor which seems in conflict with it.

*But that's what geotourism's supporters claim, **in spite of the fact that** this is an apparent contradiction.*

With certain subordinating conjunctions, a pronoun subject + the verb *be* can be left out or replaced by an *-ing* form or past participle. These include *after, before, since, if, when, while, until, once, unless* and *although*. This happens in certain fixed expressions.

***If necessary**, we'll pay more for a more environmentally friendly holiday.*
***Unless told otherwise**, I'll assume you'll be on the ten o'clock flight.*
***When in doubt before buying a ticket**, thoroughly investigate travel offers that seem too good to be true.*

EXERCISES

1 Choose the correct options to complete the sentences.

1 *In spite of the fact that / Because* we're trying to save money, we didn't have a holiday this year.
2 The tour company cancelled the trip to the village *given that / even though* the locals said they were welcome.
3 I always travel with a map *in case / unless* I get lost.
4 You can stay in the country for three months *until / provided* that you have a visa.
5 *As far as / Although* using our own minibuses is concerned, everything is going very well indeed.
6 *Regardless / In view* of the fact that the reviews were negative, our experience at the lodge was excellent.

2 Match the two parts of the sentences.

1 Since we didn't have enough people,
2 Provided that we can get more than fifteen people,
3 Regardless of the fact (that) we asked for a local guide,
4 In the event that anyone gets separated from the group,
5 The next time we visit Brazil,
6 Whenever we can,

a return to the hotel.
b we stop and take photos.
c we'll go ahead with the trip.
d we cancelled the trip.
e we plan to spend a week living with a local tribe.
f the tour leader was from a different city.

3 Choose the correct position (a or b) for the word or expression in bold. Add any necessary punctuation.

1 **in spite of the fact that**
   (a) _____ many people expressed an interest in the museum
   (b) _____ very few people actually visited.
2 **so that**
   (a) _____ we'd like you to answer some questions
   (b) _____ we can figure out what went wrong.
3 **when**
   (a) _____ we think people learn a lot about themselves
   (b) _____ they travel.
4 **provided that**
   (a) _____ we save enough money
   (b) _____ we're going to take a holiday abroad next year.
5 **considering that**
   (a) _____ the tourists want to have an 'authentic' experience
   (b) _____ it's surprising that they complain about the lack of comfort.
6 **unless**
   (a) _____ no one will know about our services
   (b) _____ we advertise.

4 Join the two sentences together using the expressions in bold.

1 The trip was bad value. It cost over $10,000. **given that**
   _____

2 Everyone wakes up on time. We should be able to leave at six o'clock. **assuming that**
   _____

3 Our groups are usually limited to six people. We can make an exception this time. **although**
   _____

4 It rains. We put on our wet-weather gear. **whenever**
   _____

5 We'll cancel the trip. There's any bad behaviour. **in the event of**
   _____

6 There has been a large number of requests. Maybe we should add a second tour. **In view of the fact that**
   _____

5 Complete the sentences with these words.

before	doubt	going
necessary	once	otherwise

1 If _____, the guide will stop for a short break.
2 Please stay in the bus unless told _____ by a guide.
3 When in _____, ask for help.
4 When _____ into the jungle, be careful!
5 _____ registered, please find your room and take your things there.
6 _____ leaving, be sure to settle your hotel bill.

6 Correct the mistake in each sentence.

1 In view the fact that he cancelled a month before the trip, we'll refund his money.
   _____

2 As long you bring a good pair of boots, the walk shouldn't be too difficult.
   _____

3 Can you let us know as soon as you'll arrive?
   _____

4 The plans look great as I'm concerned.
   _____

5 Even the tourists weren't properly dressed for the weather, they had a great time.
   _____

6 This is the exit you use in case there will be an emergency.
   _____

FUTURE IN THE PAST

When we talk about the future from the perspective of the past, we use a range of structures, depending on whether we are talking about predictions or intentions, and on the level of certainty and immediacy.

would + infinitive without *to*

We use *would* and *would have* to:

- report ideas held in the past about the future
  In the 1970s, some experts believed the world **would** be much colder by 2000.
  We thought Joe **wouldn't** arrive until midnight, but he came at eleven.

- to describe something in the past as if seen as a future prediction
  The 20th Century **would** be a time of extraordinary change.

- hypotheses about different outcomes if the situation had been different, using the third or mixed conditionals
  Airships and balloons **would have** become more common if hydrogen gas hadn't been so dangerous.
  I **wouldn't have** called you, but I didn't know who else to ask for help.

This construction is also used in the passive voice.

  You **would have been offered** the job, but you'd already taken another one.

bound to + infinitive without *to*

We use *be bound to* to talk about past beliefs about what was almost certain to happen in the future:

  Cars **were bound to** become more popular as the price went down.
  I **was bound** to find a job eventually.

It also can be used in the passive voice.

  The problem **was bound to be discovered**.

about to + infinitive without *to*

We use *about to* to talk about things in the past that were going to happen in the immediate future, or on the point of happening.

  The climbers were **about to** give up when they realized they'd reached the top of the peak.
  I **was about to** buy an MP3 player when a newer model came out.

It is also commonly used in the passive voice.

  The world record **was about to be broken**.

likely/unlikely to + infinitive without *to*

We use *be likely / unlikely to* to talk about things in the past that were seen as probable or not probable.

  They had no idea when Jim **was likely to** arrive.
  It **was unlikely to** be cold, so we didn't take any warm clothes.

In the passive, it is formed like this:

  The idea **was likely to be sold** for a lot of money.

was/were going to + infinitive without *to*

We can use *was/were going to* in the following ways to talk about the future in the past:

- to make a prediction based on available information which may or may not have been fulfilled
  It **was going to** be a very profitable investment.

- to talk about an intention which may or may not have been fulfilled
  I **was going to** take a job as a bus driver, but I decided to go to university instead.

- to talk about a plan or arrangement which then changed
  We **were going to** meet for lunch, but then Dave became ill.

- to report a thought
  I knew **I was going to need help**, but I didn't know who to ask.

- in reported speech
  I told you it **was going to** be sunny today!

This construction is also used in the passive voice.

  The rumour went around that a big discovery **was going to be made**.

was/were to

We can use *was/were to*:

- instead of *was going to* or *would* to talk about something in the past as if seen as a future prediction
  The 1900s **were to** bring even more world-changing events.

- with *have* + past participle, to talk about a past plan or expectation, especially one that wasn't fulfilled
  I **was to have** travelled to Stockholm, but the trip was cancelled at the last minute.
  They **weren't to have** arrived until midday, but the flight was early and came in at 10:30.

- to report a past instruction
  They said we **were to** let them know what time we were arriving.

EXERCISES

1 Match the two parts of the sentences.

1 I was about to call Rick
2 Anna was bound to get lost
3 Vincenzo had no idea
4 It was going to
5 It was unlikely
6 They were going to

a when he was likely to arrive.
b buy an old car and drive across the USA
c on her way home.
d be a cold day, so we dressed warmly.
e when my phone rang.
f to end well.

2 Choose the correct options to complete the sentences.

1 As he left, Sam insisted he *would* / *will* wait ten minutes for Muriel, but no more.
2 Ben *is* / *was* unlikely to be in the office, but we tried phoning anyway.
3 From the start, it was *going to be* / *being* a very difficult project.
4 We didn't think we *have* / *would have* time to stop for lunch, so we took sandwiches with us.
5 I was about *to start walking* / *starting to walk* when the bus arrived.
6 Lisa was bound *to be* / *being* late, so we delayed the start of the meeting.

3 Complete the sentences with these words.

| bound | have | to be |
| unlikely | weren't | would |

1 Had we known you were coming, we _____ have waited for you.
2 The project was _____ to succeed because the team were the best in the business.
3 _____ you about to quit when the pay increases were announced?
4 We thought he was _____ to win the award, so we were delighted when he did.
5 It was going _____ a long and happy working relationship.
6 A grant was to _____ been given for the idea with the most potential.

4 Put the words in the correct order to make sentences.

1 at / have / met / midday / to / we / were
_____

2 a / be / built / going / laboratory / to / was
_____

3 finish / on / they / time / to / unlikely / were
_____

4 about / announced / be / invention / the / to / was
_____

5 best / bound / decision / make / she / the / to / was
_____

6 become / CEO / had / have / I / I / if / stayed / would
_____

5 Complete the second sentence using the words in bold, using future in the past, so that it means the same as the first.

1 The car probably wasn't going to start. **unlikely**
The car was unlikely to start.

2 It was almost time for us to leave. **about**
_____

3 I was sure we would find the wallet. **bound**
_____

4 It was probably going to rain. **likely**
_____

5 We expected him to arrive soon. **would**
_____

6 He had a plan to start a business. **going to**
_____

6 Correct the mistake in each sentence.

1 The party was bound being a success.
_____

2 At eight o'clock, we thought Jim won't arrive for another two hours, but he was there soon after nine.
_____

3 We were about start filming when Marta suddenly lost her voice.
_____

4 They're going to have a goodbye party for Sheila last Friday, but she didn't want one.
_____

5 When I saw the house, I knew Greg will like it.
_____

6 It was obvious that Amir is going to get a promotion after all his hard work.
_____

Audioscripts

Unit 1

🎧 3

P = Paul, L = Lea, E = Ella, F = Fred

P: So we've set the date, we've got the time off work. We need to talk about what we're going to pack.

L: Definitely. We'll have two canoes, and with the tents and sleeping bags, I'm guessing we probably won't have a huge amount of extra space, so we might want to keep it to the bare minimum.

E: It might not be a bad idea to have a couple of phones with us, in case we get separated.

F: I'm no expert, but I don't think that we can expect to have a phone signal, especially as we'll be in a canyon most of the time.

L: Good point. Personally, I feel that we don't want to be weighed down with too much stuff, so maybe we should just bring one phone, in case of emergency.

P: Right. We only need one phone, no more.

E: I don't know about you, but I don't think we'll want a lot of devices on this trip. Can I just suggest we leave our other electronics at home?

P: OK, so we shouldn't bring any tablets or MP3 players.

F: Since it's summer, I think it's reasonable to assume that we're not going to need a lot of warm clothing – maybe just a jumper each, for night time?

L: Sounds good. If we get cold or wet, we should be able to build a fire and we can dry things that way.

E: All I know is that I'm going to want at least three pairs of socks. I can't stand having wet feet!

P: So let's agree, everyone should bring three pairs of socks and a spare pair of shoes.

F: Fine. And it seems to me that we should probably take along a few torches and some spare batteries. It will be dark out there after the sun goes down.

L: Definitely. I wonder if we should consider leaving the camping stove behind? We'll be able to cook over the fire, won't we?

F: I don't think there's a law against fires, but we should check the rules. I can do that.

E: Thanks. As for the camping stove, we might possibly want it if we have rainy weather. At least then, we could cook in the tent, right?

P: Let's bring the stove. But speaking of cooking – what about food?

E: I've actually made a menu already, but it might not be a bad idea for all of us to look at it together.

🎧 4

1 We need to talk about what we're going to pack.
2 I'm guessing we probably won't have a huge amount of extra space.
3 It might not be a bad idea to have a couple of phones with us.
4 Maybe we should just bring one phone, in case of emergency.
5 We only need one phone, no more.
6 We shouldn't bring any tablets or MP3 players.
7 I think it's reasonable to assume that we're not going to need a lot of warm clothing.
8 Everyone should bring three pairs of socks and a spare pair of shoes.
9 It seems to me that we should probably take along a few torches and some spare batteries.
10 Let's bring the stove.

🎧 5

1 I'm no expert, but I don't think that we can expect to have a phone signal.
2 Personally, I feel that we don't want to be weighed down with too much stuff.
3 I don't know about you, but I don't think we'll want a lot of devices on this trip.

4 Can I just suggest we leave our other electronics at home?
5 All I know is that I'm going to want at least three pairs of socks.
6 I wonder if we should consider leaving the camping stove behind?
7 We might possibly want it if we have rainy weather.
8 It might not be a bad idea for all of us to look at it together.

Unit 2

🎧 12

W = Woman, M = Man

W: How was the job interview?

M: I guess it was OK.

W: Not so great, huh?

M: I don't know. Maybe I'm just getting tired of interviews, but none of them seem to be going all that well. I think I need to work on my image. On paper, everything looks great, but I don't think I stand out face-to-face very much, or I'm just not comfortable. The other day I showed up in a suit for an interview with a software company, and the people who interviewed me were all wearing jeans and T-shirts. So obviously I didn't look like I would fit in. It really knocked my confidence and by the end of the interview, I just wanted to disappear.

W: That's a tough one. Have you considered asking about the 'unspoken dress code' at the office? Every company has one.

M: Unspoken dress code?

W: Sure. In every office everywhere, there's a usual way of dressing – like the obvious 'jeans rule' at your software interview. I would seriously consider asking about how people usually dress, and then going to interviews dressed just a little bit more formally than the unspoken dress code.

M: That's an interesting idea.

W: Another thing. Have you asked for feedback from the interviews? It doesn't always help, but someone might come up with something you could really improve on. You just might be doing something that you're not aware of that's putting people off slightly.

M: Yeah …

W: You might want to pay for an interview coach, too.

M: An interview coach?

W: Yeah. That's someone who you can do practice interviews with. They're great at spotting details you can change to really improve your image. You can definitely improve these things with some practice.

M: That might be worth a try. Could be expensive, though.

W: If you don't want to spend the money on a coach, why not try getting a book? I'm sure you could find something at the library. Could be a good place to start, anyway.

M: I like that idea. Thanks!

W: You know, most people go for ten or fifteen or even twenty jobs before they find something that's right. You mustn't lose heart. Remember, it's all practice for the one that finally works out!

M: That's a good way of looking at it. Thanks a lot!

🎧 14

1 Doing some relaxation exercises might be a good idea.
2 I would seriously consider getting some new shoes.
3 One other thing to consider: it's good for you to ask questions, too.
4 Remember, it's not unusual to go to thirty interviews before you get a job.
5 It can seem really difficult, but don't give up.

Unit 3

🎧 16

6 The marathon grew. So did our political problems. But for every disaster we had, the marathon found ways to bring people together.

17

1 It's good communication skills that start-up founders need.
2 What causes problems is poor communication.
3 The thing that co-founders need to have is a clear legal agreement.
4 It's personal conflict that causes businesses to fail.
5 What's important is to find a solution when communication breaks down.
6 The person you need to be honest with is your business partner.

A = Anna, B = Bob, C = Cath

A: Hi, Bob. Hi, Cath.
B: Hi, Anna.
C: Hello Anna.
A: Thanks for coming. Now, we've got three options here for the new logo. Do you have any views on any of them?
B: I don't know about you, but Option C really stands out for me.
C: Hmmm. I'm not so sure.
A: What are your thoughts, Cath?
C: Well, C is the most artistic, I guess you could say, but actually, would you want that guy to come to your door? I think that's an important consideration. It's the same with Option B. He looks like a kid. Do you want a kid to come and fix your pipes? I think Option A shows who we are a lot better.
B: I see what you mean about Option B, Cath. I'm not sure I like that one, either. And I agree that the guy in Option A looks friendly. But is he a brand? I think if we have a great-looking logo – which I think Option C is – people will notice it, but they won't think it's supposed to look like one of our plumbers. But what about you, Anna?
A: Actually, Option B was my idea. I agree with Cath that Option C looks a bit … too serious – alarming? Threatening, even? And I agree with you, Bob, that Option A is a nice picture, but not so much a brand. In fact, I don't want to negotiate on Option A. I really don't think it works as a logo. So Option B gets my vote. It's a lot of fun, I think.
B: OK, so we've got three options, and we each like different ones. I think one way of looking at that is to say that none of the options really works. What we need is a logo that works for all of us. So I think we need to completely rethink it.
C: Well, I think you're right about that, Bob. I'm afraid we need to go back to the drawing board with this.
B: OK. If we don't agree on how the plumber should be presented, then can we resolve this by agreeing that we don't need to show a plumber at all? After all, people know what a plumber is.
C: Exactly. So here's the real question: Which *style* of logo do we like the best?
B: Anna?
A: Well, if we're just talking about style and not about what it shows, I think Option C works well – the colours and the feel of it. I'd accept that style so long as it doesn't show a person.
C: Yeah, I can go with that. Thinking about it, logos don't usually look like photographs, do they?
B: Right. And I said at the start that Option C jumps out at me. So why don't we go back to the designer and say we want something in the style of Option C, but on the condition that it doesn't show a plumber? We want a clear, simple image …

Unit 4

20

Pretty good, until about ten minutes before my turn, when my whole body rebelled, and this wave of anxiety just washed over me. Now, when you experience fear, your sympathetic nervous system kicks in. So you have a rush of adrenaline, your heart rate increases, your breathing gets faster. Next your non-essential systems start to shut down, like digestion.

So your mouth gets dry, and blood is routed away from your extremities, so your fingers don't work anymore. Your pupils dilate, your muscles contract, your Spidey sense tingles, basically your whole body is trigger-happy. That condition is not conducive to performing folk music. I mean, your nervous system is an idiot.

22

A: About how many hours a day are you away from a device – your phone or tablet or computer?
B: You mean when I'm awake? Zero. I'm on or near a device more or less all day long – communicating.
A: That sounds kind of extreme. Is it absolutely necessary, or is it your choice?
B: Good question! To do my job, I have to respond to hundreds of emails every week. And I'm responsible for my company's social media presence, so I re-tweet some interesting link or other or write a new tweet every hour or so. And I update our Facebook status at least twice a day.
A: What time do you switch off?
B: Usually elevenish, but sometimes later, if I'm catching up on my personal messages.

23

1 About how many hours a day are you away from a device?
2 I'm on or near a device more or less all day long.
3 That sounds kind of extreme.
4 I have to respond to hundreds of emails every week.
5 I retweet some interesting link or other or write a new tweet every hour or so.
6 I update our Facebook status at least twice a day.
7 Usually elevenish, but sometimes later.

Conversation 1
A = Assistant, O = Oscar

A: Can I help?
O: Yes, hi, I hope so. I just bought this phone – it's my first smart phone – and I don't even know how to make a call. I clicked on the icon to open the map app, but I don't know to turn that off – how to get out of that.
A: OK, let's have a look. Any time you want to exit an app, you just have to press the home key.
O: The home key?
A: That's this one here at the bottom.
O: OK.
A: And to make a phone call, first you have to tap the phone icon, then along the bottom menu here you select keypad to dial or you can choose a number from your contacts.
O: You've lost me. Would you mind giving that to me one more time?
A: Sure. Here, you take the phone.
O: OK.
A: Now tap the phone icon.
O: OK.
A: Then choose either 'keypad' or 'contacts'.
O: OK, I can see how the keypad works. But can you explain why I would need to choose 'contacts'?
A: Sure. You can add people's names and phone numbers to a list in the phone, then you don't have to dial the number each time.
O: Oh, great. So are you saying I can enter my friends' numbers in the phone?
A: Exactly. Would you like me to give you a hand with that?
O: That would be great!

Conversation 2

L = Lydia, A = Assistant

L: Excuse me?

A: Yes?

L: I bought this watch earlier today, and I can't figure out how to set the date.

A: Let me see. Ah, yes. You just need to press the 'mode' button

L: Which one is that?

A: This one here, and then the 'select' button to scroll through the year, then the month, then the date.

L: Sorry, I didn't quite catch that. Could you run it by me again?

A: Sure. You start with the 'mode' button here. Press it.

L: OK.

A: Then you see the year. You can change the year with the 'select' button.

L: I'm probably just being a bit slow, but am I supposed to hold the 'mode' button?

A: No, just click it once.

L: Ah, OK. And then I click it to change the year, right?

A: You've got it.

Conversation 3

D = Dave, C = Carla

D: Carla, what's the trick to unlocking this door? I have the passcode, but I can't get the door open.

C: OK, it is a bit tricky. You need to press 'lock' and then press and hold 'enter code' for about three seconds. Then you use the number keys to enter the passcode but then that's followed by the star key and then you have to press 'lock' again.

D: Would you mind backing up for a second? I missed that last bit.

C: OK, after you enter the passcode, you press the star key and then 'lock'.

D: Sorry, I'm a bit confused. Did you say I start by pressing 'lock' or do I just enter the passcode?

C: You start by pressing 'lock', then you press and hold 'enter.'

D: I'd better write that down!

Review 2 (Units 3 and 4)

26

In 2007, environmental scientist Catlin Powers was carrying out climate research when a local asked her why researchers were so interested in outdoor air pollution when indoor air pollution was such a serious problem. When she measured the air in a local home – which happened to be the tent of nomadic tribespeople – it turned out to be ten times more polluted than the air in one of the world's most populous capital cities, Beijing. Through further research, Powers discovered that every year, around four million people globally were dying because of the smoke from the stoves they used indoors. Part of the problem was the fuel: cattle dung and wood, which produce a lot of smoke. In addition, depending on these sources of fuel creates other problems: it means animal waste is no longer available to fertilise the soil and leads to the illegal cutting down of trees.

Powers immediately began trying to figure out ways to make indoor cooking cleaner. While she was exploring possible alternative fuel sources, someone mentioned a teacher who had helped locals dig wells, repair machinery and build greenhouses, and had taught basic engineering skills to people in the area. Powers was introduced to Scot Frank and the two immediately hit it off. They began talking about ways to solve the dual problems of indoor air pollution and fuel scarcity.

They realized the solution lay in using the cleaner, more environmentally friendly energy of the sun. Having decided that solar power was the way to go, Frank and Powers, and engineer Amy Qian began working with university students in the Himalayas to collect feedback on the design features needed for a sun-powered cooker. Though some models of solar cooker had been introduced to the region by aid organizations, they weren't easy to pack and move, and so weren't suitable for nomads. The team came up with a design that looks something like an umbrella or a satellite dish – a shape called a parabola. When sunlight hits the reflective inner curve of the disc, it bounces off and can be focused onto the bottom of a pot or pan, which is held in place by a lightweight frame. On a clear, sunny day, SolSource can boil a litre of water in about ten minutes. On cloudy days, it's slower, but as long as you can see your shadow, SolSource can cook.

Two years later, Powers, Frank and Qian had perfected their solar cooker and started a company called One Earth Designs to produce it. Since then, SolSource has won numerous awards including a Dutch award for products that reduce greenhouse-gas emissions, and has successfully raised more than a hundred and forty thousand US dollars to promote SolSource and expand the business. As a result, SolSource has reached customers in eighteen countries around the world and is continuing to grow.

Unit 5

Ω8

4 I am here to tell you that we have been lied to about disability.

5 I've lost count of the number of times that I've been approached by strangers wanting to tell me that they think I'm brave or inspirational.

29

A = Adam. B = Ben, L = Lisa

A: Hilary's leaving us in three weeks, and I think it would be really nice to organize a farewell party for her.

B: Definitely. I for one am really going to miss her!

L: Yes, she deserves a good send-off. We need to come up with a great idea – something really special and different.

B: We shouldn't hang about, though. We don't have much time, so it shouldn't be anything that needs too much preparation.

L: Let's just throw out some ideas and I'll make notes. Any thoughts on food?

B: I really fancy the idea of Japanese food.

L: Hilary loves seafood. Any votes for sushi?

A: Could be expensive, but ... sure, I'd go along with that.

B: How about Mexican food?

A: Or we could do a barbecue?

B: Yeah, that would be good fun!

L: We could think about asking everyone to bring something to cook. Why don't we look into reserving some space at one of the parks?

A: Weather could be a problem, though.

L: Good point. But let's not exclude anything yet.

B: What about entertainment? Any bright ideas?

A: I've just had a brainwave: Karaoke! Hilary loves it!

L: ... Or we could have a band.

B: Yeah, who doesn't like live music!

L: Good point. Other ideas?

B: I'm not too sure about this, and it isn't exactly entertainment, but how about fancy dress? We could have a 1980s theme?

L: 1980s? That's an original idea ...

A: Maybe it's a bit too original?

L: Anyway, let's put it on the list. We could [fade out] hire someone who can ...

...

A: OK, this list is huge.

B: So, which ideas can we reject?

L: Well, let's face it. Money is a factor. Sushi isn't especially cheap.

B: We should probably opt for the barbecue instead of sushi. It will be much cheaper if people bring their own food.

A: Right. And the same goes for a band. Live music wouldn't be so easy to get on a budget.

B: Do we really need entertainment? I mean, when was the last time you went to a leaving party with entertainment. People just like talking, right? Why don't we just keep it simple and have the barbecue.

A: All right. That sounds like a plan!

Unit 6

🎧 **33**

3 OK, I'm going to give you a bit of a demonstration. Would you like to see that?

4 So let's look at the applications. Traditionally, in a crisis, what do we do? We ship water. Then, after a few weeks, we set up camps.

5 So here is the 'thinking different' bit. Instead of shipping water, and using man-made processes to do it, let's use Mother Nature.

🎧 **34**

A: We should leave in about ten minutes so as not to be late to the meeting.

B: You're right. And we should take East Street to avoid the road works in the town centre.

A: Well remembered. But I think the council has actually closed part of East Street, too, to prevent too much traffic building up in that area, so we'll need to go via Mill Lane.

B: That's the long way round. To be on time, we should have left five minutes ago!

A: Why don't you text Raymond so that they know we may be delayed because of the road works?

B: Great idea.

🎧 **35**

D = Dom, I = Ian, K = Kate

D: This definitely isn't the right way.

K: You're right. There's no path here. We've lost the path.

I: We should have been at the camp by now.

D: Hmm. I think we have about an hour of daylight left.

I: I guess we aren't where we thought we were.

K: Well, what are our options?

D: We could go back the way we came. We were definitely on the trail an hour ago.

K: I suppose so. But won't we be going in the opposite direction from the camp?

I: That's what we don't know. If we knew which way the village was, we wouldn't be lost.

D: We could split up. Maybe one of us would find the path?

K: I'm not too sure about that. I'd rather stick together.

I: Kate's right. That's one of the basic rules of hill walking.

D: Let's just take stock of what we have first. Did anyone bring a torch?

K: Not me. I didn't expect to be out at night.

I: There's one on my phone. It's pretty small, and I don't have much battery power left.

D: OK, how about water?

K: I have about a litre.

D: Me, too. About a litre.

I: OK. I've got about half a litre. Anyway, if we have to stay out all night, we'll have enough water.

K: Good. We may not have any choice. What about fire? Do you two have any matches?

D: I've got a few. If we're careful, it should be enough to start a fire.

I: We might be pretty close to the camp now without knowing it. How about if we just call out?

D: It's worth a try. But it doesn't feel to me like we're near the camp.

K: That's because we're lost!

I: Let's try it.

D: OK, sure, what have we got to lose?

All: Hello? Jack! Maya! Can you hear us? Hello? [Wait for reply]

K: Hmmm. Did you hear anything?

D: No, I …

Voice: Dom! Kate! Is that you?

K: Jack! Hey! We're here!

D: Come on. I think it's that way …

Unit 7

🎧 **37**

1 I painted for 10 years, when I was offered a Fulbright to India. Promising to give exhibitions of paintings, I shipped my paints and arrived in Mahabalipuram.

2 This fishing village was famous for sculpture. So I tried bronze casting. But to make large forms was too heavy and expensive.

🎧 **38**

I went for a walk on the beach, watching the fishermen bundle their nets into mounds on the sand. I'd seen it every day, but this time I saw it differently – a new approach to sculpture, a way to make volumetric form without heavy solid materials.

🎧 **39**

I've been living in London for ten years, but I think I'd been living here for four years when I met Ella for the first time. We'd both been going to the same Spanish class for several weeks. We'd said hello to each other a few times, but never actually had a conversation. One week she wasn't there, and I realized I'd been daydreaming about seeing her and maybe asking her out. I was suddenly afraid she'd never come back again, and I thought I'd better do something if I ever saw her again! When she came to class the following week, I finally started a conversation with her, and I asked her out. We've been going out together ever since then, and in about six months, we'll be getting married.

🎧 **41**

M = Max, L = Lucy, D = Davina

M: Have you seen this picture?

L: Yeah, it's really weird, isn't it? Where was it taken?

M: In Belgium, near a place called Chatillon.

D: What do you think happened there?

M: I'm not really sure.

L: That's odd. There might've been some natural disaster – a forest fire, maybe? Or an earthquake that completely destroyed the road?

D: Something like that. I imagine the cars were just abandoned. It looks as though people had to get away from their cars quickly for some reason.

L: And they can't've been able to go back for them, right? Why would people leave so many cars and not go back for them?

M: I guess whatever happened, the cars couldn't be moved afterwards. Or it might not have been practical to move them.

D: How long have they been there?

M: They'd been there for about seventy years when this picture was taken.

L: Maybe something happened very suddenly. What if it was an alien invasion, and all the people were taken from their cars? That may have been why they could never go back!

M: Well, I hadn't thought of that, but …

D: Here's another idea, though. Maybe the cars weren't put there all at once.

M: What do you mean?

D: It looks like a traffic jam now, but maybe someone just dumped an old car in the forest, and then someone else added one. And the trees may have grown up around them. It might not have been a wooded area before.

L: I can imagine that. One by one, people just kept taking old cars out there and leaving them, perhaps.

D: So are the cars still there? Can people go and see them?

M: No, they're not. They were taken away a few years ago.

Unit 8

🎧 44

4 Kids get instant feedback about what works and what doesn't work.

5 business students are trained to find the single right plan, right? And then they execute on it. And then what happens is, when they put the marshmallow on top, they run of time and what happens? It's a crisis. Sound familiar? Right. What kindergarteners do is that they start with the marshmallow and build prototypes.

🎧 46

J = Jane, R = Rudy, H = Helen

J: Shall I get us started? ... OK, the product promotion for the organic drinks started to run last week, and we all know there were a lot of … issues. Big challenges, which we've talked about a lot already. I think we all agreed that coordination was the biggest challenge. Even though we were working on the same thing at the same time, we weren't always working together. We didn't have an administrator to support the project manager, and this led to some real problems. The leadership was there, but the teamwork was missing. I'd be interested in hearing your views about how we can do better next time. Rudy?

R: I think next time, the project manager really needs to facilitate more communication – especially when we develop a campaign or promotion. I'd really like to analyse …

H: Before you continue, can I just say ...

J: I know you're dying to jump in, but can we just let Rudy finish?

H: Sure. Sorry.

R: I'd really like to analyse the way we do meetings.

J: Meaning … ?

R: We have really long meetings once a week, on Monday morning, and then everyone goes off and works all week. What if we had shorter meetings more often? Maybe even standing up meetings, so they don't last too long.

J: Interesting idea. What's your take on that, Helen?

H: That's just what I was going to say! I think the long meetings kill creativity. If we're going to work well as a team, we need more open, relaxed communication.

R: Yes, exactly. I'd like to suggest we start by focusing on administration …

…

J: Any more thoughts on improvements for next time, Rudy? Helen?

R: I think we've covered it.

H: No. Thanks. I think that's everything.

J: OK, if no one has anything else, I think we can stop there.

Review 4 (Units 7 and 8)

🎧 48

I love Boxcycle, mostly because the idea is just so simple. If you need cardboard boxes – say you're moving house – you can go on the Boxcycle website, type in your location and find used cardboard boxes that are available nearby. The site gives you a list that says roughly where the boxes are located, their size, and the price – which is cheaper than you would pay for new boxes. If you have boxes you don't need anymore, you just enter a description of them, the price, and your zip code, and people who want boxes can contact you via a message on the website. It couldn't be simpler, and it's great that you get a little money for your trouble! It's so much more energy efficient than using the boxes once and then sending them to the paper recycling centre, or worse, throwing them away.

Hipcycle is one of my absolute favourite online stores. All of the products on the site are things that have been made from materials that would otherwise have been thrown away. I recently bought some drinking glasses there that were made from old-style, green cola bottles. They're very heavy duty, and super stylish. The stuff on Hipcycle is appealing for so many reasons: it's handmade; it's made from junk that in many cases would have gone into landfill; and best of all, the products have a huge amount of character, unlike so much of the factory-produced stuff people sell these days. On the Hipcycle website, you can shop by material – old vinyl records, bicycle parts, glass, e-waste and so on – or you can shop by category – household goods, clothes, school and office supplies, et cetera It's such a great idea!

I was very impressed when a company called Marriott Construction did a project near my home. It was a fairly big job, and my wife and I were concerned that it was really going to be disruptive with all the workers, materials and equipment coming and going. They were turning an old factory building into modern flats, but in the process, they had to knock down quite a few bits of the old building. Well, I can't say it wasn't a noisy, dusty project, but I think they did a great job, and were as considerate as possible of the people living in the area. I used to work in construction myself, and we always used to haul away loads of old material from sites like this, then bring in new material. But Marriott has a zero waste policy. One thing they did that really impressed me was that they crushed the material from the demolition and turned it into the temporary roadway they needed to build for the project, for the lorries to come and go. Keeping the material onsite meant a lot less lorry traffic in and out of the area – which meant less noise and less air pollution – and no doubt it saved the project money. We need to see more sensible solutions like this.

Unit 9

🎧 49

It taught me – it gave me a greater appreciation, an understanding for the present moment.

🎧 50

In fact, we spend more time looking after our cars, our clothes and our hair than we — OK, maybe not our hair, but you see where I'm going.

🎧 51

1 But when you sit down and you watch the mind in this way, you might see many different patterns. You might find a mind that's really restless and – the whole time.

2 You might find a mind that's very dull and boring, and it's just, almost mechanical, it just seems it's as if you're getting up, going to work, eat, sleep, get up, work.

🎧 53

Conversation 1
W1 = woman 1, M1 = Man 1

W1: Have you got a minute?

M1: Sure. What's up?

W1: I have a favour to ask.

M1: OK.

W1: I don't suppose you'd be willing to let me borrow that black leather jacket of yours? I'm going to a work party tomorrow night, and it would look really cool over my new dress …

M1: Tomorrow, huh … ?

W1: I can have it cleaned for you, if you want.

M1: That's a bit tricky, I'm afraid … . I was planning to wear it myself tomorrow night …

W1: Hmmm. All my jackets are either too warm or too summery. I wonder if that denim jacket of yours would …

M1: Yeah, I love that one. Unfortunately, a friend borrowed it a few weeks ago and hasn't returned it, so I can't …

Conversation 2

W2 = Woman 2, M2 = Man 2

W2: Could I have a word?
M2: Sure. What's on your mind?
W2: I have to apologize.
M2: For what?
W2: I said I was going to take care of the arrangements for Mr. Miyazaki's visit – I promised I'd do it yesterday and let him know, but I didn't get round to it.
M2: Don't worry, we still have some time. Can you deal with it today?
W2: Sure. I can sort it out straightaway.
M2: OK, do that, and let me know what you come up with …

Conversation 3

W3 = Woman 3, M3 = Man 3

M3: Sorry, but if you have moment …
W3: Sure. What can I do for you?
M3: Actually, I've got a confession to make …
W3: A confession?
M3: The thing is … I left an office laptop on the train this morning. I've reported it as lost, but so far, no one has handed it in.
W3: Hmmm … that's a bit awkward.
M3: I know. There's a lot of stuff in there that we really don't want to share.
W3: You're right about that! OK, well, you did the right thing letting me know. But we're going to have to get in touch with the police and let them know what's happened. Would you please get on the phone as soon as possible …

Conversation 4

W4 = Woman 4, M4 = Man 4

W4: Excuse me?
M4: Yes?
W4: Sorry, but your van is blocking my way. The thing is, I need to get my car out. Would you mind … ?
M4: Oh, sorry, I'm just doing a delivery. I'll be here another five minutes.
W4: Would it be too much trouble to move your van two metres so I can get my car out?
M4: I won't be five minutes …
W4: Look, I'm sorry, but I'm running late and I really need to get going.
M4: Will you relax?
W4: I will when you've moved your van.
M4: All right, all right …

Conversation 5

M = Manager, D = David

M: What's on your mind, David?
D: It's my pay.
M: What about it?
D: Well, it hasn't been increased.
M: I see. We talked a bit about this when we had your six-month appraisal, but maybe the situation wasn't made clear to you at that time. The point is, you haven't had a pay increase *yet*.
D: I'm sorry, but I just don't think it's fair. Look, everyone can tell you don't like me. That's why you haven't given me a pay rise.
M: Whoa, hang on a second, David … It's a shame you feel unfairly treated, but this has nothing to do with my personal feelings. The thing is, you've been late to work every other day for the past six months. And not just a little late, but sometimes up to half an hour late. We've already spoken about this.
D: Well, I really don't think I've been late that often, but the point is I've done my job. I've done what I was supposed to do.
M: Not really, David. The thing is, being in the office during work hours is part of what you're supposed to do. Listen, we can work through this. Let's start tomorrow. Arrive on time – or a little early – every day for a month, then we'll meet again. That's the only way you're going to get anywhere with this. Agreed?
D: OK.

Unit 10

🎧 55

My job at Twitter is to ensure user trust, protect user rights and keep users safe, both from each other and, at times, from themselves. Let's talk about what scale looks like at Twitter. Back in January 2009, we saw more than two million new tweets each day on the platform. January 2014, more than 500 million. We were seeing two million tweets in less than six minutes. That's a 24,900-per cent increase.

🎧 56

Now, the vast majority of activity on Twitter puts no one in harm's way. There's no risk involved. My job is to root out and prevent activity that might. Sounds straightforward, right? You might even think it'd be easy, given that I just said the vast majority of activity on Twitter puts no one in harm's way. Why spend so much time searching for potential calamities in innocuous activities? Given the scale that Twitter is at, a one-in-a-million chance happens 500 times a day. It's the same for other companies dealing at this sort of scale. For us, edge cases, those rare situations that are unlikely to occur, are more like norms.

🎧 57

A = Alex, C = Clare, J = Jenny

A: OK, the next part of the risk assessment is seating. Clare, you're taking care of that one, right?
C: Yes.
A: OK, so what have you got for seating? Is it *really* a hazard?
J: Well, it is if you fall off! … Seriously, can't we just order some regular office chairs?
C: Right, well, according to the Health and Safety Executive, seating is considered a workplace hazard because it can lead to back pain, and also to problems with arms – especially seating that isn't adjustable.
J: Well, that makes sense – it's easy to see how the wrong chairs could be bad for people. How high is the risk of people having back or arm problems?
C: For people working all day at a computer, the risk of back problems is actually fairly high if the seating isn't appropriate. So we need to choose our chairs carefully.
A: Well, we definitely want to get this right. What are the options?
C: I've been looking into the best computer chairs, and there are some pretty interesting options to choose from. Possibly the most obvious one is a conventional desk chair design – as long as it's good quality, and adjustable, which almost all of them are these days. If each worker can adjust their own chair, this lowers the risk of back and arm problems. People are used to this sort of chair, so they're popular.
J: OK, so that's basically what I said before, right? We just order some standard-issue office chairs?
A: Clare, what are the other options?
C: Ball chairs are big right now.
A & J: Ball chairs?
C: They're big balls filled with air, and you sit on them.
J: And this is a huge improvement on the office chair design that's been used successfully for hundreds of years around the world?
C: It's claimed that they make your lower back stronger and improve your sitting position. But a lot of the research says that there really isn't a big benefit with these and the risk of back pain is about the same as a standard chair.
A: So, in light of the research, ball chairs probably aren't the best option.
C: Agreed.
J: Well, I guess that leaves us with just plain old everyday office chairs, like I said before?
C: Not quite. Now, since sitting a lot increases the risk of back and arm problems, I looked into two standing options. The first is

basically a very high stool that you lean against. It's very basic and super lightweight, so on the plus side, the high stool isn't that expensive. The other isn't a chair at all, it's a standing desk.

J: But we wouldn't expect people to work standing up all day, would we?

C: No. Standing up regularly is very healthy, but actually, one downside of standing desks is that they increase the risk of leg problems – because you're on your feet all day. And of course a lot of people just don't like the idea of working all day standing up.

J: OK, good. So that's out. Which I guess brings us back to standard office chairs?

C: Not quite, Jenny. A final option that might do the job is kneeling chairs. A lot of people really like them.

J: You're kidding, right?

C: They're said to be good for keeping your back straight.

A: Any possible problems?

C: One drawback of these is that you become uncomfortable more quickly. Though they're pretty good for backs and arms, there's some risk of leg problems with these.

J: That doesn't sound very good.

C: On the plus side, they're adjustable. But a lot of people really don't like them just because they're so different.

A: Thanks, Clare. That was incredibly thorough.

J: It certainly was! All things considered, don't you think the choice is obvious?

🎧 58

1 I love the idea of doing some fitness activities. I'd like to see yoga, aerobics, kung fu …

2 For ball sports, we should choose basketball, football or rugby.

Review 5 (Units 9 and 10)

🎧 59

The global financial crisis which began in 2007 eventually led to the failure of banks around the globe. It also resulted in changes in laws regulating the finance industry, to avoid such a catastrophe happening again. Since that time, an increasing number of the customers who felt betrayed by the banking system have taken their business out of the mainstream and into the sustainable – also called the ethical – banking sector. Today, we'll look at one sustainable banking success story: Triodos Bank.

Triodos opened for business in the Netherlands in 1980, and has since expanded to Belgium, Germany, Spain and the UK. Like any bank, it's a business and therefore needs to make a profit to survive. However, the company believes that they shouldn't earn income from any activity that harms the environment, promotes social inequality or injustice, or harms communities. This means that the company actively invests its customers' money in small to medium-sized businesses that the bank believes are a positive force in the world: fair trade enterprises, social housing, green energy projects, organic agriculture, and so on. Equally, it doesn't invest in businesses that can be linked to social or environmental harm, such as weapons manufacturers or producers of fossil fuels.

In the past, the relationship between ethics and profits was seen as either/or – a bank could be ethical, or it could be profitable, but it couldn't be both. But ethical banking has come of age, especially since the financial crisis. Nowadays, the financial returns from sustainable banking are competitive and the social, cultural and environmental returns are better understood and more greatly appreciated.

One key feature of Triodos is that its customers know how their money is being used. I'll tell you about three of them, just to give you a flavour.

Belle Vue Farm, in Wiltshire, UK, is owned by Joe and Izzy Dyke, who are the third generation to work on the 110-acre farm. In addition to raising organic produce, they offer holiday tents and weekly tours explaining the benefits of organic farming.

Key Driving Competences of Leuven, Belgium, knows that driving is essential in some businesses. Given the necessity of driving, the company believes that drivers can still reduce their impact on the environment by learning to drive more economically – and more safely. They've developed an in-car electronic monitoring system that measures drivers' behaviours and can help them alter their driving to reduce fuel consumption by up to 30%.

Graduates of Escuela del Actor, an acting school in Valencia, Spain, have performed in local, regional and national productions. In addition to training actors, the school also serves the community by organising shows and workshops for everyone, from young children to seniors.

In very practical ways, Triodos makes money work for positive change in society, the environment and culture – and everyone wins.

Unit 11

🎧 62

But what does it look like to grow up in a place like that? I am an example of that. I was born in a little village called Gando. In Gando, there was no electricity, no access to clean drinking water, and no school. But my father wanted me to learn how to read and write. For this reason, I had to leave my family when I was seven and to stay in a city far away from my village with no contact with my family. In this place I sat in a class like that with more than 150 other kids, and for six years.

🎧 63

1 Although geotourism brings benefits to both the visitors and the hosts, some environmentalists feel that some parts of the world should be completely closed to tourism.

2 Considering that the local Masai people in Kenya have become a tourist attraction themselves, it may be worth re-thinking ecotourism.

3 By the time thousands of divers have visited a popular diving spot, damage has been done that can never be repaired.

🎧 64

C = Carly, M = Mike

C: Today, Mike, I'd like you to think about – and talk about – the future. But allow your thoughts free rein. I want to encourage you to explore what your dreams might be. So to begin with, we'll just forget about where you are now, and we won't worry about what feels reasonable or responsible or realistic or possible, we'll just get some ideas out there. I'd just like to hear a bit about some things that really excite you, or things you could envisage yourself doing in the future. Maybe think back to when you were a kid and you talked about what you wanted to do when you grew up. Think with that kind of freedom, that kind of openness.

M: OK, sure. Er … I've always fancied doing something with my hands. You know, making things?

C: OK, good. What sort of thing can you see yourself making?

M: You know, somehow I could see myself making furniture. I've never tried woodworking, so I have no experience with it, but I very much admire well-made furniture.

C: Forget about whether or not you'd be good at it. Let's just focus on the idea of making furniture.

M: OK.

C: So if money were no object, you think you might like to learn about furniture making?

M: Well, yeah. You know, if money were no object, I'd love to study furniture making … if we're not really thinking about what seems feasible or sensible.

C: OK, good.

M: One other thing: I could see myself spending some time in another country. I think languages are really interesting, and I'd love to learn to speak another language well. Going overseas would be a great way to do that.

C: Yes, I can see the appeal of that. Is there a language you're especially interested in?

M: Good question, and I'm not sure of the answer. I learned some Spanish at school, but I didn't carry on with it – my parents didn't really think it was important. … Wouldn't it be great to learn something really different from Spanish, like Chinese?

C: Chinese, wow! I can see you like a challenge!

M: Well, you said not to worry about what's actually possible, right?

C: Yes, right. And I wonder if you've ever thought about something like going abroad to study a craft? How about looking into woodworking courses in Spain or something like that?

M: I'd never thought about it, but why not?

Unit 12

 66

So wouldn't it be amazing if our phones could see the world in the same way that we do, as we're walking around being able to point a phone at anything, and then have it actually recognize images and objects like the human brain, and then be able to pull in information from an almost infinite library of knowledge and experiences and ideas.

70

Conversation 1

L = Linda, P = Phil

L: Hello?

P: Hi, Linda. Phil.

L: Oh, hi. How you doing?

P: Fine, thanks. You all right?

L: Yeah, fine, thanks. Busy.

P: Linda, I was wondering if you could make a meeting next week? We need to plan the summer street party.

L: This is great timing. I was supposed to have a work trip then, but it's been cancelled, so I'm around.

P: Would Wednesday work for you?

L: That should be OK. What time?

P: Evening? Eight o'clock? Here at my place.

L: Yeah, I can make that.

P: Great. See you then.

L: OK, bye.

Conversation 2

MD = Mr Dean, P = Phil

MD: Hello?

P: Hello, Mr Dean. This is Phil Johnson.

MD: Oh, hello Phil. How are you?

P: I'm very well, Mr. Dean. How are things with you?

MD: I can't complain. Now, what can I do for you?

P: As you know, I'm trying to organize a meeting with you and Linda Smith to plan the summer street party. Would next Wednesday at eight work for you?

MD: Wednesday? Weren't we going to meet on Tuesday night?

P: Yes, we were supposed to, but something came up for me, and now I can't make Tuesday.

MD: I'm afraid Wednesday won't work for me. I'm away overnight that night. We're going to see my daughter in Bristol. I could make Thursday.

P: Hmmm. Tuesday's definitely out for me, but Thursday would work. I'll have to get back to Linda, though. She was fine with Wednesday, but I'm not sure about Thursday. Anyway, let's pencil it in.

MD: That sounds good, Phil. Thank you.

P: Thank you, Mr Dean. Goodbye.

Conversation 3

L = Linda, P = Phil

L: Hello?

P: Linda, hi, Phil again.

L: Oh, hi, Phil.

P: I just spoke to Mr Dean. He can't make Wednesday next week, but he can make Thursday. Is that any good for you?

L: Hmmm. Thursday. Not ideal, to be honest. I was going to pick up some things in town, when the shops are open late. But if we make it nine instead of eight, I can manage that.

P: Nine next Thursday, my place … . OK, I think that'll work. I'll just have to confirm with Mr Dean. And I'll put an agenda together and email it through.

L: Sounds great, Phil. Thanks.

Communication activities

Unit 4.3 Exercise 9, page 46
Student A

Choose two of the products. Decide how you could market them in your country. Think about:

- local tastes
- a product name that would be successful
- possible slogans (in English)

Try to convince your partner to buy your products. You may need to be highly creative to persuade them!

Tako ice – octopus-flavoured ice cream from Japan

Mototaxi – a three-wheeled taxi from El Salvador

Nón lá – a conical farmer's hat from Vietnam, for sun protection

Unit 4.4 Exercise 5, page 49

Student A

1 Explain this process to Student B, but don't show the picture.

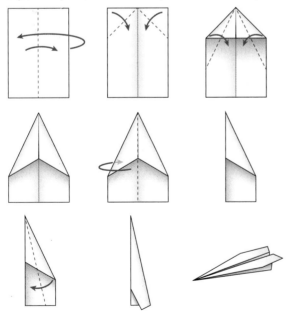

2 Listen to and follow Student B's instructions. Ask for clarification as necessary.

Unit 5.3 Exercise 7, page 58
Answers to the puzzles

1 The digits that make up this number are in alphabetical order according to how they're spelled: 8 (eight), 5 (five), 4 (four), etc.
2 If you take the first letter from each word and move it to the end of the word, you get the same word, spelled backwards.
3 The river is frozen.

Unit 6.3 Exercise 1, page 68
One of many possible solutions to the nine-dots puzzle

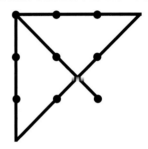

Unit 12.3 Exercise 9, Page 134
Student A

1 Read the scenario. You are an optimist. Try to convince your partner that it's a good idea for Matthew and Helena to buy the house. Consider:

- the size
- the price
- their salaries in the future
- holidays and other luxuries
- starting a family

Matthew and Helena are newlyweds who want to buy a house. They have found a three-bedroom house that they love. The price is only €250,000, which fortunately is the maximum possible loan they can get considering their current combined salaries. Paying back that amount would mean they would need to limit the cost of holidays and other luxuries, but it will be worth it. They don't have a family now, and it will probably be a few years before they want one. They're not sure whether they should buy the house, or look for something different.

2 Can you and your partner agree on a 'realistic' course of action for the couple?

TED Talk Transcripts

The transcripts use British English for all the talks, irrespective of the nationality of the speaker.

Any grammatical inaccuracies in the talks have been left uncorrected in the transcripts.

Unit 1 Less stuff, more happiness

0.19 What's in the box? Whatever it is must be pretty important, because I've travelled with it, moved it, from apartment to apartment to apartment. (*Laughter*) (*Applause*)

0.35 Sound familiar? Did you know that we Americans have about three times the amount of space we did 50 years ago? Three times. So you'd think, with all this extra space, we'd have plenty of room for all our stuff. Nope. There's a new industry in town, a 22 billion-dollar, 2.2 billion sq. ft. industry: that of personal storage. So we've got triple the space, but we've become such good shoppers that we need even more space. So where does this lead? Lots of credit card debt, huge environmental footprints, and perhaps not coincidentally, our happiness levels flat-lined over the same 50 years.

1.22 Well I'm here to suggest there's a better way, that less might actually equal more. I bet most of us have experienced at some point the joys of less: college – in your dorm, travelling – in a hotel room, camping – when you've got basically nothing, maybe a boat. Whatever it was for you, I bet that, among other things, this gave you a little more freedom, a little more time. So I'm going to suggest that less stuff and less space are going to equal a smaller footprint. It's actually a great way to save you some money. And it's going to give you a little more ease in your life.

2.02 So I started a project called Life Edited at lifeedited.org to further this conversation and to find some great solutions in this area. First up: crowd-sourcing my 420 sq. ft. apartment in Manhattan with partners Mutopo and Jovoto.com. I wanted it all – home office, sit-down dinner for ten, room for guests, and all my kite surfing gear. With over 300 entries from around the world, I got it, my own little jewel box. By buying a space that was 420 sq. ft. instead of 600, immediately I'm saving 200 grand. Smaller space is going to make for smaller utilities – save some more money there, but also a smaller footprint. And because it's really designed around an edited set of possessions – my favourite stuff – and really designed for me, I'm really excited to be there.

2.56 So how can you live little? Three main approaches. First of all, you have to edit ruthlessly. We've got to clear the arteries of our lives. And that shirt that I hadn't worn in years? It's time for me to let it go. We've got to cut the extraneous out of our lives, and we've got to learn to stem the inflow. We need to think before we buy. Ask ourselves, 'Is that really going to make me happier? Truly?' By all means, we should buy and own some great stuff. But we want stuff that we're going to love for years, not just stuff.

3.33 Secondly, our new mantra: small is sexy. We want space efficiency. We want things that are designed for how they're used the vast majority of the time, not that rare event. Why have a six burner stove when you rarely use three? So we want things that nest, we want things that stack, and we want it digitized. You can take paperwork, books, movies, and you can make it disappear – it's magic.

4.01 Finally, we want multifunctional spaces and housewares – a sink combined with a toilet, a dining table becomes a bed – same space, a little side table stretches out to seat ten. In the winning Life Edited scheme in a render here, we combine a moving wall with transformer furniture to get a lot out of the space. Look at the coffee table – it grows in height and width to seat ten. My office folds away, easily hidden. My bed just pops out of the wall with two fingers. Guests? Move the moving wall, have some fold-down guest beds. And of course, my own movie theatre.

4.43 So I'm not saying that we all need to live in 420 sq. ft. But consider the benefits of an edited life. Go from 3,000 to 2,000, from 1,500 to 1,000. Most of us, maybe all of us, are here pretty happily for a bunch of days with a couple of bags, maybe a small space, a hotel room. So when you go home and you walk through your front door, take a second and ask yourselves, 'Could I do with a little life editing? Would that give me a little more freedom? Maybe a little more time?'

5.16 What's in the box? It doesn't really matter. I know I don't need it. What's in yours? Maybe, just maybe, less might equal more. So let's make room for the good stuff.

5.35 Thank you. (*Applause*)

Unit 2 Who am I? Think again

0.11 Hetain Patel: (*In Chinese*)

0.22 Yuyu Rau: Hi, I'm Hetain. I'm an artist. And this is Yuyu, who is a dancer I have been working with. I have asked her to translate for me.

0.33 HP: (*In Chinese*)

0.38 YR: If I may, I would like to tell you a little bit about myself and my artwork.

0.44 HP: (*In Chinese*)

0.50 YR: I was born and raised near Manchester, in England, but I'm not going to say it in English to you, because I'm trying to avoid any assumptions that might be made from my northern accent.

1.06 HP: (*In Chinese*)

1.15 YR: The only problem with masking it with Chinese Mandarin is I can only speak this paragraph, which I have learned by heart when I was visiting in China. (*Laughter*) So all I can do is keep repeating it in different tones and hope you won't notice.

1.38 HP: (*In Chinese*)

1.43 YR: Needless to say, I would like to apologize to any Mandarin speakers in the audience.

1.53 As a child, I would hate being made to wear the Indian kurta pyjama, because I didn't think it was very cool. It felt a bit girly to me, like a dress, and it had this baggy trouser part you had to tie really tight to avoid the embarrassment of them falling down. My dad never wore it, so I didn't see why I had to. Also, it makes me feel a bit uncomfortable, that people assume I represent something genuinely Indian when I wear it, because that's not how I feel.

2.29 HP: (*In Chinese*)

2.35 YR: Actually, the only way I feel comfortable wearing it is by pretending they are the robes of a kung fu warrior like Li Mu Bai from that film, *Crouching Tiger, Hidden Dragon*.

3.34 OK. So my artwork is about identity and language, challenging common assumptions based on how we look like or where we come from, gender, race, class. What makes us who we are anyway?

3.57 HP: (*In Chinese*)

4.03 YR: I used to read Spider-Man comics, watch kung fu movies, take philosophy lessons from Bruce Lee. He would say things like –

4.12 HP: Empty your mind. (*Laughter*) Be formless, shapeless, like water. Now you put water into a cup. It becomes the cup. You put water into a bottle, it becomes the bottle. Put it in a teapot, it becomes the teapot. Now, water can flow or it can crash. Be water, my friend. (*Applause*)

4.41　YR: This year, I am 32 years old, the same age Bruce Lee was when he died. I have been wondering recently, if he were alive today, what advice he would give me about making this TED Talk.

4.59　HP: Don't imitate my voice. It offends me. (*Laughter*)

5.07　YR: Good advice, but I still think that we learn who we are by copying others. Who here hasn't imitated their childhood hero in the playground, or mum or father? I have.

5.24　HP: A few years ago, in order to make this video for my artwork, I shaved off all my hair so that I could grow it back as my father had it when he first emigrated from India to the U.K. in the 1960s. He had a side parting and a neat moustache.

5.46　At first, it was going very well. I even started to get discounts in Indian shops. (*Laughter*)

5.56　But then very quickly, I started to underestimate my moustache growing ability, and it got way too big. It didn't look Indian anymore. Instead, people from across the road, they would shout things like –

6.11　HP and YR: *Arriba! Arriba! Ándale! Ándale!* (*Laughter*)

6.15　HP: Actually, I don't know why I am even talking like this. My dad doesn't even have an Indian accent anymore. He talks like this now.

6.23　So it's not just my father that I've imitated. A few years ago I went to China for a few months, and I couldn't speak Chinese, and this frustrated me, so I wrote about this and had it translated into Chinese, and then I learned this by heart, like music, I guess.

6.49　YR: This phrase is now etched into my mind clearer than the pin number to my bank card, so I can pretend I speak Chinese fluently. When I had learned this phrase, I had an artist over there hear me out to see how accurate it sounded.

7.06　I spoke the phrase, and then he laughed and told me, 'Oh yeah, that's great, only it kind of sounds like a woman.'

7.14　I said, 'What?'

7.15　He said, 'Yeah, you learned from a woman?'

7.19　I said, 'Yes. So?'

7.21　He then explained the tonal differences between male and female voices are very different and distinct, and that I had learned it very well, but in a woman's voice. (*Applause*)

7.42　HP: OK. So this imitation business does come with risk. It doesn't always go as you plan it, even with a talented translator. But I am going to stick with it, because contrary to what we might usually assume, imitating somebody can reveal something unique. So every time I fail to become more like my father, I become more like myself. Every time I fail to become Bruce Lee, I become more authentically me.

8.22　This is my art. I strive for authenticity, even if it comes in a shape that we might not usually expect. It's only recently that I've started to understand that I didn't learn to sit like this through being Indian. I learned this from Spider-Man. (*Laughter*)

8.47　Thank you. (*Applause*)

Unit 3　Making peace is a marathon

0.12　I come from Lebanon, and I believe that running can change the world. I know what I have just said is simply not obvious.

0.23　You know, Lebanon as a country has been once destroyed by a long and bloody civil war. Honestly, I don't know why they call it civil war when there is nothing civil about it. With Syria to the north, Israel and Palestine to the south, and our government even up till this moment is still fragmented and unstable. For years, the country has been divided between politics and religion. However, for one day a year, we truly stand united, and that's when the marathon takes place.

1.06　I used to be a marathon runner. Long-distance running was not only good for my well-being but it helped me meditate and

dream big. So the longer distances I ran, the bigger my dreams became, until one fateful morning, and while training, I was hit by a bus. I nearly died, was in a coma, stayed at the hospital for two years, and underwent 36 surgeries to be able to walk again.

1.46　As soon as I came out of my coma, I realized that I was no longer the same runner I used to be, so I decided, if I couldn't run myself, I wanted to make sure that others could. So out of my hospital bed, I asked my husband to start taking notes, and a few months later, the marathon was born.

2.14　Organizing a marathon as a reaction to an accident may sound strange, but at that time, even during my most vulnerable condition, I needed to dream big. I needed something to take me out of my pain, an objective to look forward to. I didn't want to pity myself, nor to be pitied, and I thought by organizing such a marathon, I'll be able to pay back to my community, build bridges with the outside world, and invite runners to come to Lebanon and run under the umbrella of peace. Organizing a marathon in Lebanon is definitely not like organizing one in New York. How do you introduce the concept of running to a nation that is constantly at the brink of war? How do you ask those who were once fighting and killing each other to come together and run next to each other? More than that, how do you convince people to run a distance of 26.2 miles at a time they were not even familiar with the word 'marathon'? So we had to start from scratch.

3.34　For almost two years, we went all over the country and even visited remote villages. I personally met with people from all walks of life – mayors, NGOs, schoolchildren, politicians, militiamen, people from mosques, churches, the president of the country, even housewives. I learned one thing: When you walk the talk, people believe you. Many were touched by my personal story, and they shared their stories in return. It was honesty and transparency that brought us together. We spoke one common language to each other, and that was from one human to another. Once that trust was built, everybody wanted to be part of the marathon to show the world the true colours of Lebanon and the Lebanese and their desire to live in peace and harmony.

4.44　In October 2003, over 6,000 runners from 49 different nationalities came to the start line, all determined, and when the gunfire went off, this time it was a signal to run in harmony for a change.

5.05　The marathon grew. So did our political problems. But for every disaster we had, the marathon found ways to bring people together. In 2005, our prime minister was assassinated, and the country came to a complete standstill, so we organized a five-kilometre United We Run campaign. Over 60,000 people came to the start line, all wearing white T-shirts with no political slogans. That was a turning point for the marathon, where people started looking at it as a platform for peace and unity.

5.51　Between 2006 up to 2009, our country, Lebanon, went through unstable years, invasions, and more assassinations that brought us close to a civil war. The country was divided again, so much that our parliament resigned, we had no president for a year, and no prime minister. But we did have a marathon.

6.25　So through the marathon, we learned that political problems can be overcome. When the opposition party decided to shut down part of the city centre, we negotiated alternative routes. Government protesters became sideline cheerleaders. They even hosted juice stations.

6.50　You know, the marathon has really become one of a kind. It gained credibility from both the Lebanese and the international community. Last November 2012, over 33,000 runners from 85 different nationalities came to the start line, but this time, they challenged very stormy and rainy weather. The streets were flooded, but people didn't want to miss out on the opportunity of being part of such a national day.

7.25　BMA has expanded. We include everyone: the young, the elderly, the disabled, the mentally challenged, the blind, the elite, the amateur runners, even moms with their babies.

Themes have included runs for the environment, breast cancer, for the love of Lebanon, for peace, or just simply to run.

7.50 The first annual all-women-and-girls race for empowerment, which is one of its kind in the region, has just taken place only a few weeks ago, with 4,512 women, including the first lady, and this is only the beginning.

8.13 Thank you. (*Applause*)

8.17 BMA has supported charities and volunteers who have helped reshape Lebanon, raising funds for their causes and encouraging others to give. The culture of giving and doing good has become contagious. Stereotypes have been broken. Change-makers and future leaders have been created. I believe these are the building blocks for future peace.

8.49 BMA has become such a respected event in the region that government officials in the region like Iraq, Egypt and Syria, have asked the organization to help them structure a similar sporting event. We are now one of the largest running events in the Middle East, but most importantly, it is a platform for hope and cooperation in an ever-fragile and unstable part of the world. From Boston to Beirut, we stand as one. (*Applause*)

9.36 After ten years in Lebanon, from national marathons or from national events to smaller regional races, we've seen that people want to run for a better future. After all, peace making is not a sprint. It is more of a marathon.

9.58 Thank you. (*Applause*)

Unit 4 How I beat stage fright

0.11 I have stage fright. I've always had stage fright, and not just a little bit, it's a big bit. And it didn't even matter until I was 27. That's when I started writing songs, and even then I only played them for myself. Just knowing my roommates were in the same house made me uncomfortable.

0.29 But after a couple of years, just writing songs wasn't enough. I had all these stories and ideas, and I wanted to share them with people, but physiologically, I couldn't do it. I had this irrational fear. But the more I wrote, and the more I practiced, the more I wanted to perform.

0.44 So on the week of my 30th birthday, I decided I was going to go to this local open mic, and put this fear behind me. Well, when I got there, it was packed. There were like twenty people there. (*Laughter*) And they all looked angry. But I took a deep breath, and I signed up to play, and I felt pretty good.

1.05 Pretty good, until about ten minutes before my turn, when my whole body rebelled, and this wave of anxiety just washed over me. Now, when you experience fear, your sympathetic nervous system kicks in. So you have a rush of adrenaline, your heart rate increases, your breathing gets faster. Next your non-essential systems start to shut down, like digestion. (*Laughter*) So your mouth gets dry, and blood is routed away from your extremities, so your fingers don't work anymore.
Your pupils dilate, your muscles contract, your Spidey sense tingles, basically your whole body is trigger-happy. (*Laughter*) That condition is not conducive to performing folk music. (*Laughter*) I mean, your nervous system is an idiot. Really? Two hundred thousand years of human evolution, and it still can't tell the difference between a sabre tooth tiger and twenty folksingers on a Tuesday night open mic? (*Laughter*) I have never been more terrified – until now. (*Laughter and cheers*)

2.14 So then it was my turn, and somehow, I get myself onto the stage, I start my song, I open my mouth to sing the first line, and this completely horrible vibrato – you know, when your voice wavers – comes streaming out. And this is not the good kind of vibrato, like an opera singer has, this is my whole body just convulsing with fear. I mean, it's a nightmare. I'm embarrassed, the audience is clearly uncomfortable, they're focused on my discomfort. It was so bad. But that was my first real experience as a solo singer-songwriter.

2.46 And something good did happen – I had the tiniest little glimpse of that audience connection that I was hoping for. And I wanted more. But I knew I had to get past this nervousness.

2.55 That night I promised myself: I would go back every week until I wasn't nervous anymore. And I did. I went back every single week, and sure enough, week after week, it didn't get any better. The same thing happened every week. (*Laughter*) I couldn't shake it.

3.13 And that's when I had an epiphany. And I remember it really well, because I don't have a lot of epiphanies. (*Laughter*) All I had to do was write a song that exploits my nervousness. That only seems authentic when I have stage fright, and the more nervous I was, the better the song would be. Easy. So I started writing a song about having stage fright. First, fessing up to the problem, the physical manifestations, how I would feel, how the listener might feel. And then accounting for things like my shaky voice, and I knew I would be singing about a half-octave higher than normal, because I was nervous. By having a song that explained what was happening to me, while it was happening, that gave the audience permission to think about it. They didn't have to feel bad for me because I was nervous, they could experience that with me, and we were all one big happy, nervous, uncomfortable family. (*Laughter*)

4.05 By thinking about my audience, by embracing and exploiting my problem, I was able to take something that was blocking my progress, and turn it into something that was essential for my success. And having the stage fright song let me get past that biggest issue right in the beginning of a performance. And then I could move on, and play the rest of my songs with just a little bit more ease. And eventually, over time, I didn't have to play the stage fright song at all. Except for when I was really nervous, like now. (*Laughter*)

4.39 Would it be OK if I played the stage fright song for you? (*Applause*)

4.51 Can I have a sip of water? (*Music*) Thank you.

5.06 (*Singing*) I'm not joking, you know, this stage fright is real. And if I'm up here trembling and singing, well, you'll know how I feel. And the mistake I'd be making, the tremolo caused by my whole body shaking. As you sit there feeling embarrassed for me, well, you don't have to be. Well, maybe just a little bit (*Laughter*) And maybe I'll try to imagine you all without clothes. But singing in front of all naked strangers scares me more than anyone knows. Not to discuss this at length, but my body image was never my strength. So frankly, I wish that you all would get dressed, I mean, you're not even really naked. And I'm the one with the problem. And you tell me, don't worry so much, you'll be great. But I'm the one living with me and I know how I get. Your advice is gentle but late. If not just a bit patronizing. And that sarcastic tone doesn't help me when I sing. But we shouldn't talk about these things right now, really, I'm up on stage, and you're in the crowd. Hi. And I'm not making fun of unnurtured, irrational fear, and if I wasn't ready to face this, I sure as hell wouldn't be here. But if I belt one note out clearly, you'll know I'm recovering slowly but surely. And maybe next week, I'll set my guitar ringin' my voice clear as water, and everyone singin'. But probably I'll just get up and start groovin', my vocal cords movin', at speeds slightly faster than sound. (*Applause*)

Unit 5 I'm not your inspiration, thank you very much

0.11 I grew up in a very small country town in Victoria. I had a very normal, low-key kind of upbringing. I went to school, I hung out with my friends, I fought with my younger sisters. It was all very normal. And when I was fifteen, a member of my local community approached my parents and wanted to nominate me for a community achievement award. And my parents said, 'Hm, that's really nice, but there's kind of one glaring problem with that. She hasn't actually achieved anything.' (*Laughter*)

0.48 And they were right, you know. I went to school, I got good marks, I had a very low-key after school job in my mum's hairdressing salon, and I spent a lot of time watching *Buffy the*

Vampire Slayer and *Dawson's Creek*. Yeah, I know. What a contradiction. But they were right, you know. I wasn't doing anything that was out of the ordinary at all. I wasn't doing anything that could be considered an achievement if you took disability out of the equation. Years later, I was on my second teaching round in a Melbourne high school, and I was about twenty minutes into a year 11 legal studies class when this boy put up his hand and said, 'Hey miss, when are you going to start doing your speech?' And I said, 'What speech?' You know, I'd been talking them about defamation law for a good twenty minutes. And he said, 'You know, like, your motivational speaking. You know, when people in wheelchairs come to school, they usually say, like, inspirational stuff?' (*Laughter*) 'It's usually in the big hall.'

1.57 And that's when it dawned on me: This kid had only ever experienced disabled people as objects of inspiration. We are not, to this kid – and it's not his fault, I mean, that's true for many of us. For lots of us, disabled people are not our teachers or our doctors or our manicurists. We're not real people. We are there to inspire. And in fact, I am sitting on this stage looking like I do in this wheelchair, and you are probably kind of expecting me to inspire you. Right? (*Laughter*) Yeah.

2.40 Well, ladies and gentlemen, I'm afraid I'm going to disappoint you dramatically. I am not here to inspire you. I am here to tell you that we have been lied to about disability. Yeah, we've been sold the lie that disability is a Bad Thing, capital B, capital T. It's a bad thing, and to live with a disability makes you exceptional. It's not a bad thing, and it doesn't make you exceptional.

3.10 And in the past few years, we've been able to propagate this lie even further via social media. You may have seen images like this one: 'The only disability in life is a bad attitude.' Or this one: 'Your excuse is invalid.' Indeed. Or this one: 'Before you quit, try!' These are just a couple of examples, but there are a lot of these images out there. You know, you might have seen the one, the little girl with no hands drawing a picture with a pencil held in her mouth. You might have seen a child running on carbon fibre prosthetic legs. So in this case, we're objectifying disabled people for the benefit of nondisabled people. The purpose of these images is to inspire you, to motivate you, so that we can look at them and think, 'Well, however bad my life is, it could be worse. I could be that person.'

4.15 But what if you are that person? I've lost count of the number of times that I've been approached by strangers wanting to tell me that they think I'm brave or inspirational, and this was long before my work had any kind of public profile. They were just kind of congratulating me for managing to get up in the morning and remember my own name. (*Laughter*) And it is objectifying. These images, those images objectify disabled people for the benefit of nondisabled people. They are there so that you can look at them and think that things aren't so bad for you, to put your worries into perspective.

4.56 And life as a disabled person is actually somewhat difficult. We do overcome some things. But the things that we're overcoming are not the things that you think they are. They are not things to do with our bodies. I use the term 'disabled people' quite deliberately, because I subscribe to what's called the social model of disability, which tells us that we are more disabled by the society that we live in than by our bodies and our diagnoses.

5.27 So I have lived in this body a long time. I'm quite fond of it. It does the things that I need it to do, and I've learned to use it to the best of its capacity just as you have, and that's the thing about those kids in those pictures as well. They're not doing anything out of the ordinary. They are just using their bodies to the best of their capacity. So is it really fair to objectify them in the way that we do, to share those images? People, when they say, 'You're an inspiration,' they mean it as a compliment. And I know why it happens. It's because of the lie, it's because we've been sold this lie that disability makes you exceptional. And it honestly doesn't.

6.17 And I know what you're thinking. You know, I'm up here bagging out inspiration, and you're thinking, 'Jeez, Stella, aren't you inspired sometimes by some things?' And the thing is, I am. I learn from other disabled people all the time. I'm learning not that I am luckier than them, though. I am learning that it's a genius idea to use a pair of barbecue tongs to pick up things that you dropped. (*Laughter*) I'm learning that nifty trick where you can charge your mobile phone battery from your chair battery. Genius. We are learning from each others' strength and endurance, not against our bodies and our diagnoses, but against a world that exceptionalizes and objectifies us.

7.06 I really think that this lie that we've been sold about disability is the greatest injustice. It makes life hard for us. And that quote, 'The only disability in life is a bad attitude,' – it's just not true, because of the social model of disability. No amount of smiling at a flight of stairs has ever made it turn into a ramp. Never. (*Laughter*) (*Applause*) Smiling at a television screen isn't going to make closed captions appear for people who are deaf. No amount of standing in the middle of a bookshop and radiating a positive attitude is going to turn all those books into braille. It's just not going to happen.

7.59 I really want to live in a world where disability is not the exception, but the norm. I want to live in a world where a fifteen-year-old girl sitting in her bedroom watching 'Buffy the Vampire Slayer' isn't referred to as achieving anything because she's doing it sitting down. I want to live in a world where we don't have such low expectations of disabled people that we are congratulated for getting out of bed and remembering our own names in the morning. I want to live in a world where we value genuine achievement for disabled people, and I want to live in a world where a kid in year eleven in a Melbourne high school is not one bit surprised that his new teacher is a wheelchair user.

8.45 Disability doesn't make you exceptional, but questioning what you think you know about it does.

8.50 Thank you. (*Applause*)

Unit 6 How to make filthy water drinkable

0.11 Good morning everybody. I'd like to talk about a couple of things today. The first thing is water. Now I see you've all been enjoying the water that's been provided for you here at the conference, over the past couple of days. And I'm sure you'll feel that it's from a safe source.

0.27 But what if it wasn't? What if it was from a source like this? Then statistics would actually say that half of you would now be suffering with diarrhoea. I talked a lot in the past about statistics, and the provision of safe drinking water for all. But they just don't seem to get through. And I think I've worked out why. It's because, using current thinking, the scale of the problem just seems too huge to contemplate solving. So we just switch off: us, governments and aid agencies. Well, today, I'd like to show you that through thinking differently, the problem has been solved. By the way, since I've been speaking, another 13,000 people around the world are suffering now with diarrhoea. And four children have just died.

1.32 I invented Lifesaver bottle because I got angry. I, like most of you, was sitting down, the day after Christmas in 2004, when I was watching the devastating news of the Asian tsunami as it rolled in, playing out on TV. The days and weeks that followed, people fleeing to the hills, being forced to drink contaminated water or face death. That really stuck with me. Then, a few months later, Hurricane Katrina slammed into the side of America. 'OK,' I thought, 'here's a First World country, let's see what they can do.' Day one: nothing. Day two: nothing. Do you know it took five days to get water to the Superdome? People were shooting each other on the streets for TV sets and water. That's when I decided I had to do something.

2.31　Now I spent a lot of time in my garage, over the next weeks and months, and also in my kitchen – much to the dismay of my wife. (*Laughter*) However, after a few failed prototypes, I finally came up with this, the Lifesaver bottle.

2.47　OK, now for the science bit. Before Lifesaver, the best hand filters were only capable of filtering down to about 200 nanometres. The smallest bacteria is about 200 nanometres. So a 200-nanometre bacteria is going to get through a 200-nanometre hole. The smallest virus, on the other hand, is about 25 nanometres. So that's definitely going to get through those 200 nanometre holes. Lifesaver pores are fifteen nanometres. So nothing is getting through.

3.23　OK, I'm going to give you a bit of a demonstration. Would you like to see that? I spent all the time setting this up, so I guess I should. We're in the fine city of Oxford. So – someone's done that up. Fine city of Oxford, so what I've done is I've gone and got some water from the River Cherwell, and the River Thames, that flow through here. And this is the water. But I got to thinking, you know, if we were in the middle of a flood zone in Bangladesh, the water wouldn't look like this. So I've gone and got some stuff to add into it. And this is from my pond.

3.54　(*Sniffs*) (*Coughs*) Have a smell of that, mister cameraman.

3.58　OK. (*Laughs*) Right. We're just going to pour that in there.

4.05　Audience: Ugh!

4.07　Michael Pritchard: OK. We've got some runoff from a sewage plant farm. So I'm just going to put that in there. (*Laughter*) Put that in there. There we go. (*Laughter*) And some other bits and pieces, chuck that in there. And I've got a gift here from a friend of mine's rabbit. So we're just going to put that in there as well. (*Laughter*) OK. (*Laughter*) Now.

4.37　The Lifesaver bottle works really simply. You just scoop the water up. Today I'm going to use a jug just to show you all. Let's get a bit of that poo in there. That's not dirty enough. Let's just stir that up a little bit. OK, so I'm going to take this really filthy water, and put it in here. Do you want a drink yet? (*Laughter*) OK. There we go. Replace the top. Give it a few pumps. OK? That's all that's necessary. Now as soon as I pop the teat, sterile drinking water is going to come out. I've got to be quick. OK, ready? There we go. Mind the electrics. That is safe, sterile drinking water. (*Applause*) Cheers. (*Applause*) There you go, Chris. (*Applause*) What's it taste of?

5.55　Chris Anderson: Delicious.

5.57　Michael Pritchard: OK. Let's see Chris's programme throughout the rest of the show. OK? (*Laughter*)

6.06　OK. Lifesaver bottle is used by thousands of people around the world. It'll last for 6,000 litres. And when it's expired, using failsafe technology, the system will shut off, protecting the user. Pop the cartridge out. Pop a new one in. It's good for another 6,000 litres.

6.25　So let's look at the applications. Traditionally, in a crisis, what do we do? We ship water. Then, after a few weeks, we set up camps. And people are forced to come into the camps to get their safe drinking water. What happens when 20,000 people congregate in a camp? Diseases spread. More resources are required. The problem just becomes self-perpetuating. But by thinking differently, and shipping these, people can stay put. They can make their own sterile drinking water, and start to get on with rebuilding their homes and their lives.

7.06　Now, it doesn't require a natural disaster for this to work. Using the old thinking, of national infrastructure and pipe work, is too expensive. When you run the numbers on a calculator, you run out of noughts. So here is the 'thinking different' bit.

7.26　Instead of shipping water, and using man-made processes to do it, let's use Mother Nature. She's got a fantastic system. She picks the water up from there, desalinates it, for free, transports it over there, and dumps it onto the mountains, rivers, and streams. And where do people live? Near water. All we've go to do is make it sterile. How do we do that?

7.50　Well, we could use the Lifesaver bottle. Or we could use one of these. The same technology, in a jerry can. This will process 25,000 litres of water; that's good enough for a family of four, for three years. And how much does it cost? About half a cent a day to run. Thank you. (*Applause*)

8.19　So, by thinking differently, and processing water at the point of use, mothers and children no longer have to walk four hours a day to collect their water. They can get it from a source nearby. So with just eight billion dollars, we can hit the millennium goal's target of halving the number of people without access to safe drinking water. To put that into context, The U.K. government spends about twelve billion pounds a year on foreign aid. But why stop there? With 20 billion dollars, everyone can have access to safe drinking water. So the three-and-a-half billion people that suffer every year as a result, and the two million kids that die every year, will live. Thank you. (*Applause*)

Unit 7 Taking imagination seriously

0.11　This story is about taking imagination seriously. Fourteen years ago, I first encountered this ordinary material, fishnet, used the same way for centuries. Today, I'm using it to create permanent, billowing, voluptuous forms the scale of hard-edged buildings in cities around the world. I was an unlikely person to be doing this. I never studied sculpture, engineering or architecture. In fact, after college I applied to seven art schools and was rejected by all seven.

0.49　I went off on my own to become an artist, and I painted for ten years, when I was offered a Fulbright to India. Promising to give exhibitions of paintings, I shipped my paints and arrived in Mahabalipuram. The deadline for the show arrived – my paints didn't. I had to do something. This fishing village was famous for sculpture. So I tried bronze casting. But to make large forms was too heavy and expensive. I went for a walk on the beach, watching the fishermen bundle their nets into mounds on the sand. I'd seen it every day, but this time I saw it differently – a new approach to sculpture, a way to make volumetric form without heavy solid materials.

1.36　My first satisfying sculpture was made in collaboration with these fishermen. It's a self-portrait titled 'Wide Hips.' (*Laughter*) We hoisted them on poles to photograph. I discovered their soft surfaces revealed every ripple of wind in constantly changing patterns. I was mesmerized. I continued studying craft traditions and collaborating with artisans, next in Lithuania with lace makers. I liked the fine detail it gave my work, but I wanted to make them larger – to shift from being an object you look at to something you could get lost in.

2.21　Returning to India to work with those fishermen, we made a net of a million and a half hand-tied knots – installed briefly in Madrid. Thousands of people saw it, and one of them was the urbanist Manuel Solà-Morales who was redesigning the waterfront in Porto, Portugal. He asked if I could build this as a permanent piece for the city. I didn't know if I could do that and preserve my art. Durable, engineered, permanent – those are in opposition to idiosyncratic, delicate and ephemeral.

3.02　For two years, I searched for a fibre that could survive ultraviolet rays, salt, air, pollution, and at the same time remain soft enough to move fluidly in the wind. We needed something to hold the net up out there in the middle of the traffic circle. So we raised this 45,000-pound steel ring. We had to engineer it to move gracefully in an average breeze and survive in hurricane winds. But there was no engineering software to model something porous and moving. I found a brilliant aeronautical engineer who designs sails for America's Cup racing yachts named Peter Heppel. He helped me tackle the twin challenges of precise shape and gentle movement.

3.54 I couldn't build this the way I knew because hand-tied knots weren't going to withstand a hurricane. So I developed a relationship with an industrial fishnet factory, learned the variables of their machines, and figured out a way to make lace with them. There was no language to translate this ancient, idiosyncratic handcraft into something machine operators could produce. So we had to create one. Three years and two children later, we raised this 50,000-square-foot lace net. It was hard to believe that what I had imagined was now built, permanent and had lost nothing in translation. (*Applause*)

4.45 This intersection had been bland and anonymous. Now it had a sense of place. I walked underneath it for the first time. As I watched the wind's choreography unfold, I felt sheltered and, at the same time, connected to limitless sky. My life was not going to be the same. I want to create these oases of sculpture in spaces of cities around the world. I'm going to share two directions that are new in my work.

5.26 Historic Philadelphia City Hall: its plaza, I felt, needed a material for sculpture that was lighter than netting. So we experimented with tiny atomized water particles to create a dry mist that is shaped by the wind and in testing, discovered that it can be shaped by people who can interact and move through it without getting wet. I'm using this sculpture material to trace the paths of subway trains above ground in real time -- like an X-ray of the city's circulatory system unfolding.

6.07 Next challenge, the Biennial of the Americas in Denver asked, could I represent the 35 nations of the Western hemisphere and their interconnectedness in a sculpture? (*Laughter*) I didn't know where to begin, but I said yes. I read about the recent earthquake in Chile and the tsunami that rippled across the entire Pacific Ocean. It shifted the Earth's tectonic plates, sped up the planet's rotation and literally shortened the length of the day. So I contacted NOAA, and I asked if they'd share their data on the tsunami, and translated it into this. Its title: '1.26' refers to the number of microseconds that the Earth's day was shortened.

6.59 I couldn't build this with a steel ring, the way I knew. Its shape was too complex now. So I replaced the metal armature with a soft, fine mesh of a fibre fifteen times stronger than steel. The sculpture could now be entirely soft, which made it so light it could tie in to existing buildings -- literally becoming part of the fabric of the city. There was no software that could extrude these complex net forms and model them with gravity. So we had to create it.

7.35 Then I got a call from New York City asking if I could adapt these concepts to Times Square or the High Line. This new soft structural method enables me to model these and build these sculptures at the scale of skyscrapers. They don't have funding yet, but I dream now of bringing these to cities around the world where they're most needed.

8.05 Fourteen years ago, I searched for beauty in the traditional things, in craft forms. Now I combine them with hi-tech materials and engineering to create voluptuous, billowing forms the scale of buildings. My artistic horizons continue to grow.

8.31 I'll leave you with this story. I got a call from a friend in Phoenix. An attorney in the office who'd never been interested in art, never visited the local art museum, dragged everyone she could from the building and got them outside to lie down underneath the sculpture. There they were in their business suits, laying in the grass, noticing the changing patterns of wind beside people they didn't know, sharing the rediscovery of wonder.

9.02 Thank you. (*Applause*)

Unit 8 Build a tower, build a team

0.12 Several years ago here at TED, Peter Skillman introduced a design challenge called the marshmallow challenge. And the idea's pretty simple: Teams of four have to build the tallest free-standing structure out of twenty sticks of spaghetti, one yard of tape, one yard of string and a marshmallow. The marshmallow has to be on top. And, though it seems really simple, it's actually pretty hard because it forces people to collaborate very quickly. And so, I thought this was an interesting idea, and I incorporated it into a design workshop. And it was a huge success. And since then, I've conducted about 70 design workshops across the world with students and designers and architects, even the CTOs of the Fortune 50, and there's something about this exercise that reveals very deep lessons about the nature of collaboration, and I'd like to share some of them with you.

1.01 So, normally, most people begin by orienting themselves to the task. They talk about it, they figure out what it's going to look like, they jockey for power. Then they spend some time planning, organizing, they sketch and they lay out spaghetti. They spend the majority of their time assembling the sticks into ever-growing structures. And then finally, just as they're running out of time, someone takes out the marshmallow, and then they gingerly put it on top, and then they stand back, and – ta-da! – they admire their work. But what really happens, most of the time, is that the 'ta-da' turns into an 'uh-oh,' because the weight of the marshmallow causes the entire structure to buckle and to collapse.

1.44 So there are a number of people who have a lot more 'uh-oh' moments than others, and among the worst are recent graduates of business school. (*Laughter*) They lie, they cheat, they get distracted and they produce really lame structures. And of course there are teams that have a lot more 'ta-da' structures, and among the best are recent graduates of kindergarten. (*Laughter*) And it's pretty amazing. As Peter tells us, not only do they produce the tallest structures, but they're the most interesting structures of them all.

2.18 So the question you want to ask is: How come? Why? What is it about them? And Peter likes to say that none of the kids spend any time trying to be CEO of Spaghetti, Inc. Right? They don't spend time jockeying for power. But there's another reason as well. And the reason is that business students are trained to find the single right plan, right? And then they execute on it. And then what happens is, when they put the marshmallow on the top, they run out of time and what happens? It's a crisis. Sound familiar? Right. What kindergarteners do differently is that they start with the marshmallow, and they build prototypes, successive prototypes, always keeping the marshmallow on top, so they have multiple times to fix when they build prototypes along the way. Designers recognize this type of collaboration as the essence of the iterative process. And with each version, kids get instant feedback about what works and what doesn't work.

3.12 So the capacity to play in prototype is really essential, but let's look at how different teams perform. So the average for most people is around twenty inches; business schools students, about half of that; lawyers, a little better, but not much better than that, kindergarteners, better than most adults. Who does the very best? Architects and engineers, thankfully. (*Laughter*) Thirty-nine inches is the tallest structure I've seen. And why is it? Because they understand triangles and self-reinforcing geometrical patterns are the key to building stable structures. So CEOs, a little bit better than average, but here's where it gets interesting. If you put you put an executive admin on the team, they get significantly better. (*Laughter*) It's incredible. You know, you look around, you go, 'Oh, that team's going to win.' You can just tell beforehand. And why is that? Because they have special skills of facilitation. They manage the process, they understand the process. And any team who manages and pays close attention to work will significantly improve the team's performance. Specialized skills and facilitation skills are the combination that leads to strong success. If you have ten teams that typically perform, you'll get maybe six or so that have standing structures.

4.30 And I tried something interesting. I thought, let's up the ante, once. So I offered a 10,000 dollar prize of software to the winning team. So what do you think happened to these design students? What was the result? Here's what happened: Not one team had a standing structure. If anyone had built, say, a one-inch structure, they would have taken home the prize. So, isn't that interesting? That high stakes have a strong impact. We did the exercise again with the same students. What do you think happened then? So now they understand the value of prototyping. So the same team went from being the very worst to being among the very best. They produced the tallest structures in the least amount of time. So there's deep lessons for us about the nature of incentives and success.

5.21 So, you might ask: Why would anyone actually spend time writing a marshmallow challenge? And the reason is, I help create digital tools and processes to help teams build cars and video games and visual effects. And what the marshmallow challenge does is it helps them identify the hidden assumptions. Because, frankly, every project has its own marshmallow, doesn't it? The challenge provides a shared experience, a common language, a common stance to build the right prototype. And so, this is the value of the experience, of this so-simple exercise.

5.54 And those of you who are interested may want to go to MarshmallowChallenge.com. It's a blog that you can look at how to build the marshmallows. There's step-by-step instructions on this. There are crazy examples from around the world of how people tweak and adjust the system. There's world records that are on this as well.

6.11 And the fundamental lesson, I believe, is that design truly is a contact sport. It demands that we bring all of our senses to the task, and that we apply the very best of our thinking, our feeling and our doing to the challenge that we have at hand. And sometimes, a little prototype of this experience is all that it takes to turn us from an 'uh-oh' moment to a 'ta-da' moment. And that can make a big difference.

6.36 Thank you very much. (*Applause*)

Unit 9 All it takes is 10 mindful minutes

0.11 We live in an incredibly busy world. The pace of life is often frantic, our minds are always busy, and we're always doing something.

0.19 So with that in mind, I'd like you just to take a moment to think, when did you last take any time to do nothing? Just ten minutes, undisturbed? And when I say nothing, I do mean nothing. So that's no emailing, texting, no Internet, no TV, no chatting, no eating, no reading, not even sitting there reminiscing about the past or planning for the future. Simply doing nothing. I see a lot of very blank faces. (*Laughter*) My thinking is, you probably have to go a long way back.

0.51 And this is an extraordinary thing, right? We're talking about our mind. The mind, our most valuable and precious resource, through which we experience every single moment of our life, the mind that we rely upon to be happy, content, emotionally stable as individuals, and at the same time to be kind and thoughtful and considerate in our relationships with others. This is the same mind that we depend upon to be focused, creative, spontaneous, and to perform at our very best in everything that we do. And yet, we don't take any time out to look after it. In fact, we spend more time looking after our cars, our clothes and our hair than we – OK, maybe not our hair, but you see where I'm going.

1.38 The result, of course, is that we get stressed. You know, the mind whizzes away like a washing machine going round and round, lots of difficult, confusing emotions, and we don't really know how to deal with that, and the sad fact is that we are so distracted that we're no longer present in the world in which we live. We miss out on the things that are most important to us, and the crazy thing is that everybody just assumes, well, that's the way life is, so we've just kind of got to get on with it. That's really not how it has to be.

2.12 So I was about eleven when I went along to my first meditation class. And trust me, it had all the stereotypes that you can

imagine, the sitting cross-legged on the floor, the incense, the herbal tea, the vegetarians, the whole deal, but my mom was going and I was intrigued, so I went along with her. I'd also seen a few kung fu movies, and secretly I kind of thought I might be able to learn how to fly, but I was very young at the time. Now as I was there, I guess, like a lot of people, I assumed that it was just an aspirin for the mind. You get stressed, you do some meditation. I hadn't really thought that it could be sort of preventative in nature, until I was about twenty, when a number of things happened in my life in quite quick succession, really serious things which just flipped my life upside down and all of a sudden I was inundated with thoughts, inundated with difficult emotions that I didn't know how to cope with. Every time I sort of pushed one down, another one would just sort of pop back up again. It was a really very stressful time.

3.12 I guess we all deal with stress in different ways. Some people will bury themselves in work, grateful for the distraction. Others will turn to their friends, their family, looking for support. Some people hit the bottle, start taking medication. My own way of dealing with it was to become a monk. So I quit my degree, I headed off to the Himalayas, I became a monk, and I started studying meditation.

3.39 People often ask me what I learned from that time. Well, obviously it changed things. Let's face it, becoming a celibate monk is going to change a number of things. But it was more than that. It taught me – it gave me a greater appreciation, an understanding for the present moment. By that I mean not being lost in thought, not being distracted, not being overwhelmed by difficult emotions, but instead learning how to be in the here and now, how to be mindful, how to be present.

4.15 I think the present moment is so underrated. It sounds so ordinary, and yet we spend so little time in the present moment that it's anything but ordinary. There was a research paper that came out of Harvard, just recently, that said on average our minds are lost in thought almost 47 per cent of the time. Forty-seven per cent. At the same time, this sort of constant mind-wandering is also a direct cause of unhappiness. Now we're not here for that long anyway, but to spend almost half of our life lost in thought and potentially quite unhappy, dunno, it just kind of seems tragic, actually, especially when there's something we can do about it, when there's a positive, practical, achievable, scientifically proven technique which allows our mind to be more healthy, to be more mindful and less distracted. And the beauty of it is that even though it need only take about ten minutes a day, it impacts our entire life. But we need to know how to do it. We need an exercise. We need a framework to learn how to be more mindful. That's essentially what meditation is. It's familiarizing ourselves with the present moment. But we also need to know how to approach it in the right way to get the best from it. And that's what these are for, in case you've been wondering, because most people assume that meditation is all about stopping thoughts, getting rid of emotions, somehow controlling the mind, but actually it's quite different from that. It's more about stepping back, seeing the thought clearly, witnessing it coming and going, emotions coming and going without judgement, but with a relaxed, focused mind.

6.04 So for example, right now, if I focus too much on the balls, then there's no way that I can relax and talk to you at the same time. Equally, if I relax too much talking to you, then there's no way I can focus on the balls. I'm going to drop them. Now in life, and in meditation, there'll be times when the focus becomes a little bit too intense, and life starts to feel a bit like this. It's a very uncomfortable way to live life, when you get this tight and stressed. At other times, we might take our foot off the gas a little bit too much, and things just become a sort of little bit like this. Of course in meditation – (*Snores*) – we're going to end up falling asleep. So we're looking for a balance, a focused relaxation where we can allow thoughts to come and go without all the usual involvement.

6.50 Now, what usually happens when we're learning to be mindful is that we get distracted by a thought. Let's say this is an anxious thought. So everything's going fine, and then we see the anxious thought, and it's like, 'Oh, didn't realize I was worried about that.' You go back to it, repeat it. 'Oh, I am worried. Oh, I really am worried. Wow, there's so much anxiety.' And before we know it, right, we're anxious about feeling anxious. You know, this is crazy. We do this all the time, even on an everyday level. If you think about the last time, I dunno, you had a wobbly tooth. You know it's wobbly, and you know that it hurts. But what do you do every 20, 30 seconds? (*Mumbling*) It does hurt. And we reinforce the storyline, right? And we just keep telling ourselves, and we do it all the time. And it's only in learning to watch the mind in this way that we can start to let go of those storylines and patterns of mind. But when you sit down and you watch the mind in this way, you might see many different patterns. You might find a mind that's really restless and – the whole time. Don't be surprised if you feel a bit agitated in your body when you sit down to do nothing and your mind feels like that. You might find a mind that's very dull and boring, and it's just, almost mechanical, it just seems it's as if you're getting up, going to work, eat, sleep, get up, work. Or it might just be that one little nagging thought that just goes round and round and round your mind. Well, whatever it is, meditation offers the opportunity, the potential to step back and to get a different perspective, to see that things aren't always as they appear. We can't change every little thing that happens to us in life, but we can change the way that we experience it. That's the potential of meditation, of mindfulness. You don't have to burn any incense, and you definitely don't have to sit on the floor. All you need to do is to take ten minutes out a day to step back, to familiarize yourself with the present moment so that you get to experience a greater sense of focus, calm and clarity in your life.

9.08   Thank you very much. (*Applause*)

Unit 10   Protecting Twitter users (sometimes from themselves)

0.11   My job at Twitter is to ensure user trust, protect user rights and keep users safe, both from each other and, at times, from themselves. Let's talk about what scale looks like at Twitter. Back in January 2009, we saw more than two million new tweets each day on the platform. January 2014, more than 500 million. We were seeing two million tweets in less than six minutes. That's a 24,900-per cent increase.

0.53   Now, the vast majority of activity on Twitter puts no one in harm's way. There's no risk involved. My job is to root out and prevent activity that might. Sounds straightforward, right? You might even think it'd be easy, given that I just said the vast majority of activity on Twitter puts no one in harm's way. Why spend so much time searching for potential calamities in innocuous activities? Given the scale that Twitter is at, a one-in-a-million chance happens 500 times a day. It's the same for other companies dealing at this sort of scale. For us, edge cases, those rare situations that are unlikely to occur, are more like norms. Say 99.999 per cent of tweets pose no risk to anyone. There's no threat involved. Maybe people are documenting travel landmarks like Australia's Heart Reef, or tweeting about a concert they're attending, or sharing pictures of cute baby animals. After you take out that 99.999 per cent, that tiny percentage of tweets remaining works out to roughly 150,000 per month. The sheer scale of what we're dealing with makes for a challenge.

2.21   You know what else makes my role particularly challenging? People do weird things. (*Laughter*) And I have to figure out what they're doing, why, and whether or not there's risk involved, often without much in terms of context or background. I'm going to show you some examples that I've run into during my time at Twitter – these are all real examples — of situations that at first seemed cut and dried, but the truth of the matter was something altogether different. The details have been changed to protect the innocent and sometimes the guilty. We'll start off easy.

3.03   Let's look at spam. Here's an example of an account engaged in classic spammer behaviour, sending the exact same message to thousands of people. While this is a mockup I put together using my account, we see accounts doing this all the time. Seems pretty straightforward. We should just automatically suspend accounts engaging in this kind of behaviour. Turns out there's some exceptions to that rule. Turns out that that message could also be a notification you signed up for that the International Space Station is passing overhead because you wanted to go outside and see if you could see it. You're not going to get that chance if we mistakenly suspend the account thinking it's spam.

3.45   OK. Let's make the stakes higher. Back to my account, again exhibiting classic behaviour. This time it's sending the same message and link. This is often indicative of something called phishing, somebody trying to steal another person's account information by directing them to another website. That's pretty clearly not a good thing. We want to, and do, suspend accounts engaging in that kind of behaviour. So why are the stakes higher for this? Well, this could also be a bystander at a rally who managed to record a video of a police officer beating a non-violent protester who's trying to let the world know what's happening. We don't want to gamble on potentially silencing that crucial speech by classifying it as spam and suspending it. That means we evaluate hundreds of parameters when looking at account behaviours, and even then, we can still get it wrong and have to re-evaluate.

4.44   Now, given the sorts of challenges I'm up against, it's crucial that I not only predict but also design protections for the unexpected. And that's not just an issue for me, or for Twitter, it's an issue for you. It's an issue for anybody who's building or creating something that you think is going to be amazing and will let people do awesome things. So what do I do? I pause and I think, how could all of this go horribly wrong? I visualize catastrophe. And that's hard. There's a sort of inherent cognitive dissonance in doing that, like when you're writing your wedding vows at the same time as your prenuptial agreement.(*Laughter*) But you still have to do it, particularly if you're marrying 500 million tweets per day. What do I mean by 'visualize catastrophe?' I try to think of how something as benign and innocuous as a picture of a cat could lead to death, and what to do to prevent that. Which happens to be my next example. This is my cat, Eli. We wanted to give users the ability to add photos to their tweets. A picture is worth a thousand words. You only get 140 characters. You add a photo to your tweet, look at how much more content you've got now. There's all sorts of great things you can do by adding a photo to a tweet. My job isn't to think of those. It's to think of what could go wrong.

6.19   How could this picture lead to my death? Well, here's one possibility. There's more in that picture than just a cat. There's geodata. When you take a picture with your smartphone or digital camera, there's a lot of additional information saved along in that image. In fact, this image also contains the equivalent of this, more specifically, this. Sure, it's not likely that someone's going to try to track me down and do me harm based upon image data associated with a picture I took of my cat, but I start by assuming the worst will happen. That's why, when we launched photos on Twitter, we made the decision to strip that geodata out. (*Applause*) If I start by assuming the worst and work backwards, I can make sure that the protections we build work for both expected and unexpected use cases.

7.20   Given that I spend my days and nights imagining the worst that could happen, it wouldn't be surprising if my world view was gloomy. (*Laughter*) It's not. The vast majority of interactions I see – and I see a lot, believe me – are positive, people reaching out to help or to connect or share information with each other. It's just that for those of us dealing with scale, for those of us tasked with keeping people safe, we have to assume the worst will happen, because for us, a one-in-a-million chance is pretty good odds.

8.02   Thank you. (*Applause*)

Unit 11 How to build with clay and community

.11 I would like to show you how architecture has helped to change the life of my community and has opened opportunities to hope.

.25 I am a native of Burkina Faso. According to the World Bank, Burkina Faso is one of the poorest countries in the world, but what does it look like to grow up in a place like that? I am an example of that. I was born in a little village called Gando. In Gando, there was no electricity, no access to clean drinking water, and no school. But my father wanted me to learn how to read and write. For this reason, I had to leave my family when I was seven and to stay in a city far away from my village with no contact with my family. In this place I sat in a class like that with more than 150 other kids, and for six years. In this time, it just happened to me to come to school to realize that my classmate died.

1.36 Today, not so much has changed. There is still no electricity in my village. People still are dying in Burkina Faso, and access to clean drinking water is still a big problem.

1.55 I had luck. I was lucky, because this is a fact of life when you grow up in a place like that. But I was lucky. I had a scholarship. I could go to Germany to study.

2.14 So now, I suppose, I don't need to explain to you how great a privilege it is for me to be standing before you today. From Gando, my home village in Burkina Faso, to Berlin in Germany to become an architect is a big, big step. But what to do with this privilege? Since I was a student, I wanted to open up better opportunities to other kids in Gando. I just wanted to use my skills and build a school. But how do you do it when you're still a student and you don't have money? Oh yes, I started to make drawings and asked for money. Fundraising was not an easy task. I even asked my classmates to spend less money on coffee and cigarettes, but to sponsor my school project. In real wonder, two years later, I was able to collect 50,000 U.S. dollars.

3.29 When I came home to Gando to bring the good news, my people were over the moon, but when they realized that I was planning to use clay, they were shocked.

3.45 'A clay building is not able to stand a rainy season, and Francis wants us to use it and build a school. Is this the reason why he spent so much time in Europe studying instead of working in the field with us?'

4.03 My people build all the time with clay, but they don't see any innovation with mud. So I had to convince everybody. I started to speak with the community, and I could convince everybody, and we could start to work. And the women, the men, everybody from the village, was part of this building process. I was allowed to use even traditional techniques. So clay floor for example, the young men come and stand like that, beating, hours for hours, and then their mothers came, and they are beating in this position, for hours, giving water and beating. And then the polishers come. They start polishing it with a stone for hours. And then you have this result, very fine, like a baby bottom. (*Laughter*) It's not photoshopped. (*Laughter*) This is the school, built with the community. The walls are totally made out of compressed clay blocks from Gando. The roof structure is made with cheap steel bars normally hiding inside concrete. And the classroom, the ceiling is made out of both of them used together.

5.37 In this school, there was a simple idea: to create comfort in a classroom. Don't forget, it can be 45 degrees in Burkina Faso, so with simple ventilation, I wanted to make the classroom good for teaching and learning. And this is the project today, twelve years old, still in best condition. And the kids, they love it.

6.08 And for me and my community, this project was a huge success. It has opened up opportunities to do more projects in Gando. So I could do a lot of projects, and here I am going to share with you only three of them.

6.28 The first one is the school extension, of course. How do you explain drawings and engineering to people who are neither able to read nor write? I started to build a prototype like that. The innovation was to build a clay vault. So then, I jumped on the top like that, with my team, and it works. The community is looking. It still works. So we can build. (*Laughter*) And we kept building, and that is the result. The kids are happy, and they love it. The community is very proud. We made it. And even animals, like these donkeys, love our buildings. (*Laughter*)

7.17 The next project is the library in Gando. And see now, we tried to introduce different ideas in our buildings, but we often don't have so much material. Something we have in Gando are clay pots. We wanted to use them to create openings. So we just bring them like you can see to the building site; we start cutting them, and then we place them on top of the roof before we pour the concrete, and you have this result. The openings are letting the hot air out and light in. Very simple.

7.59 My most recent project in Gando is a high school project. I would like to share with you this. The innovation in this project is to cast mud like you cast concrete. How do you cast mud? We start making a lot of mortars, like you can see, and when everything is ready, when you know what is the best recipe and the best form, you start working with the community. And sometimes I can leave. They will do it themselves. I came to speak to you like that.

8.34 Another factor in Gando is rain. When the rains come, we hurry up to protect our fragile walls against the rain. Don't confound with Christo and Jeanne-Claude. It is simply how we protect our walls. (*Laughter*) The rain in Burkina comes very fast, and after that, you have floods everywhere in the country. But for us, the rain is good. It brings sand and gravel to the river we need to use to build. We just wait for the rain to go. We take the sand, we mix it with clay, and we keep building. That is it.

9.19 The Gando project was always connected to training the people, because I just wanted, one day when I fall down and die, that at least one person from Gando keeps doing this work. But you will be surprised. I'm still alive. (*Laughter*)

9.39 And my people now can use their skills to earn money themselves. Usually, for a young man from Gando to earn money, you have to leave the country to the city, sometimes leave the country and some never come back, making the community weaker. But now they can stay in the country and work on different building sites and earn money to feed their family. There's a new quality in this work.

10.15 Yes, you know it. I have won a lot of awards through this work. For sure, it has opened opportunities. I have become myself known. But the reason why I do what I do is my community.

10.36 When I was a kid, I was going to school, I was coming back every holiday to Gando. By the end of every holidays, I had to say goodbye to the community, going from one compound to another one. All women in Gando will open their clothes like that and give me the last penny. In my culture, this is a symbol of deep affection. As a seven-year-old guy, I was impressed. I just asked my mother one day, 'Why do all these women love me so much?' (*Laughter*) She just answered, 'They are contributing to pay for your education hoping that you will be successful and one day come back and help improve the quality of life of the community.' I hope now that I was able to make my community proud through this work, and I hope I was able to prove you the power of community, and to show you that architecture can be inspiring for communities to shape their own future.

11.57 Merci beaucoup. (*Applause*) Thank you. Thank you. Thank you. Thank you. Thank you. Thank you. (*Applause*)

Unit 12 Image recognition that triggers augmented reality

0.12 So wouldn't it be amazing if our phones could see the world in the same way that we do, as we're walking around being able to point a phone at anything, and then have it actually recognize images and objects like the human brain, and then be able to pull in information from an almost infinite library of knowledge and experiences and ideas?

0.31   Well, traditionally that was seen as science fiction, but now we've moved to a world where actually this has become possible.

0.36   So the best way of explaining it is to just show it. What you can see over here is Tamara, who is holding my phone that's now plugged in. So let me start with this. What we have here is a painting of the great poet Rabbie Burns, and it's just a normal image, but if we now switch inputs over to the phone, running our technology, you can see effectively what Tamara's seeing on the screen, and when she points at this image, something magical happens.

1.01   (Laughter) (Bagpipes) (Bagpipes) (Applause) (Bagpipes) Voice: Now simmer blinks on flowery braes ...

1.16   Matt Mills: Now, what's great about this is, there's no trickery here. There's nothing done to this image. And what's great about this is the technology's actually allowing the phone to start to see and understand much like how the human brain does. Not only that, but as I move the object around, it's going to track it and overlay that content seamlessly. Again, the thing that's incredible about this is this is how advanced these devices have become. All the processing to do that was actually done on the device itself.

1.47   Now, this has applications everywhere, whether in things like art in museums, like you just saw, or in the world of, say, advertising, or print journalism.

1.57   So a newspaper becomes out of date as soon as it's printed. And here is this morning's newspaper, and we have some Wimbledon news, which is great. Now what we can do is point at the front of the newspaper and immediately get the bulletin.

2.09   Voice: ... To the grass, and it's very important that you adapt and you, you have to be flexible, you have to be willing to change direction at a split second, and she does all that. She's won this title.

2.20   MM: And that linking of the digital content to something that's physical is what we call an aura, and I'll be using that term a little bit as we go through the talk.

2.28   So, what's great about this is it isn't just a faster, more convenient way to get information in the real world, but there are times when actually using this medium allows you to be able to display information in a way that was never before possible.

2.41   So what I have here is a wireless router. My American colleagues have told me I've got to call it a router, so that everyone here understands – (Laughter) – but nonetheless, here is the device. So now what I can do is, rather than getting the instructions for the device online, I can simply point at it, the device is recognized, and then –

3.03   Voice: Begin by plugging in the grey ADSL cable. Then connect the power. Finally, the yellow ethernet cable. Congratulations. You have now completed setup.

3.15   (Laughter) MM: Awesome. Thank you. (Applause)

3.20   The incredible work that made that possible was done here in the U.K. by scientists at Cambridge, and they work in our offices, and I've got a lovely picture of them here. They couldn't all be on stage, but we're going to bring their aura to the stage, so here they are. They're not very animated. (Laughter) This was the fourth take, I'm told. (Laughter)

3.45   OK. So, as we're talking about Cambridge, let's now move on to technical advancements, because since we started putting this technology on mobile phones less than twelve months ago, the speed and the processor in these devices has grown at a really phenomenal rate, and that means that I can now take cinema-quality 3D models and place them in the world around me, so I have one over here. Tamara, would you like to jump in?

4.14   (Music) (Dinosaur roaring) (Laughter) MM: I should leap in. (Music) (Dinosaur roaring) (Applause)

4.33   So then, after the fun, comes the more emotional side of what we do, because effectively, this technology allows you to see the world through someone's eyes, and for that person to be able to take a moment in time and effectively store it and tag it to something physical that exists in the real world. What's great about this is, the tools to do this are free. They're open, they're available to everyone within our application, and educators have really got on board with the classrooms. So we have teachers who've tagged up textbooks, teachers who've tagged up school classrooms, and a great example of this is a school in the U.K. I have a picture here from a video, and we're now going to play it.

5.09   Teacher: See what happens. (Children talking) Keep going.

5.17   Child: TV. (Children react)

5.21   Child: Oh my God.

5.22   Teacher: Now move it either side. See what happens. Move away from it and come back to it.

5.28   Child: Oh, that is so cool.

5.31   Teacher: And then, have you got it again?

5.34   Child: Oh my God! How did you do that?

5.38   Second child: It's magic.

5.41   (Laughter) MM: (Laughs) So, it's not magic. It's available for everyone to do, and actually I'm going to show you how easy it is to do by doing one right now.

5.50   So, as sort of — I'm told it's called a stadium wave, so we're going to start from this side of the room on the count of three, and go over to here. Tamara, are you recording? OK, so are you all ready? One, two, three. Go!

6.01   Audience: Whooooooo!

6.05   MM: Fellows are really good at that. (Laughs) (Laughter)

6.08   OK. Now we're going to switch back into the Aurasma application, and what Tamara's going to do is tag that video that we just took onto my badge, so that I can remember it forever.

6.21   Now, we have lots of people who are doing this already, and we've talked a little bit about the educational side. On the emotional side, we have people who've done things like send postcards and Christmas cards back to their family with little messages on them. We have people who have, for example, taken the inside of the engine bay of an old car and tagged up different components within an engine, so that if you're stuck and you want to find out more, you can point and discover the information.

6.47   We're all very, very familiar with the Internet. In the last twenty years, it's really changed the way that we live and work, and the way that we see the world, and what's great is, we sort of think this is the next paradigm shift, because now we can literally take the content that we share, we discover, and that we enjoy and make it a part of the world around us. It's completely free to download this application. If you have a good Wi-Fi connection or 3G, this process is very, very quick.

7.15   Oh, there we are. We can save it now. It's just going to do a tiny bit of processing to convert that image that we just took into a sort of digital fingerprint, and the great thing is, if you're a professional user, — so, a newspaper — the tools are pretty much identical to what we've just used to create this demonstration. The only difference is that you've got the ability to add in links and slightly more content. Are you now ready?

7.34   Tamara Roukaerts: We're ready to go.

7.35   MM: OK. So, I'm told we're ready, which means we can now point at the image, and there you all are.

7.40   MM on video: One, two, three. Go!

7.46   MM: Well done. We've been Aurasma. Thank you. (Applause)

Communication activities

Unit 4.3 Exercise 9, page 46
Student B

Choose two of the products. Decide how you could market them in your country. Think about:

- local tastes
- a product name that would be successful
- possible slogans (in English)

Try to convince your partner to buy your products. You may need to be highly creative to persuade them!

Viper – a poisonous snake sometimes eaten in Australia

Ugli fruit – a tropical fruit from Jamaica, a bit like an orange

Wooden bicycle – a form of basic transport popular in East Africa

(handwritten notes) transportation may never been so colourful. ، Bicywood!

↓
The cheapest form of transport in the world.

Unit 4.4 Exercise 5, page 49

Student B

1 Listen to and follow Student A's instructions. Ask for clarification as necessary.
2 Explain this process to Student A, but don't show the picture.

Unit 6.3 Exercise 4, page 69

Suddenly, the girl saw a way out. Moving quickly, she reached into the bag, grabbed a stone, and then immediately dropped it on the path. 'Oh, I'm so clumsy!' she said. 'Oh well,' she continued, 'we can see which stone remains in the bag, and then we'll know which one I took.' Suddenly, the old man had a problem. He didn't want to lose the girl or the money, but it would be far worse to reveal himself as a cheat. He was forced to show that the remaining stone was white, and so the girl didn't have to marry him, and he had to forgive the debt.

Unit 10.3 Exercise 1, page 112
Answers

1 e Being struck by lightning in your lifetime (1 in 3,000)
2 b Being injured by a toilet this year (1 in 10,000)
3 a Being killed by a bee sting (1 in 6 million)
4 d Being attacked by a shark (1 in 11.5 million)
5 c Being killed by an asteroid impact (1 in 74,817,414)

Unit 12.3 Exercise 9, Page 134
Student B

1 Read the scenario. You are a pessimist. Try to convince your partner that it's a bad idea for Matthew and Helena to buy the house. Consider:

- the size
- the price
- their salaries in the future
- holidays and other luxuries
- starting a family

Matthew and Helena are newlyweds who want to buy a house. They have found a three-bedroom house that they love, but it's expensive at €250,000. This amount is the maximum possible loan they could get considering their current combined salaries. Paying back that amount would mean they would need to limit the cost of holidays and other luxuries – and they both love traveling and relaxing. They don't have a family now, but they probably want to start one in the next few years. They're not sure whether they should buy the house, or look for something different.

2 Can you and your partner agree on a 'realistic' course of action for the couple?

Keynote Advanced
Student's Book
Lewis Lansford

Publisher: Gavin McLean

Publishing Consultant: Karen Spiller

Development Editor: Stephanie Parker

Editorial Manager: Alison Burt

Head of Strategic Marketing ELT: Charlotte Ellis

Senior Content Project Manager: Nick Ventullo

Manufacturing Manager: Eyvett Davis

Cover design: Brenda Carmichael

Text design: Keith Shaw

Compositor: MPS North America LLC

National Geographic Liaison: Leila Hishmeh

Audio: Tom Dick and Debbie Productions Ltd

DVD: Tom Dick and Debbie Productions Ltd

Cover Photo Caption: Beatrice Coron speaking at TED2011: The Rediscovery of Wonder, February 28 - March 4, 2011, Long Beach, CA. Photo: © James Duncan Davidson/TED.

The author would like to say a big thank you to Liz Driscoll, Paul Dummett, Gavin McLean, Stephanie Parker, Jess Rackham, Sarah Ratcliff, Karen Spiller and Helen Stephenson.

Student's Book ISBN: 978-1-305-80015-9
Student's Book + Online Workbook Code ISBN: 978-1-305-88062-7

National Geographic Learning
Cheriton House, North Way, Andover, Hampshire, SP10 5BE
United Kingdom

Cengage Learning is a leading provider of customized learning solutions with employees residing in nearly 40 different countries and sales in more than 125 countries around the world. Find your local representative at **www.cengage.com**.

Cengage Learning products are represented in Canada by Nelson Education Ltd.

Visit National Geographic Learning online at **ngl.cengage.com**

Visit our corporate website at **www.cengage.com**

CREDITS

The publishers would like to thank TED Staff for their insightful feedback and expert guidance, allowing us to achieve our dual aims of maintaining the integrity of these inspirational TED Talks, while maximising their potential for teaching English.

The publisher would like to thank all the reviewers who took part in the piloting and development of the material.

Although every effort has been made to contact copyright holders before publication, this has not always been possible. If contacted, the publisher will undertake to rectify any errors or omissions at the earliest opportunity.

The publishers would like to thank the following for permission to use copyright material:

Cover: © James Duncan Davidson/TED.

Photos: 6 (tl, tr, ml, br) © James Duncan Davidson/TED; 6 (mr) © Ryan Lash/TED; 6 (bl) © TED Conferences, LLC; 7 (tl, tr, mr, br) © James Duncan Davidson/TED; 7 (ml) © Dafydd Jones/TED; 7 (bl) © Ryan Lash/TED; 8–9 © by Huang Qingjun; 8 © James Duncan Davidson/TED; 10 © James Duncan Davidson/TED; 15 © Yadid Levy/Photolibrary/Getty Images; 16 © Skip Brown/Getty Images; 17 (t) © Patryk Kosmider/Getty Images; 17 (b) © Maskot/Getty Images; 18 © Pavel Oskin/National Geographic Creative; 19 © James Duncan Davidson/TED; 20 © James Duncan Davidson/TED; 25 (l, r) © Jordyn Taylor for the New York Observer; 26 (l) © Robert Kneschke/Shutterstock.com; 26 (ml) © Bevan Goldswain/Shutterstock.com; 26 (mr) © Zdenka Darula/Shutterstock.com; 26 (r) © PanicAttack/Shutterstock.com; 28 © The Real Junk Food Project Images; 30 © Daniel Renhardt/EPA; 31 © James Duncan Davidson/TED; 32 © James Duncan Davidson/TED; 37 © Zachary Scott/Getty Images; 40–41 © Steve McCurry/Magnum Photos; 40 © Ryan Lash/TED; 42 © Ryan Lash/TED; 47 © RosaIreneBetancourt 1/Alamy; 48 © Marco Vacca/Photographer's Choice/Getty Images; 50 © One Earth Designs; 52 © Matt Propert/National Geographic Creative; 53 © TED Conferences, LLC; 54 (all) © TED Conferences, LLC; 59 "Where Good Ideas Come From" by Steven Johnson. Published by Riverhead, an imprint of Penguin Publishing Group, a division of Penguin Random House LLC; 60 © Ghislain & Marie David de Lossy/Getty Images; 62–63 © Annie Griffiths/National Geographic Creative; 62 © James Duncan Davidson/TED; 64 © James Duncan Davidson/TED; 69 © mark wragg/Getty Images; 70 © Yellow Dog Productions/Getty Images; 72 © Tetsu Espósito, courtesy of Sonidos de la Tierra; 74–75 © age fotostock/Alamy; 74 © James Duncan Davidson/TED; 76 © James Duncan Davidson/TED; 79 © Keystone-France/Gamma-

Keystone/Getty Images; 81 © Digital Vision/Getty Images; 82 (l) © Exclusivepix Media; 82 (r) © Universal History Archive/Getty Images; 84–85 © Mitchell Kanashkevich/Getty Images; 84 © James Duncan Davidson/TED; 86 © James Duncan Davidson/TED; 89 (tl) © Alvaro Leiva/Getty Images; 89 (tr) © Ariel Skelley/Getty Images; 89 (ml) © Leren Lu/Getty Images; 89 (mr) © john finney photography/Getty Images; 89 (bl) © Chris Ryan/Getty Images; 89 (br) © Paul Bradbury/Getty Images; 91 © Cultura Creative (RF)/Alamy; 92 © Ffooter/Shutterstock.com; 94 © Hipcycle.com; 96 © Lebedev Artur/ITAR-TASS Photo/Corbis; 97 © Dafydd Jones/TED; 98 © Dafydd Jones/TED; 103 © Digital Vision/Getty Images; 104 © PathDoc/Shutterstock.com; 106 © Susana Gonzalez/Bloomberg/Getty Images; 107 © James Duncan Davidson/TED; 108 © James Duncan Davidson/TED; 113 © Colin Anderson/Getty Images; 114 © Stephen Simpson/Getty Images; 116 © Sijmen Hendriks/Hollandse Hoogte/Redux; 118 © SIHASAKPRACHUM/Shutterstock.com; 119 © Ryan Lash/TED; 120 © Ryan Lash/TED; 123 © steve estvanik/Shutterstock.com; 125 (t) © Romolo Tavani/Shutterstock.com; 125 (ml) Photograph by © Alfred Manner - Courtesy Friends of Peace Pilgrim; 125 (mr) © Marco di Lauro/Reportage by Getty Images for CNN/Turner Broadcasting System; 125 (bl) © Everett Kennedy Brown/epa/Corbis; 125 (br) © Ramin Talaie/Corbis; 126 © Raul Arboleda/AFP/Getty Images; 127 (t) © Leland Bobbe/Getty Images; 127 (b) © ARENA Creative/Shutterstock.com; 128–129 © Julien Vidal; 128 (l) © James Duncan Davidson/TED; 128 (r) © James Duncan Davidson/TED; 130 © James Duncan Davidson/TED; 135 (l) © Mateo_Pearson/Shutterstock.com; 135 (r) © Sharon Day/Shutterstock.com; 136 © Ruskin Photos/Alamy; 138 © Mellowcabs PTY Ltd; 172 (tl) © Akio Suga/EPA/Newscom; 172 (tr) © Mike Von Bergen/Shutterstock.com; 172 (b) © jethuynh/Shutterstock.com; 183 (tl) © TommyIX/Getty Images; 183 (tr) © Smneedham/Getty Images; 183 (b) © Michael Runkel/Robert Harding Picture Library/Age Fotostock.

Illustrations & Infographics: 12, 22, 34, 38, 39, 44, 56, 66, 78, 88, 100, 110, 122, 132 emc design; 114, 172, 183 MPS North America LLC.

Infographics: 12 based on: http://www.economist.com/blogs/freeexchange/2010/08/consumption; 22 Sources: idtheftedu.com, forbes.com; 34 Source: blogs.msdn.com; 44 Source: fastcompany.com; 56 based on: http://www.pinterest.com/pin/292734044498582108/]; 66 based on: http://lifehacker.com/use-this-flowchart-to-identify-what-type-of-procrastina-1615614759; 78 Sources: sciencedaily.com, english.chosun.com; 88 Source: cipd.co.uk/binaries; 100 Sources: http://en.wikipedia.org/wiki/Holmes_and_Rahe_stress_scale; 110 Sources: totalprosports.com, advancedphysicalmedicine.org, thebmc.co.uk; 122 Source: huffingtonpost.com; 132 Sources: bbc.co.uk/news, saturdayeveningpost.com, farm8.staticflickr.com.

Printed in China by RR Donnelley

Print Number: 01   Print Year: 2016